MW00635076

Rhonda Hetzel is a retired journalist and technical writer best known for her award-winning blog, 'Down to Earth'. Rhonda lives with her husband, Hanno, on the Sunshine Coast, where they happily tend a food garden, gather eggs and occasionally look after grandchildren. Rhonda is a keen volunteer worker and often presents simple-living workshops in her community. She is the author of the bestseller *Down to Earth: A Guide to Simple Living* and the Penguin Special *The Simple Life*. In 2014 Rhonda won *Green Lifestyle* magazine's Local Green Hero Award.

down---to---earth.blogspot.com.au

ALSO BY RHONDA HETZEL

Down to Earth: A Guide to Simple Living

The Simple Life: Penguin Special

RHONDA HETZEL

the
simple
home

A month-by-month guide to self-reliance,
productivity and contentment

PHOTOGRAPHY BY JULIE RENOUF

VIKING
an imprint of
PENGUIN BOOKS

For my grandchildren Jamie, Alex and Eve,
my sister Tricia's grandchildren, Johnathan and Alana,
and for all grandchildren now and in the future.

This book is one of the breadcrumbs I'll leave behind in a trail
that leads to home. I won't always be here to remind my children
and grandchildren that time will change the world and things
won't stay the same. My trails will take my family to a familiar
place because they always start and end at home;
the most important place for all of us.

INTRODUCTION

I am a woman who has been profoundly changed by my home and the work I do there. After spending much of my working life being 'busy' earning a living, I was exhausted, disappointed and in need of a change. Time passed, that change happened and I discovered the significant joys and rewards of a simple home.

When I first put on my apron to make bread and cook real food every day, I could clearly see the benefits. When I linked the from-scratch cooking to preserving, stockpiling, shopping and backyard food production, that in turn was connected to budgeting, paying off debt and living on less than we earned. Our health improved because we were eating fresh, local food, we had virtually eliminated preservatives from our diet and we had contact with fewer chemicals by making our own soap, laundry products and cleaners. Instead of being just a group of housekeeping projects, connecting the dots between all these activities showed me that we had built a holistic system, with each part relating to the others and paving the way to a simpler life.

In those early months, I went to bed each night exhausted from the work I'd done but impatient for the new morning to break so I could do it all again. I had control over what I was doing and I felt happy and satisfied. What was going on! People were supposed to be excited about going out and spending money, being out in the wide world and part of the hustle and bustle, and here I was being made whole again by planting saved seeds, mending, preserving, menu planning and drinking tea in the shade of an elder tree. My home mended my broken spirit.

I made up for lost income by working smarter and towards different goals, redefining what I wanted from life and what I believed success to be. I shopped for groceries in a different way, bought ingredients instead of products, stock-piled and stopped wasting food - not just once, but always. It didn't take any extra cash; in fact it took much less. And so, over a decade later, Hanno and I are still here, evolving into older age and wondering why living this way isn't talked about more, or taught in schools. I might be making the transition from mainstream living sound easy and quick – it wasn't, but it wasn't difficult either. Anyone can do it.

And that is why this book is so relevant now. With all the talk of financial uncertainty, sky-high property prices and rents and increasing energy costs, I know this book can help people, young and older, live well in difficult times. There needs to be a way forward that gives ordinary folk the power to choose family and home life instead of intense consumerism and the bleak conse-quences of it. Living simply can be that way forward.

The Simple Home is set out as twelve monthly chapters showing how tasks can fit into the year. For instance, we're concentrating on organising the home and finances in January and February, cooking real food in March, and in April, May and June we're gardening, giving our laundry some love and learning more about food storage and stockpiling. When it's cold and windy outside in July and August, we're baking and working on crafts, and in spring, when milk is at its best, we focus on homemade dairy foods and spring cleaning. There is time for self-reflection in November while we think about health and wellbeing, and in December we gather our friends and family around us while we celebrate and relax.

The topics have been timed according to the seasons of the southern hemi-sphere, but I've provided an alternative, northern hemisphere chapter order at the end of the book. Wherever you live, you can use the book however you choose. You might read the entire book and then dip in and out of the months as you need them. I'm sure there will be other readers who use *The Simple Home* as a recipe book, and that's fine too. My hope is that the book will serve whatever your purpose is and support you and the work you do in your home.

Simplifying your life will make you more involved in the day-to-day running of your home, and that might look like hard work to you. But look more closely, disregard the rubbish we've been fed about shopping to boost the economy, stop listening to advertising, forget the pangs of envy you sometimes feel when reading magazines. Instead, smell the bread baking, reuse what you might once have thrown away, taste the first ripe raspberry of the season, crack a fresh egg from the backyard, feel the satisfaction of organised cupboards and clean clothes, enjoy entertaining family and friends and discover life without debt. When you have experienced all that, you'll know how life can be made better by the work you do in your home.

This is not an all-or-nothing way of living: we all choose our own starting point, and that could be food, cleaning, debt reduction or whatever, and then it's small steps while you build on your successes and move towards the next stage. There is a splendid life waiting when you slow down and move beyond consumerism. Life lived when debt is reducing instead of increasing is better than a hundred trips to the shops. You can see the big picture and where you fit into it. When that happened to me, I knew I was on the right path, and now, looking back, I wonder how I could have been fooled into believing so many wrong things were right. Being in charge of your own life and making decisions based on what you want to do rather than what you have to do will give you a rare kind of contentment and show you that every ordinary day offers magnificent opportunities.

INVITATION TO JOIN THE DOWN TO EARTH FORUMS

We have a thriving international online community of people who discuss and ask questions about their own simple lives. I invite you to join us at simpleliving.forums.net and look forward to seeing you there soon.

january

ORGANISE THE YEAR AHEAD

*'Give me six hours to chop down a tree and I will
spend the first four sharpening the axe.'*
— ABRAHAM LINCOLN

ORGANISING LIFE AT HOME

When the new year starts, I sometimes feel like I'm living in a bubble. Most people are on holidays, school's out, and my attention moves from daily work and getting things done to a contented calmness sustained by the sound of ice cubes in cold drinks, cricket on the radio, knitting needles and holiday visitors. For Hanno and me, it's a beautiful time of year when we relax, spend time with our family and friends and make the most of the warm summer days. We didn't achieve this seasonal slowness overnight – we work at it every year and feel thankful when the pace slows and we start to unwind. After the rush of Christmas, when you've had a few days of serious relaxing, it's the ideal time to think about the year ahead and how you will approach it.

No matter what year it is, you can count on change. Some will be changes that you know about and have prepared for; some will be unexpected and sudden. You'll put yourself in a better position if you've thought about potential changes and have a strategy to deal with them. Planning early in the year will help move life in the direction you want it to go. Things won't always go according to your plan, but when the unexpected happens, it will be easier to get back on track if there is a plan to return to.

I prefer to share the ins and outs of how we live rather than lecture on the rights and wrongs of it. But I know when people are in a muddle and don't know where to start, sometimes another voice offering suggestions can help, even if those suggestions seem so obvious they are barely worth writing down.

I hope my lists inspire you to come up with your own. Developing your own independence and applying many of the practical activities we'll be discussing later in the book will help you stop relying on those ever-present whispers from social media, fashion, well-meaning friends or anyone else who tells you what to do and how to do it. I hope I can encourage you to live your life your way and if you find one or two or twenty things in this book and modify them to suit you, I will be happy.

Make time in January to mark up your calendar and diary with all the important days for the year such as birthdays, anniversaries, school and work holidays, training days, family trips and get-togethers. Some cultures celebrate saints' days such as St Patrick's Day, some families hold the winter and summer solstices as special days, and Halloween is becoming more popular with young families. If any of these events are important in your family, mark them on your calendar, and if they need extra money, add them as an item in your budget as well. If you have school-aged children, when you receive the first few school newsletters and register for after-school activities you'll probably be able to add dates such as pupil-free days, school camps, excursions, sports days, concerts, award ceremonies, practice sessions and game schedules. If you have a baby or preschoolers, you'll need to add vaccination dates and clinic check-ups. Also add reminders for your pets' tick and flea treatments and vaccinations.

I rely on my computer to keep me organised and on track. It suits me to add reminders to my calendar in the form of alerts and emails. If you mark up all your relevant dates on your computer calendar, then sync it with your phone, you'll have your current calendar with you all the time and will be able to check dates when you're out and about. Alternatively, you could use a paper calendar to mark up the year, then write all those dates into a diary you can carry with you.

Once your calendar is set, there are many more things you can organise during January that will help keep you on track later in the year.

THE HOME FOLDER

One organisational system I'd encourage you to try is a home folder. I wrote about this in *Down to Earth*, but since then my folder has evolved. If you do this thoughtfully, your folder will develop into a comprehensive reference manual customised specifically to you, your family and your home.

When I first started living as I do now it took me a very short time to realise that unless I organised myself and recorded all the new tasks I was hoping to do, I would sink like a stone. I had downloaded recipes, ideas, patterns and project plans, but needed to gather all my printed materials together and keep them in one place. Enter my home folder. It's an old three-ring binder that I covered in fabric. I also added a few plastic sleeves left over from my old office. Try to make do with what you have when you put your home folder together – a filing drawer or a concertina folder are good alternatives to a binder.

Your home folder will hold the written information you need to run your home efficiently. I found that when I had added a lot of printed material to my home folder, it was difficult to find things quickly. It needed dividers that I could stick labels on. Now my home folder is divided into two sections: Indoors and Outdoors. It is then broken down into sections with labelled tabs. Here are some ideas for topic headings that might help you set up your home folder. Remember, make your folder reflect *your* family life, and don't be too specific with your titles otherwise there will be dozens of sections and sub-sections.

Indoors

INSPIRATION

Start your home folder with a quote that summarises how you feel about your life and home now, or a statement about what you want your life to be or changes you intend to make. Even a small mood board of your ideal kitchen or garden will help you think about what you hope to achieve.

Add a printout of this year's calendar with important events already filled in. When you update your calendar during the year, update your printout too.

CONTACTS

Even though your contacts will be recorded elsewhere, list your personal contacts in your home folder too in case you lose your phone or address book. All business numbers should be easily found online or in the phone book.

HEALTH

This could be a large section or a very small one, depending on your health and that of your family. Some of the items you may decide to include are:

- Vaccination records and schedules for you and your children
- Information sheets included in any medications you or your family are taking
- Exercise sheet as recommended by your physiotherapist
- Information about illnesses in your family
- Information about support groups for issues particular to your family
- Your doctor's details, including opening hours and after-hours contact number
- Details of a local after-hours doctor who does home visits
- Details of your health insurance if you have private cover, and list of what you're covered for

FOOD

- Menu plans
- Recipes for breakfast, lunch, dinner and snacks
- Packed lunch ideas
- Baking recipes – bread, cakes, biscuits
- Preserving and fermenting recipes
- Drinks recipes
- Seasonal fruit and vegetable list for your area (which you can find online)
- Table of volume, weight and temperature conversions

FOOD SHOPPING

- Current grocery flyers
- Details of online shopping accounts and passwords (or just hints so they remain secure)
- Contact or website details of the local food sellers you deal with (butchers, fishmongers, farmers' markets, bulk food stores)

BUDGETING

- Your budget
- Old water, gas, electricity and phone bills to compare with the next bill that comes
- Meter readings for water and electricity if you do your own readings
- Cost estimates and plans for future projects

CLEANING

- Recipes for green cleaning products
- Special washing instructions for clothes or household linens
- Spring-cleaning checklist that you can add to during the year as you think of other tasks you need to do

CRAFTS, SEWING, CROCHET AND KNITTING

- Knitting and crochet patterns
- List of knitting abbreviations
- List of knitting needle sizes
- Printouts of online patterns
- Contact or website details of your favourite yarn or fabric suppliers
- Details of free local craft classes
- Details of your online craft accounts such as Ravelry, Knitty or Pinterest

APPLIANCES

- Manuals
- Warranty documents
- New appliance receipts

An inventory of what you own is a very good list to have. It will give you a realistic idea of how much to insure your possessions for. Take photos of the high-cost items and jewellery, and group them in a document you can print out. Record the serial numbers of the electronics.

- Household goods such as furniture, dinner and cutlery sets, glasses, bowls, books, lamps, linen, blankets and doonas
- Appliances such as fridges, TVs, irons, toasters, microwaves, air conditioners and fans
- Electronics and technology such as computers, laptops, tablets, phones, games consoles, cameras and chargers
- Outdoor equipment such as garden tools, mowers, outdoor furniture and pool filters
- Sports equipment such as tennis racquets, surfboards, cricket gear, bikes and gym gear
- Clothes, shoes and jewellery

GIFTS

- List of gifts you will give this year (including names and dates)
- List of gifts already in the cupboard
- Ideas for gifts

SCHOOL AND AFTER-SCHOOL

- School newsletters and info
- Reports
- Term dates for school and extracurricular activities
- Receipts for things like levies, fees, excursions.
- Invitations and cards received

Outdoors

- A drawing of your garden plan
- Seasonal planting guide for your area
- Ideas for the next planting season
- Moon planting calendar
- Seed catalogues
- Fruit and nut tree catalogues
- Record of planting (fruit trees and vines, vegetables)
- Record of rainfall
- Record of your vegetable, fruit and egg harvests
- Mower maintenance record and upcoming dates

PETS AND LIVESTOCK

- Contact details or websites of local vet and feed supply companies
- A sheet for each animal with relevant information such as date of birth, record of vaccinations and dates for upcoming tick and flea treatments
- A record of how much and when your animals should be fed each day
- Recipes for pet food
- List of hens' names and when they were added to the flock

Your home folder will change as you progress, and you'll probably update it quite often. That's good! It shows you're changing and thinking about your changes as you go. All our home folders will be different because, ideally, they'll reflect the stage of life we're at, the way we live, the number of people in our family and all the hopes and plans we have for the future.

FOOD PLANNING

Another thing you can do during January is write a set of summer menu plans. We'll come back to this again in March and do the rest of the year then. But now, to see you through the rest of summer and into autumn, do eight weeks of summer menu planning, or a four-week cycle that you can repeat.

The idea behind menu planning is that it removes the stress of daily meal preparation because you've already decided what you'll be eating and made sure all the ingredients are in the fridge and pantry. It makes you much less likely to run out of ideas or time and find yourself phoning for takeaway. Other benefits are:

- Saving money because you can buy food that is on special
- Saving time because you can shop once a week and pick up everything you need
- Eating fewer preservatives and artificial additives by cooking from scratch
- Eating more local and seasonal foods because you've planned them into your menu and aren't relying on what the supermarket is trying to push
- Providing the opportunity to involve your children in choosing healthy food options

Plan breakfasts, lunches – including packed lunches – dinners, snacks, drinks and special events, such as birthdays. Also plan to use leftovers for at least one meal each week, or if you have none, include a casual weekend meal like homemade pizza or toasted sandwiches. The leftovers meal should be the last meal you cook before you shop again. It might stretch your imagination, because you'll be trying to use up whatever's in the fridge that won't last much longer. Don't forget this leftovers meal – it will help you stop wasting food, and that's something we should all be doing.

The best way to menu plan in January is to make some time just before your regular shopping trip. Start with some of your popular meals, then add a few new meals for variety; recipes that will be easy to prepare mid-week and that you know your family will eat, if you're cooking for a family. Research online or flick through your recipe books. Involve the family in menu planning; it's a good opportunity to discuss budgets, food prices and nutrition. For a general guide to menu planning, see the March chapter.

Be mindful that fruit and vegetables are cheaper and better quality when they're in season. If what you want isn't in season and you have to have it, is there a frozen or canned local alternative? If you grow vegetables and fruits, incorporate your own produce in your meal plans and only buy the vegetables you can't grow or don't have enough of.

Put some time into researching the best place for you to shop. Are there local farmers' markets, a dairy, a good family butcher or nearby roadside fruit and vegetable stalls? Can you barter something you produce, such as eggs, for honey or homemade soap? Choosing local merchants over the big supermarkets is often a cheaper alternative, and it will keep your money within the local community.

If your only choice is to shop at the major supermarkets, they all have free downloadable apps that give details on store locations, hours, specials and recipes, often using that week's specials. Most of them have a shopping-list facility that you can add to whenever you think of something you need, and you can scan barcodes so you don't have to keep typing in the products you always buy.

January is a good time to start thinking about school and work lunches. They need to be nutritious and satisfying but also able to withstand being jostled around in a bag. Write all your ideas down, even those you haven't tried yet. If you have time during the month, test recipes and combinations.

TIP: Lunches are more likely to be eaten if they're still fresh and in one piece at lunchtime. If you've been using just a sandwich bag to pack lunches, look around for a sturdy container. There's such a good range of lunchboxes now, in a wide variety of materials. These boxes can be washed every day, and if you buy one with separate compartments you'll probably be able to stop using plastic wrap and bags.

CUSTOMISE YOUR WORK SPACES

Most homes are set up to look good rather than to support the people who live there or the housework they do. When I started considering how I worked in certain areas and moved furniture around to accommodate functionality, things flowed more smoothly. A home needs to be customised to the unique needs of its inhabitants. You might discover that a spare bedroom works better as an ironing and craft room. Moving a few things around in your laundry may give you the ideal space to make soap and cleaners. If you make a lot of hot drinks, organise a small tea and coffee station near the kettle and teacups. You'll have everything you need right there and will only have to fetch milk from the fridge.

I encourage you to wander around your home and think about how you can change spaces and rooms to suit your family and how you work. You might find that these small adjustments will result in big gains in time management and productivity.

The drop zone

This is the area where things are inevitably dumped when everyone comes home from school and work. I tried to move this area over the years but was never successful. Whatever I said was forgotten, and hats, cases, schoolbags and keys were dropped as soon as my husband and sons entered the house. If this is the case with your family, work with it. Organise the area so that it's tidy and, if you have room, give everyone their own space for what they take to school and work.

Your climate and the age of your children, if you have them, will play a big part in how you arrange the space. If you live in a cold climate, you'll need hooks for coats, hats and gloves, and, ideally, a seat to sit on to put on and take off boots. If you're in a warmer region, you might just need hooks for hats and bags. Below each hook, have a basket for each person in which they can put what they need the next day at school or work. If you have less space, a small hall table for phones and keys, with a basket underneath for backpacks and library bags, might be enough to make a difference. If anyone in your house cycles, they'll need a rack outside for their bike and a hook for their helmet.

If you live alone, you can drop your things anywhere and no one will complain. But if you drop your phone and keys in the same place every day, and place your bag and coat on a hook right there, it will be easy for you to get out the door without searching for what you have to take with you.

If you can set up a drop zone that works for you and your family, it will save hours of searching for keys, phones and hats during the year. I promise you, your mornings and afternoons will improve if everyone knows where to leave these items and where to find them in the morning. It's a very worthwhile project to get the family involved in.

The charging station

Most of us have phones and other devices that need daily charging. It's a good habit to attach your phone to the charger when you come home. Setting up a charging station close to the drop zone reminds everyone to charge their phone and take it with them the following morning. See the Resources for a DIY charging station.

The home admin station

This area is probably going to be close to your computer or writing desk. It's for all the paper bills, letters and newsletters that come into the home. Start with an in-tray that will hold the mail you receive. You don't have to deal with it straight away; if it's all in one place, you'll be able to go through it when you have the time.

You might like to have three tiers to your in-tray or just find three large bulldog clips to hold documents in these categories:

- **To pay** – bills
- **To do** – letters to reply to, school permission slips to sign
- **To file** – paid bills, letters you've finished dealing with

You might want to have stationery items and stamps there as well so you can send out letters that can't be returned by email.

After setting up the home admin station in January, try to allow one hour a week for dealing with your paper admin and keeping on top of the filing.

ROUTINES: GETTING THE WORK DONE

January is the ideal time to think about how you can work smarter in the months to come. Working to a routine, or a few different routines, can be useful when things are very busy. It doesn't matter what the work is; once it's started, it usually provides motivation to do more.

A routine is a sequence of events that happen in the same order, or close to it, every day, week or month. It's simply the habit of repeating ordinary tasks. There are certain household tasks that are constant. For me, and possibly for many of us, they are making the bed, baking bread, cleaning the kitchen, washing up, sweeping the floors and cooking. I do those tasks almost every day, and so incorporate them into my daily routine. There are other tasks that are done weekly, like changing the bed linen, washing, vacuuming and deep cleaning. Others still, such as gardening, organising, sewing, knitting, soap-making, preserving and shopping, are occasional pastimes that I do either when I feel like doing them or when they're needed.

> TIP: I want the work I do in my home to make family life better and to enrich my spirit. I don't expect to be drained and depleted by housework. I try to organise my days so I'm doing work I don't like along with the work I love. So if I have to clean the toilet or do the ironing, I'll reward myself afterwards with morning tea on the front verandah or an hour's knitting. This works well for me.

Start thinking now about the routines you'll use during the year. If you've never worked to a routine, start by either doing the work or estimating how long it would take you to do it. You need to know your timeframes so you can group certain tasks together. Depending on your circumstances, you might need several routines, such as:

- Mornings
- Before bed
- General house tidying

- Cleaning
- Laundry
- Shopping (including your weekly/monthly shopping and picking up fresh milk during the week)
- Cooking and family mealtimes
- Weekends

I believe the easiest and best routines to establish are those that happen in the early morning and just before you go to bed, as they help you set up and finish each day effectively. I call this the before bed–morning combo, and it's ideal for those with schoolchildren and workers going out in the morning. If you have kids, you'll probably be busy every evening because you'll be helping them with homework, preparing the evening meal and trying to get everyone showered and ready for bed. When you can manage it, though, try to do the following:

- Wash the dishes after dinner
- Make lunches and drinks for the following day (most lunches can be prepared the night before and will be fine in the fridge until morning)
- Set the table for breakfast (or have one of the children do it)
- If you're having oats for breakfast, soak them overnight
- If you're having cereal, get the plates ready with cereal boxes next to them
- If it will be tea and toast, put out the spreads, cups and plates so all you have to do in the morning is make the tea and toast

Whatever you can do in the evening will be one less thing to do in the morning. Ideally there will be time to sit with everyone at breakfast, and you'll make that more likely if you stick to your routine in the evening.

Routines can work for school-aged children too; it will teach them day-to-day organisational skills. Sit with each child and help them write up a routine that happens every day. An after-dinner routine might look something like this:

- Finish homework and put it in schoolbag
- Give Mum/Dad school newsletter/note from teacher/birthday invitation
- Check on calendar what is happening at school tomorrow and get relevant gear ready (e.g. books for library)
- Have shower and clean teeth

Depending on whether you work from home, have small children, live alone, work in a full-time job, look after elderly parents or a disabled child, pick some of the suggested routines or add your own unique routines that will help you get through each week. Of course, you might pick only one routine and find that by doing that every day you can carry on with the rest of your work. Or you might choose all of them. Whatever you do, work out what your routine is, write it down, and pin the sheet up where you can see it. Even if you have reminders on your computer, phone or calendar, that sheet will be the physical reminder that starts you working and, if you make space for it, gives you a checklist to tick off as you go.

> TIP: If you want to start small, just choose two tasks to do each day. When I was getting started on my simple-life journey, I found that carrying out two daily tasks helped focus me on what I wanted: a sustainable and productive home. Your two tasks can be anything that you should do every day, but sometimes miss out on doing. My two tasks were making the bed and baking a loaf of bread. Each of them didn't take long to do, but doing them every morning kept me on track all day during those early months. I felt that if I had done just those two things, then I was progressing on the right path, and it usually motivated me to continue with more work.

When you work to any routine that takes a long time to complete, plan for your own relaxation time as well. This is important. It helps support you in your work and it helps you take care of yourself and your health. Even if it's only a 15-minute break to have a cup of tea halfway through a task, take it. You'll return to your work with a clear head and without the resentment that can build up when there's a lot of work and you're the only one doing it.

But if you *are* the only one doing it, why are you? If you're part of a family, January is a good time to discuss housework and work out a few routines so everyone can help. You'll be teaching valuable skills to your children by showing them how to clean, cook and organise. Start when they're young, because most young children love helping, pleasing their parents and feeling they've accomplished something. We all know what would happen if, out of the blue, you asked a teenager who had never been expected to help before to tidy and vacuum a room. A child of about three has the capacity to pick up toys and put a hat and shoes in a certain place. As they grow older, add more small tasks that are appropriate for their age, and explain how housework is done for the benefit of the entire family and that everyone has a responsibility to help. This is not a burden; it is a gift.

Looking after yourself

Whether you're a woman or a man, working in your home full-time or part-time, be careful not to lose your sense of yourself because of the needs of the family. It is important to look after yourself too, no matter how busy you are. It might be a nap when the baby has a sleep, or putting your feet up for fifteen minutes with a cup of tea and a book.

Don't be afraid to serve something really easy for dinner when you've had a tough day. If you have a casserole or soup in the freezer, that will do fine, but it could just as well be baked beans or eggs on toast. The family will survive, and it's better for them to have a sane and happy mum and dad than a perfect house, with everything put away and the perfect meal on the table. Perfection is overrated and unnecessary.

Don't lose touch with your friends or your extended family, either. Strive to be a role model, have an opinion, think about what's best for you or your family and work to achieve that. It will be easier to do all of this if you are well connected to your friends and extended family, and remain active in your community.

Plan time in your schedule to socialise, even if it's just an hour for coffee a couple of times a month. If you can't get out by yourself during the day, make arrangements to meet your friends when your partner is at home after work. If you would prefer to spend time at a craft class, a knitting circle or a men's shed, do it. If you want to go for a walk or to the gym, plan it. Having your own time is important. Getting out and being social will keep you in touch. No doubt you want the best for your family and your home, but you have to include yourself in that too.

ORGANISING AND LOOKING
AFTER YOUR THINGS

Living simply isn't only about saving, reducing waste and slowing down, it's also about looking after what you already own. January is the ideal time to set up systems that will help you do that in the months that follow.

Mending and repairing

Unless you set yourself up to do the household mending, it won't get done. Usually you won't have time to mend a rip or missing button the moment you find it, but if you have a basket or box for all your mending, it will happily sit there until you're ready. If you put aside an hour or two for a mending session, you'll be able to gather all your equipment and work your way through the pile. I'm sure you'll have a feeling of satisfaction when you're finished. When you choose a container to hold the mending, make up a small sewing kit to keep there as well. Many of your repairs and mends will be stitching a hem, sewing on a button or darning a hole. These are all old skills many of us have lost but they're so easy and simple that it won't take long at all to learn how to do them. If you need help getting started, look in the August chapter for some step-by-step guides.

Tagging your children's school things

If you have school-aged children, put aside two or three hours over the last few weeks of January to organise and tag their back-to-school supplies and uniforms. If you have more than one child, you'll be passing on school uniforms to younger children as they grow into them, so it's wise to mark school clothes just with the family name.

Don't forget to mark stationery items, too, as well as lunchboxes, drink bottles, hats and backpacks.

A YEAR OF GIFT-GIVING

When you step away from your old life and begin to settle into simple living, you'll realise that some rituals are the same but you go about them in a different way. Gift-giving is a good example. Of course you may buy some gifts, but most of them will be handmade. This form of gift-giving emphasises the shift in mindset – moving from commercial worth to the thought, love and time that goes into handmade gifts.

Having a plan for gifts and cards will help you save money and reduce anxiety during the year when these dates come up. January is the perfect time to start on that plan. Make sure you add it to your home folder so you can refer to it during the year. You should also make notes as you go, adding ages and interests of children to make it easier next year.

If you know there will be gifts that can't be handmade, make a list of what you need, along with relevant details about who you're buying for. Make sure you've made this an item in your budget. Only buy what's on your list. Don't be tempted by what you see just because it's cheap.

In Australia, the sales carry on right through January, so as long as you have a secret place to store the gifts and you won't be tempted to give them too early, buy them now and save. Remember, there will be mid-year stocktake sales as well, so if gifts are due in the second half of the year, you can wait until then to shop for them.

TIP: For interesting homemade gift ideas, search Pinterest or Google. Many blogs have excellent tutorials for gift-making, so even if you've never done any, you can be guided by what you find online. Alternatively, ask a crafty friend or find a gift-making book at the local library.

READY TO DIVE IN?

Organisation is the ultimate simplifying tool. Living simply gives you a real reason to be organised because it helps you to do everything you want to do. If you're prepared for what will come during the year, running a busy household while working full-time or part-time and connecting with family and friends will be easier. You can enjoy life, knowing you are organised and your home is prepared for most things.

There is no correct way to organise a home. It must suit you and your family and the way you live. I've suggested that you set your calendar, then use the time in January to make up a home folder, work out your routines and menu plans, do a few small modifications to make your home function well all through the year, and prepare for returning to school and work. This may be a starting point for you, or it might reinforce what you're already doing. Even if you're coming to this later in the year, you don't have to wait until next January to get stuck into these tasks – you can plan for the remaining months of the year.

Whenever you're ready, I encourage you to sit and think about your home and work life and plan for the events unique to you and your situation. Be guided by what is in this chapter, but more importantly by your own knowledge of what you and your family need and what has to happen in your home for it to function as the family hub. Whatever it is, organising your year and planning as much as you can will make life better during the months ahead.

february

YOUR MONEY AND YOUR LIFE

'*We make a living by what we get, but
we make a life by what we give.*'
— Winston Churchill

A NEW WAY TO LIVE

Hanno and I made the transition from a frenzied working life to a more simple and beautiful one about fifteen years ago. Our lives now encompass saving what we can, caring for what we own and constantly being aware of what we can mend, recycle, reuse or repurpose. Using these principles, we have transitioned from thoughtless spenders who bought everything we wanted, to mindful, self-reliant people living on a fraction of what we once did. We are also happier than we were before.

Living well on a small amount of money is important for those of us who don't have a lot. It's also important for those who have more than enough but choose a simple, frugal life. If you're debt-free or close to it, you can start reclaiming your life, free to do what you want to do. By taking control of your finances and paying off your debts, you give yourself choices. If you haven't yet made that important adjustment in your life, I hope that reading this book will encourage you in that direction.

We all need a place to live, food to eat, clothes to wear, education and interests to live a rich life, and we need money to do that. At the start of the year, money is high on the priority list because if you don't get the money right, you'll find it harder to manage day-to-day life, no matter how much you earn. So much relies on being financially stable. If you can get some systems set up early in the year, and then monitor what you do in the months to come, you can relax and get on with the real business of living.

Over the years, many of us have realised that promises of unlimited economic growth have turned us into curators of our own junk. Clothing, furnishings and knick-knacks are so cheap now, it's easy to buy what we don't need and to just put it on the credit card. That brings stress when the monthly statement arrives and we have to juggle our finances and decide which bill to pay. Sometimes we think about creating a better work–life balance, but then we're tempted by advertising and by what our friends have, and those thoughts turn towards earning more to pay for it all. We work hard, buy products we are convinced we need, rush around and wonder why we don't feel fulfilled.

Politicians tell us that spending supports the economy, and, conversely, that we should all be saving more. I tend to be swayed by the saving argument; I believe we still support the economy when buying and renting our houses, furnishing them, buying groceries and working for a living. Supporting the economy by buying things we don't need is wasteful and focuses on one aspect of our nation's viability at the expense of many others. Of course we need a healthy economy, but we should also be thinking about quality of life, with time for our families, work–life balance and satisfaction.

Creating a simple life

I remember spending a lot of time walking through shops looking for things to buy. Back then I thought it was 'normal' to do that – and I guess it was, for me and most of my contemporaries. But now I see how wasteful it was in terms of money, time and my abilities. I was capable of much more than passively shopping my time and money away. Now that I have put all that behind me, I spend my time with my family and friends, or learning what I want to know, and, of course, there is the work I choose to do. At the moment, that work is writing this book in the hope of encouraging others to live their own unique life, but there is also cooking, baking, mending, recycling, reading, knitting, gardening and tending the chooks, and so much more.

And that is the real point of these thoughts about frugality. If you think about money in terms of the hours you or your partner spent earning it, you will realise that how you spend your money has a direct relationship to how you spend your time. Being mindful in your spending will reduce your dependence on an ever-increasing income, freeing up the most valuable thing of all: your time.

There are so many options, so many things you could be doing instead of working to pay for a thousand things you don't need, if that's what you do now. You could spend more time with your family, help care for a loved one, volunteer in your community, start a small business, join a craft group, go to university to learn about your interests, travel, learn to play a musical instrument, or follow my lead and use your talents to live contentedly and sustainably in your own home. If you love working but your job is stressful, you could look for another job, possibly on a lower salary, that gives you pleasure and less stress. Or if you are already on a low income, taking control of your finances could help reduce the stress of your situation and possibly open up new options.

Developing the right attitude

Working to lower the cost of living is as much a psychological exercise as it is a physical one. It's important to have the right attitude and I hope your new attitude will help you change your ideas about what success is. I used to think success meant having enough money to buy whatever I wanted. Now I feel I'm successful if I remain independent, self-reliant and active, and if my family is safe, happy and close. I want to do my fair share of the work needed to live the way we do, and now that I've retired, that work gives me countless reasons to get up in the morning. There is a different feeling tied up in the work you do for yourself. Often it doesn't feel like work because you see direct links between the effort and the rewards.

But if you struggle with the changes you're making, you're not alone: I did too. I knew I had to make changes, but in those early days it was difficult. I felt competent doing the work in my home and backyard, but budgeting and saving were much more difficult for me to understand and live with. I doubted myself and was constantly reading about how to manage money to live simply. Then I realised that personal responsibility plays a big part in this, and that the reading had to stop so the doing could start. I had to do the work to create the life I wanted.

If you can let go of the idea that you need everything everyone else has;

if you know deep down in your bones that your real worth is not determined by what you own, then you're well on your way to breaking out of the restrictions of mainstream life. It can take a while to get your head around thrift and to discover the joy of having enough, even if that's just a fraction of what you used to have. There is real liberation in disconnecting from the insatiable desires of over-consumption. When you start seeing the changes in your life brought about by what you're doing, it gets easier, life gets richer and if you keep going, you'll be living the life you dream for yourself.

There is an important aspect of this thriftier way of life that needs to be highlighted before we go any further. Being frugal doesn't mean being cheap. Changing this aspect of your life is intended to open you up to what life has to offer, and you won't see that if you're miserly or selfish. This life has helped me introduce generosity, kindness and thoughtfulness into my everyday life, and while I'm prudent and careful when spending for myself, I make sure I'm openhearted and generous whenever the opportunity arises. I invite friends around for home cooking, send them home with fresh eggs and vegetables, and I'm available if they need me. I became a better friend when I stopped spending.

Being frugal also doesn't mean being miserable. If there is something you're doing now that means a lot to you and makes you happy, don't stop doing it if you can afford it. Paying off a mortgage (the biggest debt most people incur) takes a number of years and you can't cut yourself off from everything while you do so. So be disciplined but plan enjoyment, appreciation and acceptance into your debt-reduction plan.

The real cost of shopping

In discussions such as this the focus is usually on recreational shopping, but I want to comment on grocery shopping too, because it's a real concern for me. When I go supermarket shopping I'm shocked that people purchase so many bottles of water and soft drink. I'm amazed at the number of disposable products and convenience foods bought. I'm not judging anyone, but I do know there is a better way to live that doesn't contribute to harming the planet we live on. Slowing down to live a more simple life will show you that in the most gentle and beautiful way.

When you're establishing how you'll live, I urge you to think about the power of your dollars. If we all use that significant power, we can bring about some of the changes we want to see in the world. Politicians aren't the answer; if you want change, use your money wisely and talk to the shop management when you're not happy with the products you see. If something is over-packaged, tell them you won't buy it until it changes; if you hate the idea of all that plastic rubbish floating in our oceans, choking marine life, stop buying bottled drinks and taking them home in plastic bags. If it breaks your heart to see chickens in cages and pigs in concrete pens they can't turn around in, buy chicken and pork that is grown humanely, or stop eating it. And then tell the shop management what you're doing and why. It's easy nowadays to contact people by email; if you start complaining about the things you don't like and use your money carefully, you and me – we can help change the world.

Customising the recipe

I don't claim to know all the answers, but I can tell you honestly that all the methods I'm about to share with you worked for us and they can work for you too. This is not rocket science; it's about strength, hard work, vision, flexibility and, most importantly, the understanding that you need to change. So take what is here and use it to help reinvent your life. Some things may not work for you; others may need modifying to suit you, your situation and your values. It's like a recipe for a meal you think you'll really enjoy, but when you cook it, you modify it. You add a few things, leave a couple of things out, and in the end, you have a meal you absolutely love because it's been customised to your taste. So just get the information in your head, be flexible and make it work for you.

Remember too that as you age, your circumstances change and you have to keep thinking about what you want from life. Don't be afraid to modify things. Remain flexible in your thinking and try to stay open to new ideas. And I hope that at every stage you actively look for the joy in life and celebrate it.

As you read through this chapter, please be mindful of the fact that I voluntarily spend a lot of time at home. Even though I still work as a writer, it's done at home and I have the time to slot in many tasks such as baking, cooking from scratch, gardening, sewing and knitting. Don't think for one minute you have to do exactly what I do. When you have more time, do more, but don't work yourself into the ground with a job, small children to look after and/or all the other responsibilities of modern life. Remember that your simple life is not just this year or next year. It's for the rest of the eighty-plus years I hope you live. There are seasons in everyone's life. There will come a day when you have more time and can then potter around at home doing everything you want to do.

By taking control of your finances and paying off your debts, you give yourself choices.

WORKING FOR A LIVING

While I knew from a young age that I would work when I was older, it didn't occur to me until much later how vital work is. Work builds character, families, neighbourhoods and nations. I can say without a doubt now that I am the person I am because of the work I've done – both in the workforce and at home. The daily effort of earning a living and keeping a home operating creates layer upon layer of experience, skill, confidence, trust, character, responsibility and many other traits. In the next section we'll look at some of the most common demographic categories in relation to working life:

1. Starting out
2. Single life
3. Living on one income and stay-at-home-parent families
4. Working couples with children
5. Retirement

There are suggestions and information unique to each period, but read all of them because you may pick up something you can modify to fit your situation.

Starting out

When you leave school and launch yourself into the workforce you give structure to your days, you develop skills and knowledge and you start contributing to the wealth of your country. The money you earn will also allow you to start acquiring assets, such as clothes, a phone, computer or iPad, and will enable you to live the way you wish to live. Slowly, over the course of many years, you'll probably save to buy a home. I didn't realise how important that was until I retired. I know now that I would feel very insecure if I was renting at this stage of life. That thought might seem a million miles away for you right now, but I encourage you to develop thrifty habits early, budget, save, do your fair share and work for what you get.

Don't expect to have everything your parents have straight away. What you've grown up with is the accumulation of your parents' working life. When they started out, things were basic and they built what they have over the years. You'll need to buy a few things for your own life along the way, and you should balance that with saving. Find a ratio that works for you, using this as a guide: spend about 60 per cent of what you earn on things you need – rent, food, transport and so on – about 20 per cent on things you want, and about 20 per cent on savings. The savings component might be divided between a few different accounts: emergency fund, house deposit and travel fund, for instance. It might be several years before your thoughts turn to buying your own home, but it's a good idea to start saving for it as early as possible. Going into home ownership with a healthy deposit puts you in a very good position, and even if it means making a few sacrifices along the way, it's well worth it.

The emphasis in this period is to establish good budgeting and saving habits. If you can go through your twenties without incurring any debt, you'll be well ahead in your thirties. That includes credit card debt, which sometimes starts off innocently but can spiral out of control because the interest rate on credit cards is very high. Always remember the transient nature of fashion and holidays – you won't like having to pay for them long after they've lost their shine.

You started this stage with no debt and if you can reach your thirties and forties with no debt other than a mortgage, you'll be in the best possible position. Anything is possible now: take advantage of it in every way you can.

ACTION PLAN

- Resist the urge to spend. Don't follow what everyone else does.
- Create a budget.
- Establish good frugal habits such as taking lunch to work, shopping at secondhand stores and using public transport.
- Do some research and ask people you know about saving for retirement.
- If you decide to get a credit card, make sure you know the amount of interest you'll pay and avoid it by paying off the full debt every month.
- When you change jobs, make sure you keep your superannuation in one fund.

Single life

Single life includes young singles, single parents and divorced singles whose children have left home (older couples are increasingly divorcing at retirement age). There are also differing levels of assets, but no matter what your age or financial status, a budget will be beneficial and you should be saving.

When you're single you don't have to take anyone else's opinion into account when budgeting; however, you won't have anyone to share the expenses with either (unless you live in a share house). Long-term plans might seem harder to make when you're on your own, but make them anyway and don't put off budgeting and saving.

And if you do form a relationship with someone, make sure their values are similar to yours. It will be almost impossible to live simply and frugally if the person you love has no issue with living beyond their means. Have those talks early. Hopefully you'll discover both of you want the same kind of future, and then you'll be able to share the enjoyment of planning a life together.

Safeguarding your future is important now, particularly if you are a single parent. Look into death and disability insurance so that if anything does happen to you, the children will be financially secure, and you'll all be protected. Young singles should start thinking about retirement, either in the form of superannuation or retirement saving. Starting early, keeping all your contributions in one fund, even when you change jobs, and adding small contributions when and if you can, should guarantee you a good nest egg. By the time you reach retirement age, there probably won't be much in the way of government assistance.

If you're newly single after having separated from your partner, consult a financial planner about the breakup of your joint assets. If you're close to retirement age, it's probably a good idea to sell the family home jointly and split the money rather than being stuck with the property. Accepting the home as your part of the settlement, while your partner takes the cash assets and superannuation, will give you a place to live but you may have to downsize to make it work. You'll know the value of the cash assets and superannuation but you won't know what you'll get from the house until it's sold. Again, talking with a good financial planner may give you a better idea about a sensible and practical way forward.

Whether you're a young single or newly single, one of the most important things to do is to look after you. All aspects of your life – family, health, finance, work, home and sustainability – can be tremendous supports for you. So take it slowly, think about the future as well as today, and enjoy life.

- Research options such as life insurance or income protection, particularly if you're a single parent.
- Newly single? Consult a financial planner about the breakup of assets and how to structure your single finances. Take control of your finances and make sure you alone have access to your bank accounts.
- All through your working life, have only one superannuation fund. Give the details of it to your new employer when you start work. This will maximise the potential of your investments and save on fees.
- Create a budget you can live with.
- See if you can get a better deal from your electricity, internet, phone and insurance providers.

Living on one income/stay-at-home parents

When I was young it was unusual for both parents to work outside the home. Usually, the man would go out to work and the woman would raise the children and look after the house. Although it's less common now, it is still an option for one partner – male or female – to continue working while the other stays at home to look after the children. It makes sense for the person who enjoys work the most and makes the most money to be the one who's employed. The at-home partner works in the home, looking after the children, shopping carefully, cooking meals from scratch, baking, making green cleaners and doing as much vegie growing, preserving, mending and recycling as possible. When your children are babies and toddlers, childcare and housework take a lot of time, often extending into the night. When the employed partner is home, they should be sharing the housework. You'll be tired at lot during this stage but working as a team will get you through it. Remember, it doesn't last forever.

Two jobs, both equally important: one in paid employment and one consciously working to save as much as possible to enable the family to live on less than they earn. Together, working like this, you can build your own healthy domestic economy.

- Research insurance options such as life insurance, death and disability or income protection.
- Make sure you're named as co-owner on every one of your family assets. Check it this month and adjust the paperwork if you need to be added.
- See if you can cut down on your food bill or get better quality at the same price. You'll find some good ideas in the next chapter.
- Teach your children to shop for food and cook, not only because they're skills they should have but also so they can give you some time out when you need it.

How you spend your money
has a direct relationship
to how you spend your time.

Working couple with kids

When both partners are working, there is a lot less time available for home-based, money-saving tasks. That's where organisation, routines and working as a team come into play. Menu planning, permanent shopping lists, family calendars, slow cooking and batch cooking will all help you live simply even when you have less time at home. If you share the same values as your partner and can do this together, it will be easier. And if you want to cut back on your working hours, use the ideas in this book to reduce your household costs so you can give yourself that option.

Figure out who will do what housework, and expect your children to help. They won't be able to contribute financially, but they can help with the house and yard work, and in doing so make a real contribution to the family. Even small children are able to assist if you give them tasks they can manage.

Make sure you allocate family time too. It doesn't have to be expensive: plan a movie night, a swim at the beach, a hike or a bike ride. Don't fall into the habit of giving your children expensive clothes, gifts or holidays, although everyone should have a small amount of pocket money to help teach the value of money. All your children want when they're growing up is to be loved and to spend time with parents who enjoy being with them. There will be a happy balance between work and family somewhere; you just have to find it.

A lot of balancing goes on in this stage of your life. You want to save or pay off your mortgage while finding joy and happiness in your everyday life. There will be highs and lows, but remember you're not alone, and that you don't have to give your children the best 'stuff' for them to be their best. Value this time – there will come a day when the kids fly the coop and it's just you and your partner again. And maybe then you can spread your wings.

ACTION PLAN

- Make up a list of frugal family entertainment ideas and schedule them on your calendar.
- During the school holidays, take your children grocery shopping and to the farmers' market to teach them about food choices.
- Go over your budget to see if there are any money leaks.
- If you've been budgeting for a while, track your money again for a month to check how much you're spending.

- Make sure all your superannuation is in one fund. Your partner should have theirs in a single fund too.
- Read next month's food chapter for time-saving ideas to help put home-cooked meals on your family's table.

Retirement

The best way to prepare for your retirement and older age is to have a home you can live in; be debt-free or close to it; know, or be ready to learn, the things you want to do after you leave work; and have family, friends and hobbies to fill your days. When you get to this point, you will ideally have paid off the mortgage or be ready to downsize to pay it off. Nothing you can do or plan for will help you in later life more than owning your home. If you're renting and know that you'll continue renting in the future, try to find a stable rental, close to family and friends. If you can get a long lease, that will be a bonus.

When you leave work for good, you'll spend a lot of time at home, so take the time to organise and declutter your home within the first few months. Make it the kind of place you feel comfortable in and want to invite family and friends around to. If you're going to be doing more cooking, or taking up a hobby, you might be able to rearrange furniture and cupboard storage to better suit what you'll now spend time on.

During this time of self-evaluation, it's a good idea to go through your budget again and make sure your calculations are correct. Work out ways of staying within your budget, because now there will be much less money coming in and you must safeguard what you have. The Australian government's MoneySmart website has useful information on planning for managing your income in retirement (web address in the Resources).

Retirement can be a joyous time if you're prepared for it and have already done the hard work of reducing your spending. All those plans and generous dreams you had while you were working can come true. Now is your time; enjoy it.

ACTION PLAN

- Up until now you've been focused on saving. Now you still have to save, but your focus will move towards management of your existing savings.
- If you haven't already done so, apply for a Seniors Card and talk to the people at Centrelink to see if there are benefits or concessions you're entitled to.
- Keep your Seniors Card or Pensioner Concession Card in your wallet so you have it with you to claim discounts and concessions.
- Make sure you know and understand your financial situation. Create a new retirement budget, taking your concessions into account.
- Talk to a financial planner if you need help with your money.

I feel I'm successful if I remain independent, self-reliant and active, and if my family is safe, happy and close.

THE GENDER GAP

Throughout the developed world, there is a significant difference between what men and women earn. In Australia the gap is currently around 17 per cent. All through their working lives, women earn less than men even when doing the same type of job; they move in and out of employment during the years they have babies, and often work part-time when they do return to work. As such, a woman's overall lifetime income is likely to be much lower than a man's. As well as being unfair, this means that women's superannuation is much lower than that of their male counterparts, putting them in a precarious situation as they age.

I wish I could advise on a solution to this problem. I wish we had politicians strong enough to stand up and work towards real change. I don't have all the answers, but I do have some suggestions:

- Retain and develop your skills by working whenever you can. If you keep up with the changes in your field, you'll be able to get back to employment or your career when you're able to or you need to.
- If you are married or in a de facto relationship, it's wise to have a joint account so you can both access the bank statements, check online what's going in and what's going out, and have financial control over the account. That is important. If you do want some money that is yours alone, have a separate account that only you can access.
- Have or share control of the budgeting so you get a full picture of your finances. List your assets, know what you spend on groceries and monthly bills, know how much you owe on your mortgage as well as how much you're paying in interest.
- You should both have life insurance with each other as the beneficiary, so that in the unfortunate situation of one of you dying early, the surviving partner and the children will have some funds to carry on.
- Make sure your name is alongside your partner's on the deed to any property you buy and that you're officially the co-owner of your car. Have your own credit card, as it will help you build a credit history. Always pay it off on time and don't get caught up with buying just because you can.

None of this will completely protect you from the financial problems that might occur if your partner dies or you separate, but it will help you get on your feet again because you won't have to start learning everything from scratch.

MANAGING YOUR FINANCIAL LIFE

If you've never felt the need to make up a budget before, or you think it's too difficult, I hope you believe in me enough to at least read through this entire chapter. I'll try to change your mind. Being honest and sensible about your own economic situation and thinking about your values and what you dream for your future is so important. If you combine that with your own customised financial plan you'll have the best way to fulfil those dreams. I wrote about this subject in depth in *Down to Earth*, but it's so much a part of the foundation of this way of living that it's well worth going over the basics again.

We all need to fully understand our own financial situation. We should know how much money is coming in, how much we owe, how much we spend, and what we spend it on. The goal is to get to the point where you can pay your bills every week and still have money to save or put aside for something you really want. This way of life is not about being miserly; it's the first step towards living well and controlling your finances instead of them controlling you. So, take a deep breath – you're about to start changing your life.

Tracking your spending

Tracking your spending is recording everything you spend money on, from the mortgage payments right down to a cup of tea at a cafe. You must know what you spend in order to make a realistic budget, but a good side benefit is that you'll also know just how much you're spending on things you don't need.

It can be a confronting exercise, especially if you're doing it with a partner in order to create a combined budget, but I encourage you to be truthful, no matter what that truth is. You also have to be thoughtful and kind – if one or both of you have been overspending, blaming each other does no one any good. Start your budgeting in a positive frame of mind and agree there will be no blame. This is a new beginning.

Here are three ways to track your spending:

1. Keep a small notebook and pen with you and whenever you spend, write it down.
2. Collect every receipt and when you come home, add them up and record the totals. Remember to include online purchases and bills, which won't give you a paper receipt.
3. Use a smartphone app. See the Resources for some options.

Once you've tracked your spending for a month, you'll be able to identify two important things: what you spend money on, and what your non-essential spending is.

Non-essential spending is money that we don't have to spend, but do. It's magazines, takeaway coffee, movies, eating out, chocolate, iTunes, shoes, clothes, accessories, taxis, fast food, alcohol, soft drinks or bottles of water. If you add up the money you spend on those non-essential things in a month, I'm sure you'll be surprised.

Cutting back non-essential spending

Changing your spending behaviour is rarely about the big things. The big-ticket items stand out and we notice them. They make us stop and question whether we can afford to buy them. The small things like coffees and magazines are such a part of modern life, we take them for granted. We buy them without thinking and it's only when we add up the cost over a month or a year that we realise just how much we're spending on throwaway products. If you can harness that money and put it towards debt repayment, or even towards the groceries you need this month, it's a step in the right direction.

Let's make one exception to this, though. The road to being debt-free is long, and we all need to enjoy life as we work towards our goals. If there's something special you enjoy or that means a lot to you, keep doing it. The occasional date night with your partner is an investment in your relationship. Coffee with a friend helps maintain that friendship. It's wise to keep those rituals going; in doing so, you feel like you're looking after yourself.

Once you've decided where you can cut back, then you go to the next step: working out a budget.

Creating a budget

When I came to this point many years ago I was in a bit of a panic. I thought a budget would restrict me. It soon became obvious that instead of restricting me, my budget showed me how much cash I had, what I needed to allow for and how much was left over for spending or saving. That budget was like a map showing me a way forward. There was no more not knowing if I had enough money but spending it anyway – it was all written down in black and white.

Here are the steps to take when creating a budget:

1. Decide what time period your budget will cover – a week, fortnight or month. Matching your budget period to your pay period will make things easier, so if you get paid monthly, do a monthly budget.

2. Write a list of all the spending categories: mortgage/rent, electricity, gas, food, fuel, entertainment, insurance and so on.

3. Estimate how much you spend on each category, using past bills and the information you gathered when tracking your spending. If you don't have past bills, make an estimate. Your first year's budget isn't always accurate but it can be adjusted as you go through the year.

4. Add it all up, and see whether it's more or less than your income for the same period.

5. Work out if there are any expenses you could manage better – your phone plans, internet and car/health/home insurance, for example – and if there are any expenses you can cut out completely, such as a second car or pay TV. Then adjust the figures, always staying realistic, until you're happy with the expenditure versus the income.

TIP: The Australian government's Moneysmart website has an excellent guide to budgeting. You can write your budget online using its forms, then print it out. See the Resources for more information.

Your budget will be your personal spending map from now on. Refer to it often to make sure it's accurate and that you're sticking to it. Update it whenever there's a change to your income (for example, pay rises, parental leave or a job gained or lost) or expenditure (changing mobile phone plans, interest rate adjustments, new loans), or every few years.

Building up an emergency fund

Unfortunately, even when we decide to follow a more frugal path, unexpected expenses still crop up. I remember when Hanno and I first became much more prudent with our spending, an emergency trip to the vet with both our dogs ended up costing us $800. Your car might need new tyres, the fridge might break down or you might have to pay for travel and accommodation if a relative becomes ill. It could be anything. Having a stash of money put aside for these emergencies will ensure you don't end up relying on your credit card to cover them. You don't want extra debt repayments when you're trying to create new habits.

Even though saving for an emergency fund might seem like an added burden, when it's established it will provide you with a feeling of comfort and security. You'll know that even if there is an unexpected emergency, you'll be able to cover it while still proceeding along your chosen frugal path. And remember – when you use some or all of your emergency fund, you'll need to rebuild it.

To get it started, decide how much you're going to save. It could be $1000 or $5000; it might be enough to cover your living expenses for a certain period of time, maybe three months. It's your decision.

Open a bank account specifically for the emergency fund, then decide how much you'll add each week or month and how you'll come up with that money. If you get any birthday money or windfalls, put that money into your emergency fund until it's at your desired level. If you don't have any extra cash, see if you can find it by giving something up.

When you have the money saved, don't be tempted to spend it. It's your safety net. It's there to help you through the sudden and unexpected things that life sometimes throws your way.

Saving

After you've built an emergency fund, it's a good time to think about saving. Some things you might want or need to save for are:

- House deposit
- Home improvements
- Car upgrade
- Time off work with a new baby
- Education (your own or your kids')
- Travel/holiday
- Retirement
- Investments

If you are disciplined in your saving and sensible in the goals you set, you'll be able to achieve these goals without increasing your debt. For example, you'll be able to pay for a modest family holiday upfront instead of putting a more lavish one on a credit card and then taking months to pay it off. You'll enjoy the holiday much more that way and be able to start saving for the next one as soon as you're home again. Or if you know you'll need to upgrade your car in a year or so, work out how much you can save in that time and make your decision about what to buy according to your budget, rather than buying whichever car you like the look of and then carrying the resulting debt burden for years.

If you manage your money really well, you can save for these things at the same time as reducing your existing debt and/or paying off a mortgage.

TIP: Keep your savings in a separate account from your everyday one and don't be tempted to dip into it for anything else. Think about whether you need an account for each savings goal.

Paying off the mortgage

There is one simple exercise that I hope will convince you about the merits of paying off your mortgage – or any large loan – early. Enter your loan amount and interest rate into an online mortgage calculator, then play around with the loan length and see how much interest you will save by paying it off faster. You can also change monthly payments to fortnightly. Now add an extra payment every three months, or an extra hundred dollars to each payment, and note the huge reduction in the amount you have to pay back.

To give you a better idea, I've done some sample calculations in a mortgage calculator. I used a hypothetical $300 000 loan with an interest rate of 5 per cent. Here are the figures:

MONTHLY REPAYMENTS	LOAN LENGTH	TOTAL INTEREST PAID
$1755	25 years	$220 256
$1855	22.5 years	$199 846
$1955	20.5 years	$179 556
$2155	17.5 years	$149 663

As you can see, increasing your repayments by $100 per month reduces the length of this loan by two and a half years, and reduces the interest paid by more than $20 000 over the life of the loan. A further $100 per month takes another two and a half years and another $20 000 off your loan. Then the extra payments start to have increasing benefits: a *further* $100 per month (that is, $300 more per month than the minimum repayment) reduces the length of the loan by a further *three* years (seven and a half years shorter than the original twenty-five years) and knocks a further *$30 000* off the total interest paid. That's a huge amount, but even an extra $20 a week makes a difference. And if you can't commit to regular higher payments, try to put any spare money – a tax rebate, for instance, or a payment for extra work you took on – towards the mortgage. Every bit helps.

Imagine being mortgage-free and living in your own home when the children are ready to go to work or university, rather than still having many years of payments ahead of you. I know people tend to have much bigger loans now, but Hanno and I paid off our twenty-five-year home loan in eight years. It was tough at times, but worth all of it when we came to that final payment. If you knuckle down to pay it off faster, you'll give yourself options. If you're not tied to a mortgage you won't be tied to a job either.

> TIP: Each bank has different loan-repayment rules. If you're applying for a new loan, make sure you choose one with the option to make extra payments, and if your current lender doesn't allow this, consider changing to one that does.

ORGANISING YOUR MONEY

Bank accounts

Most of us will have two types of spending: the regular bills that we pay monthly, quarterly or yearly, such as electricity, phone, internet and insurance, and the more irregular expenses such as groceries, fuel, transport and so on. We pay the former online by direct debit, BPAY, PayPal or credit card, and use cash for the latter. If you have a computer, it's worth the effort to sit down and organise automatic direct debits, regular payments and a list of regular payees to make your bill payments as efficient as possible so you avoid incurring late fees. A late mortgage payment might mean a strike against you on your credit rating. Make sure that never happens.

It's easier to manage money if you have one account just for your spending (bills, debit card and cash withdrawals) and a separate one (or several) for your savings. Leave enough money in the spending account for the bills you need to pay this month, as well as the quarterly, six-monthly and annual bills you're putting aside money for. This is the account to have your pay deposited into. From your budget you should have a set amount to save each pay period, so when all the bills are paid and money set aside for other expenses, transfer that amount to your savings account.

Cash and cash envelopes

Many people use debit or credit cards to spend their money – there is no problem with that if it works for you and you're not incurring fees. I have always found that I have a better idea of what I'm spending if I use cash instead of cards. When I have to hand over a fifty-dollar note, I feel it, but I don't when I hand over a card to pay the same amount. If you're struggling with your budget or if you're still over-spending, I encourage you to put the cards away for a while and try working with cash.

One problem with cash is that it's a temptation when you have it in your purse. To avoid this problem, when we withdraw cash from the bank every month we put it into envelopes or zip-lock bags earmarked for particular budget categories – groceries, petrol, garden supplies and so on. My budget tells me how much to put into each bag. When I go shopping, I take money from these envelopes and then return any change. During the month, I can see the amount getting smaller and I know exactly how much I have left to spend. We can also take money we haven't used from one envelope to pay for something else that may have been more expensive than expected that month. Whatever is left in the envelopes at the end of the month – and there always is some left over – can be added to our savings.

It will take you a few months to have this system rolling along effortlessly, but when it does, it works very well.

Life is made wonderful by living splendidly within our means.

THE BIG JOYOUS PICTURE

I have found that my sense of contentment increases when I want less and have less to look after. I hope that reading this chapter will help you discover that too. Life is made wonderful by living splendidly within our means, not by the possessions we surround ourselves with. If you have a steady income, be it from a job, a business, investments, a pension or welfare, and can consistently live on less than your income, you'll be doing okay. If you can manage to save the extra, you'll be doing even better. Once you've made the shift from spender to saver, I hope you see the wisdom in what you're doing, from financial, health and environmental perspectives, as well as from a lifestyle one. And don't downplay the lifestyle angle: everyone wants to feel they're living well and being productive, no matter how their income is derived.

When you see your friends in a new car, or changing with the fashions, you'll most likely want to remind yourself that your life provides plenty of satisfaction and that even though you like the new things your friends have, you don't want them; the cost is too high, no matter what it is. Your debt is reducing, not going up, and that will give you a measure of satisfaction and accomplishment that no amount of new clothes or travel can match.

Much of what I suggest is aimed at both reducing spending and increasing contentment: thrift connects so much of what we do in our simple lives. Figure out how to cut your costs, stick to a budget and pay off your debts. These things take time, so enjoy everything that life offers as you live it. Don't close yourself off to the people around you. Remain interested, take chances, learn new things, develop the person you want to be. This can be tough at times, and not everything will go according to plan, but keep your eye on where you're heading and know that all this work, caution and forethought will pay off. Your reward won't just be living debt-free, it will be the choices and options that will give you, as well as all the joy you find along the way.

march

A FOOD REVOLUTION

*'One cannot think well, love well, sleep well,
if one has not dined well.'*
– Virginia Woolf

GOING BACK TO BASICS

I want to focus on food early in the year because we all need a plan to manage our food and a budget with which to buy it. If you think about your food strategy in the early months, it will set you up to wisely manage your food shopping, cooking, storage and budgets in those that follow.

Of all the activities we deal with in simple life, food is the one that all of us know about and spend money on. We may not all be making cheese, keeping chickens, gardening, sewing, recycling, riding bikes or budgeting, but we are all eating. Food keeps us alive.

Food has undergone a splendid revolution in the past decade, which, for many of us, has changed what we eat, how we cook and where we buy. There's been a big move towards grow-your-own, too, and there are many more vegetable gardens, chickens and bees in backyards. An ever-growing group of people wants to know where their food comes from, and the ethics of food and animal husbandry now play a big part in whether or not food is purchased. But there is still a long way to go. Animals and poultry are still kept in shameful conditions and given food that encourages growth rather than health. Preservatives and artificial additives have become a common part of processed food, even though research hasn't been able to eliminate the possibility of negative repercussions for all those secret decisions made about the food we eat. My hope is that we'll know more in the coming years. In the meantime, I'll continue to cook from scratch.

The choices we make about the food we buy are still largely driven by cost, and while for many people this is unavoidable, the strategies in this book outline many ways to reduce food waste and lower the cost of food by shopping for ingredients rather than for convenience foods. I hope that food shopping will continue to move away from supermarkets and out into the communities where greengrocers, farmers' markets, fishmongers, family butchers, spice merchants, Asian grocers, delicatessens and community gardens are waiting to offer value for money. That is where you'll find the good food, and if you start supporting the sellers who are the primary producers, or those associated with them, in time there will be more of those independent provedores, and supermarkets will begin to lose their powerful grip on our purses and wallets.

Currently, supermarkets dictate what we eat. They tell farmers and food companies how to produce what they want to sell, and in doing so, they control the variety and quality of food. And if you believe what you read about primary producers not getting a fair price for their produce – and I do – then all of us who care about our food chain should do something about it. It's not difficult to help: we just need to shop at the businesses we value and support them with our dollars.

Cooking from scratch

I've been cooking from scratch on and off since I started cooking nearly fifty years ago. It makes sense to me because it's tastier, it's cheaper and I know what's in our food. Years ago, I went through my 'convenience phase' of adding gravy powder to my gravy, buying pastry cases and making stock with stock cubes, but none of these habits lasted long. My gravy didn't taste as good, the pastry I bought was capable of sitting on the shelf for weeks (and tasted like it), and I remembered that making stock with bones and herbs was much more satisfying than boiling water and stirring in a cube of who-knows-what. I am much more cautious of synthetic food preservatives and additives than I am of the fungus and bacteria they prevent. If I want to provide my family with healthy and safe meals, I prefer to use fresh food, add only natural seasonings and cook it from scratch. We want to eat real food.

When you cook your own meals from scratch, I doubt you will add sulphites, nitrates, gums, MSG, artificial colourings or flavours; yet they're common ingredients in foods on supermarket shelves. They have to be, because many of those foods have to sit on the shelf for long periods before they're purchased. They're added to keep food 'fresh', to enhance colour and flavour, and to replace certain food properties that are removed during processing. Some additives are harmless and some cause problems, so if you buy processed foods or pre-prepared meals, it's wise to read the labels and have some understanding of what you're reading.

I've noticed many internet sites claiming to use basic recipes and from-scratch cooking, but they're still using packets of soup mix, jars of commercial sauce and many of the other convenience foods available on supermarket shelves. That isn't cooking from scratch. You can see how many additives are in a packet of soup mix just by reading the label. As far as I'm concerned, cooking from scratch is the basic cooking our grandmothers did, which uses fresh ingredients and nothing that contains preservatives or artificial colours or flavours. So bread, cakes and biscuits are made with basic flour, fruit or cocoa rather than with pre-mixes, cake mixes or frozen commercial cookie doughs. Flavour is built up in savoury food by caramelisation, spices and herbs. Raw foods such as salads are made using the freshest in-season produce and dressed with ingredients you mix at home. Soups are made with marrow bones; grains are soaked; yoghurt, sauces, relishes and cordials are made from scratch. You might be a long way from that now, but small steps will get you there.

When I speak to the people I meet at my library talks and workshops, the most common complaint I hear is that cooking from scratch takes too much time. And yes, I agree that if you make a meal every night from scratch, you'll spend a lot of time at the stove. So you have to be smart about it and work out a few shortcuts and time-savers. My sanity is saved by double-batch cooking and my slow cooker. Once-a-month cooking is also popular, but I'm not motivated enough to do it for just the two of us. If you are, it's a great way to eat home-cooked food every night. See the Resources for more information.

Batch cooking

A wonderful habit to get into is doing some batch cooking on the weekends. If you have a spare couple of hours, have a cooking session and then you'll have three or four meals in the freezer for during the week. In the morning, transfer one meal from the freezer to the fridge. When you come home from work, or when you've finished your home chores, you know the meal is there; all you have to do is warm it up. If there is someone around to help, get them to set the table and prepare some drinks. Goodbye, takeaways and convenience foods! But I know that many of you don't have that spare time on the weekends, and even if you do, you're so tired that cooking is the last thing you want to give two hours to.

There is another way to squirrel away a meal or two without going to much extra effort: many meals that you can cook on a weeknight can easily be doubled up. You'll eat half straight away, and freeze the other half for later. Curry, stew, soups, pizza, stroganoff and meatballs in sauce can all be made in a double batch and the second half frozen. You can also be creative and turn one meal into a different meal, such as using meat sauce for pasta one night and tacos the next. Any roast meat or chicken can be eaten as a hot roast one night and turned into a quick curry, hash or stir-fry the following night, or stored in the freezer with your increasing stash of home-cooked meals. If one chicken is enough for your family for one meal, then cook two at a time, save the second in the fridge or pick the meat off the bones and store it in portions in the freezer. It saves electricity/gas, time and effort. If you can get into this habit of cooking double batches, and you seal them and mark them correctly, you'll have a meal waiting in the freezer on those nights when you run late or you're just too tired to cook everything from scratch.

Slow cooking

Another cooking method that will save your sanity and time is slow cooking. Just load the slow cooker in the morning before you go to work, turn it on low, make sure it's on a sturdy surface and that the cord is safety tucked away, and you can leave it all day to cook. All stews, soups, or curries can be made this way, and corned beef is soft and tender after a few hours of slow cooking. If you have a large slow cooker, make a double batch and freeze half of it.

I don't often recommend buying new appliances, but if you don't have a slow cooker and you're a family who likes soups and casseroles, it would be wise economy to buy one.

SHOPPING FOR FOOD

I've gone from being an ordinary housewife, using my food budget to provide as much as I can for the money I have, to being someone who looks for fresh food that's been produced locally and ethically. Now I buy free-range, and if I can't get that, I'll go without and use something else. It's easily done. I always check labels, and never buy products from compromised locations such as China and Thailand. I only want to be a part of a food chain that considers kindness and quality of life along with nutritional values and profit.

It gives me a feeling of purpose to select, prepare and serve food for Hanno and me. I see it as an important part of my homemaking to provide food that will keep us healthy and support our values. I love when our family gets together and we sit around the kitchen table and share a meal. That is the time when we catch up with each other's news, forge strong connections and solidify our family ties. Serving food that reflects our values fits very well into that scenario.

Making the most of your food budget

I have no doubt that if you do all your food and grocery shopping at the supermarket, you'll miss some of the bargains that can be found out in the community. Ask your friends and neighbours if they shop at the local butcher, greengrocer, dairy or fishmonger. Find out which local markets are the best. Many markets are open every weekend, and if you find a good one, you may be able to shop there for fruit, vegetables, fish and meat.

If you have good neighbours or close friends, you might do some bulk-buying with them to make real savings. Don't rule out bulk-buying even if you're single or there's just the two of you. All you need is a chest freezer. Sometimes we buy a side of pork or lamb or a forequarter of beef and have it cut and packed to order by the butcher, including sausages and mince if we want them. If you bulk-buy meat you'll pay the same reduced price per kilo for the whole side or quarter. That price varies, but often it's about half what you'd pay in the supermarket. Find a butcher near you and phone them for a quote. If you live in a city and you're close to the fruit and vegetable markets or fish markets, you might be able to do the same thing there.

Living well on a small amount of money is not about the big choices. It's a series of consistent decisions to live on the budget you've defined for yourself. It's about shopping for bargains and making as much at home as you can. If you have the time to make some of the things you now buy, you'll save money, and probably get a better product. If you can reduce your grocery bill, you'll be able to make savings every time you shop.

When you look at the savings you're making on your groceries, you could choose to reduce your food budget and use the saved money for debt reduction, or keep your budget at the same level and buy organic produce. The choice is yours to make.

I just want to remind you that it is rare to make big savings doing this. It's all about consistent, regular small savings when you do the grocery shopping, but menu planning, shopping for bargains, stockpiling and buying less food because you grow it and make it yourself, will all make a difference. So don't think small savings aren't worth it; they add up. When you look back over a year, you'll be surprised just how much you were able to save by sticking to your plan.

> TIP: Don't always rely on meat as your main protein. Legumes, grains, fish, eggs and tofu can all be part of a well-considered menu plan.

Other things you could do to provide healthy, thrifty food include:

- Shop for ingredients rather than convenience foods, including washed salads, sliced or grated cheese, bottled sauces or packets of prepared spices. By doing the work of washing, grating and so on, you'll save a lot of money and develop your skills in the kitchen.
- Make your own seasoning mixes.
- Fruit juice can be expensive. It's much better to grow your own or buy oranges or pineapples in season and squeeze your own juice. Squeezed juice stores very well in the freezer.
- Buy in season: fruit and vegetables in season are usually cheaper and fresher.
- Buy cheaper cuts of meat, like shoulder of lamb or pork instead of the leg, and chuck steak, skirt steak, gravy beef and shin beef. All these cuts contain cartilage that breaks down with long slow cooking to give you natural gelatine in your food. That is very good for you. There's much more to be read about this in the excellent book *Nourishing Traditions* (see the Resources).
- Use your leftovers. Learning how to deal with leftover food can stretch one dinner into two, or at the very least provide lunch the following day.
- Pack lunchboxes for work or school with food cooked from scratch.
- 'Don't eat anything your great-great-grandmother wouldn't recognise as food,' food expert Michael Pollan says in his excellent *New York Times Magazine* article, 'Unhappy Meals'. Forget the expensive and over-processed Corn Flakes or Coco Pops and go for rolled oats or semolina instead. Don't buy instant oats (or instant anything); buy rolled or steel-cut oats or barley. They will usually be cheaper and provide at least the same, if not better, nutrition.

TIP: There is a wonderful app called Paprika that helps you browse and collect recipes and store them in an organised way. You can drag and drop recipes into a calendar for your menu plan, and it makes up a shopping list with ingredients you need. I don't like recommending things to buy, but this app saves time, it's easy to use and it helps with menu planning, recipe collection and shopping lists more than anything else I've tried. See the Resources for more details.

Menu planning

If you can put aside some time to plan a month's menus, you'll go a long way towards saving money when you do your shopping, you'll cut down on food wastage, and you'll feel more in control. Start your menu list with your family's favourite meals and then add a few new ones you want to try. Make up your week's shopping list according to what you need for your first week. That's all you need to do to start, and when you're halfway through your first week, add more meals to your second week. It's fine to repeat easy and favourite meals.

I encourage you to start menu planning in an organised way. You have to deal with recipes, calendars and shopping lists, so if you can combine them all in one app, book or spreadsheet, it will make the task much easier.

There are two common ways to menu plan: you can shop with a list and buy what is on special and in season, then menu plan when you have your supplies. Or you can collect supermarket flyers and plan the menus before you go shopping. I think the second method is the safest, because you will be able to shop for everything you need if you already know what you'll be making. Remain flexible, and if you see something that isn't on your list, buy it for the following week if it will keep, or change one of your meals to include what you find.

Whichever way you do it, here are some points worth remembering:

- Check your fridge and pantry to see what you have on hand and what needs to be used in the next day or so. Plan the next meal to use those foods.
- Be flexible. Write your shopping list according to your meal plans, but if you see an ingredient at a good price or something seasonal that you want to try, don't restrict yourself just because you have your meals already listed.
- Plan to use leftovers. Cooking one large meal such as a roast or double the amount of pasta sauce, casserole or soup will feed everyone for two nights.
- If you're growing food in the backyard, use your fresh harvests in your meal plans.
- Plan with seasons in mind. Food only available during a particular season will add interest and variety to your meals.
- Include your family or flatmates in the menu planning and share the cooking as well as the planning.

Permanent shopping list

Menu plans don't work for everyone – that's when a permanent shopping list comes in handy. This is a list of all the groceries you regularly buy. It lives in your computer and you print one off before you go shopping, and just tick the items you need that week. It's much easier than compiling a weekly shopping list because you're not trying to remember brand names and sizes, and if it's not you who does the shopping that week, you know you'll still have the products you usually buy. Remember to include brand names and sizes if they're important to you. I don't care about brand names for their own sake, but I do want to buy Australian-grown and Australian-made, so we check that on the label before we buy.

It takes a while to build a permanent shopping list. Start off with headings, and as you think of certain products, add them to the list under a heading. Update the list when you buy something not listed. Here is a general example:

BAKING	BATHROOM	BREAD
Bread flour – white and rye	Toothpaste	Toast bread
Dry yeast	Toilet paper	Rye bread
Self-raising flour	Tampons	Crumpets
Plain flour	Razor blades	
Baking powder	Shaving cream	
Cocoa	Organic body lotion	
Vanilla		
Pecans or walnuts		
Choc chips		
Coconut		

CANNED FOOD	CLEANING	CONDIMENTS AND SPREADS
Baked beans	Borax	Mustard
Diced tomatoes	Bicarb soda	Tomato sauce
Tuna	Washing soda	Hoisin sauce
Salmon	Lux flakes/soap	Soy sauce
	Caustic soda	Cider vinegar
	Coconut oil or copha	Malt vinegar
	Dishwashing liquid	Mayonnaise
	Dishwasher powder	Vegemite
	Essential oils	Peanut butter
	White vinegar – 2 litres	

DAIRY

Milk
Cheese
Yoghurt

DRINKS

Coffee
Tea

DRY GOODS AND GRAINS

Rolled oats
Rice
Cannelloni beans
Chickpeas
Lentils
Pasta

FRESH FISH

2 pieces snapper
2 pieces salmon

FROZEN FOOD

Peas
Berries
Ice cream

FRUIT

Apples
Peaches
Strawberries
Oranges
Lemons

MEAT

2 kg topside mince
1 kg pork sausages
1 free-range chicken
1 kg bacon
2 kg piece of silverside
(for cold cuts)

ODDS AND ENDS

Candles
Light bulbs
Matches

OILS

Extra virgin olive oil – 4 litres
Extra virgin olive oil spray
Sunflower oil

PAPER PRODUCTS/BAGS

Tissues
Sandwich bags
Freezer bags
Aluminum foil
Baking paper

PETS

Dog food
Fish food
Chicken food

SEASONINGS AND SPICES

Sea salt
Pepper
Chilli flakes
Curry powder
Cumin
Celery salt
Onion powder

SUGARS

Brown sugar
Raw sugar
Golden syrup
Honey

VEGETABLES AND HERBS

Tomatoes
Lettuce
Carrots
Onions
Celery
Garlic
Potatoes
Pumpkin
Beans
Cauliflower
Parsley
Sage
Rosemary

OTHER

Stockpiling groceries

The thing that will support you cooking from scratch more than anything else is to have the ingredients you need on hand. Whether you're in a large family or live alone, stockpiling groceries will give you the convenience of having a cupboard full of groceries available to you twenty-four hours a day. If children come home from school and hand you a note saying they need to have some cupcakes for the school fair the next day, no problem. If someone drops by out of the blue for dinner, you won't be frantic wondering what you'll feed them. And it's a great time-saver, too. When you have filled that cupboard to the capacity you want, you won't have to shop every week. You'll keep scanning the sales flyers and shop only when you see a bargain, or to pick up fresh milk, fruit and vegetables. We'll talk more about stockpiling in the June chapter.

> TIP: A pantry and stockpile serve difference purposes. A pantry is full of the foods you've opened and are currently using. Generally everything will be in a sealed container. A stockpile is a cupboard full of goods not opened, waiting to move to the pantry when they're needed.

Grow some of your own produce

If you have some land or a space in the sun to place containers, another food strategy that will save money, as well as give you the best organic fruit and vegetables, is to grow your own. If you do this, you'll have to learn when to harvest and how to manage your harvests so you don't waste anything. Often that means you'll learn how to preserve in jars and freeze your produce too. I wrote extensively about backyard produce in *Down to Earth*. In April we'll look more closely at growing in containers, so please refer to that chapter for more information.

Choosing local or organic

There has been a sharp rise in the number of products labelled 'organic' on supermarket shelves in the past few years. Often I am asked if the weekly shopping should include organic fruit, vegetables, meat and chicken, as well as the newer organic products we're seeing now – butter, cheese, wine and tinned goods. It's tricky to answer these questions as we're all so different; we have different needs, tastes and incomes, and we all know that 'organic' comes at a price.

I know I'm lucky to live in Australia – and to pinpoint it more closely, in the hinterland of the Sunshine Coast. Not only do we have a beautiful climate and adequate rainfall here to grow a wide variety of backyard food all year long, we also have a lot of producers' markets and small local markets. Within a short distance of where I live there is an organic supermarket and butcher and a food co-op with a lot of organic produce such as milk, cheese, grains, flour, dried fruit, chocolate, tea and coffee.

So for me, it's not a question of, *Where do I find organic food?* It's easy to find. The question here is, *Do I buy it?*

Like many of us, I didn't question whether to choose organic when I first came to this way of living. It was premium and what I wanted to buy. But in the years since then, I've thought a lot about what organic means and if I should tweak my budget, and go without other things, to buy mainly organic food. The answer for me now is no. When I have a choice, I prefer to buy fresh and local.

The term 'organic' means different things in different places. Here in Australia, producers apply for organic certification, undergo a series of inspections and, all things going well, get their certification and operate according to those standards. There are also producers who say they're organic, and might very well be, but are not certified. There's a diverse understanding of the term. Some people think that organic produce has been grown without the use of fertilisers and insecticides. But there are a number of 'natural' fertilisers and a short list of acceptable insecticides used to grow organic produce.

When I consider whether I should buy organic food now, I think not only of the synthetic chemical means of production but also social factors and logistics. It's not only a question about how food is grown; it's much more than that. Do I want to buy organic food if the people producing it are paid next to nothing? Is organic food the best option if it's been flown across the world from place of production to place of sale? Shouldn't food miles play a part in my food choices? Should I still buy organic apples, potatoes and onions if they have been stored for months in a coldroom?

I have had a shift in thinking, and now I don't just rely on a label to tell me something is organic. When we buy our food, I think we should not only look at the health component, which takes in whether it was grown organically or not, but we should also consider how far it's travelled from point of production to our door, how it's packaged, and where that packaging came from. We should consider the means of production and the workers who produced it. As a term that we use to describe the top choice, 'organic' should mean more than chemicals and price. I think it should also include social justice and sustainability.

We need to think about animals slaughtered for our food. I want the eggs and meat I eat to come from creatures that have lived a decent life. I'd rather never eat those products again if buying them meant I was supporting and helping to perpetuate cruelty in the form of caged poultry, gestation pens or whatever else. For me, genuine free-range, fresh and local are premium and outweigh organic from another country, or even another state.

It may sound like I'm trying to complicate buying a bag of potatoes and a pork chop, but I believe it's important to shop ethically, and that using our consumer dollars thoughtfully is one of the best ways we have to bring about the changes we want to see. I know I'm lucky to live where there is a wide variety of healthy food, in addition to our backyard produce, but that variety and choice brings important decision-making with it. I encourage you to think about what is important to you, and to make your food choices according to those ideas.

HOME COOKING

Food fads

There are fashions in foods as well as clothes. At the moment the food fads seem to be kale, bone broth, any 'new' grain or seed such as quinoa, spelt or amaranth, kimchee and other ferments, and coconut oil. I'm sure there are others I've failed to notice. I'm not a follower of fashion. I think it cheats us. It makes us want something, then when we have it, it says we can't like it any more. *Throw out the old and buy this; it's better.* When you've been around as long as I have, you'll realise that most things go in and out of fashion and you should just like what you like, regardless.

If you think I don't care for any of the food fads I've mentioned, think again, because I think they're all great foods. I just don't see them as something new. Like most of our ancestors, yours included, I've been using all of them for many years and will continue to, even when they've gone out of fashion again. If you could phone your great-grandma right now and ask her about food, she may not know what Big Macs, Pop-Tarts or yoghurt tubes are but she would know most of the foods supposedly in fashion now. She might know kimchee as sauerkraut or fermented cabbage, but she'd probably also be able to show you how to make it. So be confident with your food choices and don't be bullied into or out of liking something.

Food waste

The rate of food wastage in many Western countries, including Australia, is shameful. The current estimate is that about 30 per cent of the food we buy is wasted. I think the main problems are buying too much, and a general lack of skills when it comes to selecting fresh food in the shops and then storing it correctly at home. Luckily, these are skills anyone can learn.

If food spoils before you've had a chance to eat it, it might be wise to rethink your food-buying and storage strategy. If food sits in the fridge until it looks unusable or the use-by date tells you it's not safe to eat, you're probably buying too much food, or at least the wrong kind of food.

Tips to reduce food waste include:

- Plan your menus every week. If you're only buying what you need for that week's meals, you'll have less waste (and more money).
- Clean out your crisper bins in the fridge before you shop. Use the vegetables and fruit that are still in there before you buy a new batch.
- Bring your shopping home as soon as you can. When you get home, put everything away immediately, starting with the cold products.
- Before putting dried goods such as flour and grains in your pantry or stockpile, place them in the freezer for two days to kill any larvae present.
- Add new products to the back of the stockpile and move older food to the front.
- Follow any particular storage instructions your foods come with.
- Don't store potatoes or onions in plastic bags as they'll rot.
- Wrap celery in aluminium foil – it will keep well for six weeks, still crisp.
- Store most vegetables in sealed plastic bags rather than just loose in the crisper.
- Have a plan for using leftovers.

Building up your recipe collection

One of the great treasures you'll develop during your years of cooking will be your recipe collection. Your family will grow up eating these recipes, and hopefully they'll continue cooking the traditional family recipes when it's their turn. You can start your collection with your childhood favourites and those you've collected over the years. I've written extra notes in a couple of my favourite cookbooks, and I hope my sons will treasure them when I'm no longer here.

One thing is for sure: you'll need some way of storing your recipes so they can build into a treasure trove. You can do that by buying a beautiful book with blank pages, a box with cards or an exercise book, or you could do what I've been doing for a few months now – collecting digital recipes in an app on my phone. Storing recipes digitally in the 'cloud' has the benefit of you being able to access them at work when you're deciding what to have for dinner, if your menu plan isn't up and running yet. If you need to pick up a few things at the shop on the way home, you'll have the recipes and ingredients list right there in your phone.

Once you've worked out how you'll store your recipes, it's just a matter of collecting them. Ask your parents, grandparents and siblings for family recipes, ask your friends for favourites you may have eaten at their homes, and spend some time browsing online or through magazines to find some you like the look of and want to try. Once you have them in your collection, work your way through and only keep those you truly love.

Once you start, you'll never stop collecting and trying recipes. But make sure you're organised from the beginning – set yourself up for success from day one and don't create a mess of clippings and notes that you'll hide in a drawer and never use.

A FEW OF MY FAVOURITE RECIPES

There is more to good home cooking than following a recipe. To consistently cook well, you need to understand how flavours develop. There are ways of developing flavour in your cooking that don't involve adding anything from a packet. They include caramelising, reducing, and using sugar, honey, herbs and spices. There is more information about this in *Down to Earth*.

Bone marrow, vegetable and barley soup

SERVES 6

Stock can be made out of most bones, but if you can add bone marrow to the mix, you've got yourself a super soup. Try to buy free-range, grass-fed or organic bones if you can, but don't fuss over it – buy what you can afford. You'll have to get the butcher to cut the bones for you, because many marrow bones are too long to fit into your stockpot. This recipe is made with bone stock, bone marrow, root vegetables and barley – my favourite grain. Roasting the bones until they're brown will add to the flavour of the soup, but isn't necessary. It's a good idea to soak the barley (and all grains), so when you start organising the bones, place a cup or two of barley in water and let it sit until you're ready to use it.

This isn't really *my* recipe; it's my family's recipe – it might even be your family's recipe. My parents made it, my grandmother made it and I have no doubt she watched as her mother and granny made it too.

You could cook the stock for a couple of days if you wanted to, but twenty-four hours will give you good stock. The larger the bones, the longer you'll need to cook them. You can turn it off overnight if you want to, and start it up the following morning. If you have a wood stove, leave it on the stove for the entire cooking time.

FOR THE STOCK

marrow bones

8 L water

½ teaspoon pepper

2 tablespoons vinegar

small bunch parsley

2 bay leaves

1 large onion, chopped

FOR THE SOUP

2 cups pearl barley

1 swede, chopped

2 parsnips, chopped

3 carrots, chopped

3 sticks celery, chopped

1 onion, chopped

1. Place the bones into a large stockpot and cover them with water. Add the pepper, vinegar (to help extract the minerals from the bones), three-quarters of the parsley, bay leaves and onion. Bring to the boil and let it slowly simmer all day. If scum develops and rises to the top, skim it off with a slotted spoon. Often the bones you use will add fat to the stock. You can get rid of it by cooling the stock in the fridge so the fat forms a solid layer on the top that's easy to scrape off with a spoon.
2. Strain the stock through a sieve to remove the bones, herbs and onion. If the bones are marrow bones, put them to the side – you'll use them again soon.
3. The night before making the soup, rinse the barley in water, place into a bowl and cover with water. The amount of barley depends on how thick you want the soup to be – the more barley, the thicker the soup.

4. To make the soup, pour your stock into the stockpot, and add the soaked barley and any meat from the bones. The gristle will break down during the cooking and add more nutrients to the soup. Bring to the boil, turn the heat down and, with the lid on, simmer for 1–2 hours to soften the meat. Add the vegetables, and salt and pepper to taste.
5. Remove as much marrow as you can from the bones and add it to the soup. You'll often find pockets of marrow that will easily slip out, but sometimes you have to dig around with the end of a spoon. Cook for another 30–40 minutes or until the vegetables are cooked, then sprinkle with the remaining parsley.

TIP: When I was growing up, there weren't cartons of stock on supermarket shelves. Bones would be saved from a roast or bought raw from the butcher, and a 24-hour slow-cooking session would result in the most nutritious stock to make into a soup. That long slow cooking brings the minerals - calcium, phosphorus, magnesium and sulphur - out of the bones, dissolves the gristle and gives you a form of glucosamine and chondroitin that is easily digestible and beneficial. You may have seen that combination being sold as a supplement to help treat arthritis; this is its natural form.

Fast potato and pumpkin soup

SERVES 4

This is a never-fail soup that can be made and on the table in 30 minutes with only 5 minutes prep. It is delicious served with toasted five-minute bread (see July's chapter). If you want a thick soup, add more pumpkin.

½ Japanese pumpkin (or ¼ large pumpkin), peeled and chopped into large chunks

1 sweet potato, peeled and chopped into chunks

1 large potato, peeled and quartered

1 large onion, chopped into large pieces

1 bay leaf

salt and pepper

parsley or chives, finely chopped

sour cream to serve

1. Place the vegetables and bay leaf in a large saucepan with 1½ L water. Season with salt and pepper. If you have homemade chicken stock in the freezer, you can use that instead of water. Bring to the boil, then simmer with the lid on for 20 minutes or until the vegetables are soft.

2. Remove the bay leaf and discard. Use a stick blender or a food processor to puree the soup. Add more salt and pepper to taste, then stir in the herbs. Serve with a dollop of sour cream.

TIP: When choosing colourful vegetables such as pumpkin, carrots and sweet potato, opt for darker rather than lighter. Usually the darker they are in their own particular colour, the more nutrients they have, and their taste will be deeper and more complex.

Chicken cacciatore (hunter's chicken)

SERVES 4–6

Because you can make it with a whole frozen chicken, this is one of those recipes I rely on when we have unexpected guests or I've forgotten to get something out of the freezer to thaw for dinner. It always produces a delicious meal, with the benefit of producing its own chicken stock. It might look complicated, but you can prepare it in small blocks of time and just let it sit cooking. It will take about 90 minutes from frozen chicken to finished meal. Serve with pasta or rice.

THE STOCK

1 whole free-range chicken *(can be frozen)*

2 bay leaves

1 tablespoon vinegar

THE SAUCE

¼ cup extra virgin olive oil

2 brown onions, peeled and chopped

2 sticks celery, diced *(optional)*

2 cloves garlic, crushed

1 tablespoon tomato paste

400 g can whole tomatoes, chopped with juices

1½ cups chicken stock

1 bay leaf

3 sprigs thyme

½ cup parsley, chopped

salt and pepper

1. Remove all the giblets from the chicken and discard. Place the chicken in a stockpot with 2 L of water, bay leaves and vinegar. Bring to the boil, and simmer for 1 hour.
2. When the flesh is beginning to fall off the bones, remove the chicken to a plate to cool and pour the chicken stock into a large jug.
3. When the chicken is cool enough to handle, strip the meat off the bones and chop into bite-size pieces. Discard the skin and make sure there are no small bones in with the meat. (The carcass can be saved to boil for chicken soup if you want another meal from it.) Put the chicken pieces in the fridge while you prepare the sauce.
4. Heat the olive oil in a frying pan and add the onion, celery and garlic. Cook for 2 minutes, making sure the garlic doesn't burn. Add the tomato paste, cook for 1 minute while stirring, then add the tomatoes and half the chicken stock. Simmer for 30 minutes to develop the flavours.
5. When the sauce has thickened slightly and the vegetables are cooked, add the chicken and enough stock to just cover it. Add the herbs and season to taste. Bring to the boil, then simmer for 15 minutes while you prepare the pasta or rice.

Cabbage rolls

SERVES 4-6

This is one of those recipes that memories are built on. It's a bit fiddly, but easy and well worth the effort. If there is stuffing left over, it's delicious wrapped in a crisp lettuce leaf for lunch the next day. Serve with steamed potatoes or egg noodles and the gravy.

1 white or savoy cabbage, cored

500 g pork mince

1 large onion, chopped

1 stick celery, chopped

1 red capsicum, chopped

1 tablespoon paprika

salt and pepper

1½ cups cooked rice

handful of parsley, chopped

2 tablespoons plain flour

1. Carefully remove about 12 full leaves from the cabbage without breaking them. Fill up a frying pan with water, bring to the boil, then place the cabbage leaves in the boiling water for a few minutes, or until wilted but still green. You'll need to do them in batches. Remove the cabbage leaves, drain and set aside to cool.

2. Heat a small amount of olive oil in the frying pan and brown the mince. Make sure it takes on a lot of brown colour without burning, as this is what adds flavour. Add the vegetables, paprika and salt and pepper, then add the rice and parsley and mix well. Cook until the vegetables are soft. Turn off the heat but keep the pan on the stove; you'll use it again to cook the stuffed rolls.

3. Place 2 heaped tablespoons of the mixture on a cabbage leaf. Turn the sides in first, then roll it up fairly tightly. It should stay firmly rolled as long as you're gentle. Repeat with all of the leaves.

4. To make a light gravy, brown the flour, seasoned with salt and pepper in the same pan the meat and vegetables were cooked in. The flour should be like a thin paste, so add a small amount of oil if you need it and stir while it browns. When the flour paste is brown, add 2 cups of cold water and stir well. Bring to the boil, making sure you scrape all the brown bits off the pan – these add a lot of flavour.

5. Place all the rolls in this gravy, put a lid on the pan and simmer for 15 minutes.

Fish curry

SERVES 4

Any firm white fish caught in local waters is suitable for this recipe. If you're not sure, tell the fishmonger you want fish for a curry. Mackerel, jewfish, blue-eye trevalla, coral trout and red emperor are all suitable. Serve with rice or steamed potatoes and a salad.

800 g firm white flesh fish, cut into bite-size pieces

salt and pepper

1 tablespoon coconut oil

2 onions, thickly sliced

2 garlic cloves, crushed

1 long red chilli, deseeded and cut into thin circles

5 cm piece ginger, skinned and grated

2 teaspoons turmeric

a pinch of ground cumin

½ teaspoon chilli powder – more if you like it hotter

400 ml coconut milk

juice of 1 lemon

handful of bean shoots

chopped parsley or coriander to serve

1. Season the fish with salt and pepper and set aside. Add the coconut oil to a heated frying pan, then add the onion, garlic, chilli, ginger and spices. Mix well and stir for 2 minutes, taking care not to burn.
2. When the onion is soft, add the fish and stir until the spice mix is completely covering it. Add the coconut milk and lemon juice. Stir until everything is coated.
3. When the sauce comes to the boil, turn down the heat and simmer for 3–4 minutes or until the fish is cooked and the sauce has reduced and thickened. Just before serving, add a handful of bean shoots and chopped parsley or coriander. Serve with rice or steamed potatoes, and a salad.

April

FOOD GARDENING
IN CONTAINERS

*'The highest reward for a person's toil is not what they
get for it, but what they become because of it.'*
— JOHN RUSKIN

STARTING SMALL

I think growing your own food is one of life's best prizes. When you crunch into a pod of peas sweeter than any you've ever bought, when you taste your first heirloom tomato, or when you pluck blueberries from the bush and walk through your garden eating them – well, that feeling is one you'll never forget. It's something you can't buy; only working the land yourself will give you that level of satisfaction and pleasure.

April is a great time to start growing food. When we had a big vegetable garden, we always started our annual planting in March and carried through to April. This is autumn in Australia and New Zealand, so many of us plant winter vegetables. Where I live it's still warm enough to grow tomatoes, cucumbers and herbs as well as the winter vegetables so we take full advantage of that. It's the ideal time to get out in the fresh air, be enriched by the surroundings and think about all those harvests ahead.

When you're starting out on your simple life journey, or if you move to a home with a bit of land, you may want to start growing your own fruit and vegetables. That's a good option for experienced gardeners, because a large, productive garden will add value and strength to your home and increase the opportunities you have to eat well, share an abundance of produce and store food that can be eaten at other times of the year. It will give you freshness that you can't find in any shop, and organic produce cheaper than any you can buy.

However, if you've never grown anything before and have to start from scratch, often it doesn't make financial sense, or you just can't afford it. You might have to buy soil or enrich virgin soil, build raised beds or fences, and buy seeds and seedlings as well as the tools to work the soil. You might spend much more on setting up than you could save on the vegetables. When you spread the set-up costs over a few years it makes more sense, but if you can't afford the set-up costs of a large garden or prefer to garden on a smaller scale, what are the alternatives?

I'm the last person to tell you not to grow vegetables, but I will advise you to start small. Food gardening requires time, hard work and constant attention. You'll need a plan, and time to implement that plan. If you've never grown anything before, learning how to grow vegetables in containers will be easier. And if the worst happens and you lose a few plants, it's not the same as losing a full kitchen garden from lack of time or experience.

The thing that many people don't understand before they start gardening is that it isn't just one set of skills to learn, it's several. You'll have to know about climate, microclimates, choosing the right plants for your conditions, sowing seeds, transplanting seedlings, fertilising, making fertilisers, mulching, optimising conditions so you get the best from your vegetables, watering, trellises, tying back, harvesting, storing and preserving food. And that's just the list if everything goes well. If you have problems, that's another story altogether. But the good news is, it's easy to learn, and when you build one skill upon another, it starts making sense.

Be prudent in the first years of vegetable gardening. By going slow you'll build up your skills, collect what you need as you need it, discover a bit each season and keep enjoying life. You won't be overwhelmed by the work that a large garden needs. And if you choose to grow the vegetables that you eat a lot of, or those you love that are expensive, you're still going to be saving money during the growing season. Starting small helps you learn the fundamentals of gardening, collect a few tools and understand the microclimate of your backyard so that when you're ready, you'll be able to start a big garden.

If you don't know much about gardening, you'll need a good gardening book suited to your climate. I've added suggestions for books to the Resources section.

DECIDING WHAT TO GROW

The first questions to ask yourself are: What do we eat a lot of? What is best fresh from the garden? What do we buy regularly that's expensive?

Here are a few suggestions. All these plants will grow in containers in their season:

- **Fruiting vegetables:** tomato, capsicum, chilli, zucchini, eggplant
- **Climbing vegetables:** climbing bean, pea, cucumber
- **Leaves:** silverbeet/chard, spinach, lettuce, Asian greens
- **Roots, tubers and bulbs:** radish, carrot, parsnip, garlic, potato
- **Herbs:** parsley, chives, Welsh onion, rosemary, sage, thyme, lemon thyme
- **Fruit:** strawberry, raspberry, blueberry, lemon, orange

Let's look more closely at growing potatoes, tomatoes, and a range of other delicious and useful plants. I've chosen these because they're commonly used vegetables and they taste much better fresh from the ground than from the supermarket. Of course there are many other vegetables and fruit that are best homegrown, but let's start with these.

Growing potatoes

You'll probably be surprised to learn that potatoes are a crop you can add to your container garden. In fact, potatoes are easy to grow and, as they're one of the crops that are generally sprayed with herbicide just before harvesting (to kill off the green tops), it's worth the time it takes to grow them.

Seed potatoes (the ones you plant to grow new potatoes from) should be available at hardware stores and nurseries when the season starts. My favourites are Dutch cream and kipfler; both are easy growers and delicious. If you can't find any seed potatoes, look for organic potatoes at the fruit shop and use them.

A bag is often more suitable than a pot for growing potatoes, as you need something large and tall. You can buy grow bags or, if you have a sewing machine, you could easily sew your own using weed mat, which allows water

and air through but is strong enough to contain the weight of the soil and potatoes. Further information about where to buy weed mat and how to sew grow bags can be found in the Resources section.

PLANTING POTATOES IN A GROW BAG

1. When fully loaded, a potato growing bag will be heavy, so put it in its permanent position and bring all the materials you need to the bag. Roll down the sides of the bag to make it easier to work with. As you build up the layers, bring up the sides of the bag with them.
2. Prepare the base: cover the bottom of the bag with a layer of straw about 50 mm thick. Place half a bucket of old manure or good compost on top of the straw. Cover that with another straw layer to a depth of about 100 mm.
3. Cover the straw with about 50 mm of potting mix and place four or five potatoes into the mix. If there are shoots on the potatoes, be careful not to break them off and plant them so the shoots are pointing upwards.
4. Cover the potatoes completely with potting mix.
5. Repeat steps 3 and 4, allowing for 100 mm between each level.
6. If you have comfrey growing, or can get hold of some, add a layer of chopped-up comfrey leaves over the potting mix. Sprinkle this layer with blood and bone and water it in.
7. Cover completely with straw to a thickness of about 100 mm.
8. Water again, making sure the straw is soaked. Check the bottom of the bag to make sure the water is draining out.

LOOKING AFTER POTATO PLANTS

Depending on how hot it is, the potatoes will need watering every second or third day. Don't fertilise the bags with nitrogen fertiliser, because you'll get a lot of green tops and very few potatoes. If you have homemade fertiliser, especially comfrey fertiliser or worm tea, water with a very weak solution once a week.

After a couple of weeks, you'll see new shoots appearing in the straw. Allow them to grow a few centimetres, then carefully cover the tops with straw again.

It will take at least three months for potatoes to mature, depending on your climate. Continue to water and fertilise the bags and, if they're well cared for, the potatoes will be ready to harvest when the green tops begin to turn brown and die. Once that happens, start digging for your treasure.

> TIP: For the best potato salad you'll ever eat, peel, quarter and boil your just-harvested potatoes in salted water. When they're cooked, drain off the water and pour a tablespoon of apple cider vinegar over the potatoes while they're still hot. When the potatoes are cold, slice them into a bowl and add homemade mayonnaise, chopped parsley, finely chopped bread and butter cucumbers or a few chopped small gherkins, two chopped poached eggs, and salt and pepper.

Growing tomatoes

Homegrown tomatoes are one of life's richest pleasures. If your climate is not too hot and not too cold, growing tomatoes should be on your to-do list. Tomatoes come in a wide variety of colours, tastes and types. As you're going to be growing in a container, buy seeds for a medium-sized (determinate) tomato, a roma or a cherry/cherry-pear tomato that you can prune back if it gets too big. The taller, non-determinate types, such as Brandywine, Grosse Lisse, Mortgage Lifter, Gardener's Delight, Green Zebra and many others, can be grown in containers but they'll need to be up against a wall so you can attach a tall trellis. The larger types can grow to 4 m. You'll get an easier crop of tomatoes from containers if you grow tomatoes on small to medium bushes, such as:

- **Cherry:** Tiny Tim, Bullseye, Tommy Toe (this one needs a trellis but it's worth growing because it's so prolific)
- **Roma** (good for cooking and bottling): San Marzano, Ballerina, Plum Fryer, Super Roma
- **Large tomatoes:** Burbank, Golden Sunrise, Kotlas, Walter (good tropical plant)

Tomatoes are a high-maintenance vegetable but the care you give them will pay off handsomely. Don't be put off. Once you taste that first homegrown tomato, you'll be hooked.

You'll grow only one tomato plant per container, so choose your seeds or seedlings and add four seeds or two seedlings to each container. That will allow you to choose the strongest plant to grow to maturity. Plant the seeds according to the instructions on the packet, or transplant the seedlings, being very careful with the roots. Water them in, and if you planted seedlings, use a weak seaweed solution as well.

> TIP: You get better results if you apply weaker fertiliser more frequently. If the bottle suggests using 2 spoonfuls in a litre of water every month, for example, mix up 1 spoonful in a litre of water and apply it fortnightly. This gives a constant weak supply of nutrients, which is better for the plant than one or two big applications over its lifetime.

LOOKING AFTER TOMATO PLANTS

Don't let the seed or seedlings dry out. Water them every second day, or daily if it's hot. The tomato bushes will need some support to grow to their full potential, so put in a climbing frame or a bamboo tripod and as the bush grows, tie it onto the frame. If you're growing an indeterminate-type tomato, it will have to be up against a wall with a trellis. The higher and bushier the plant grows, the more you'll have to tie it back to the support. As you're attaching the tomato to its support, snip off those little shoots that will grow between the main stem and the side branches. If the tomato grows too tall, you can cut off the top of the main stem. That should stop it increasing in height.

Growing herbs and green onions

I think it makes good sense to grow the herbs you commonly eat. A bunch of herbs will cost a few dollars at the supermarket, and it can become quite costly to buy several different herbs every week. Herbs are easy to grow and look after, so they're ideal for new gardeners. Think about which ones you eat most – basil, thyme, oregano, coriander, sage, rosemary? – and plant up small herb bushes. The rosemary will grow bigger than the others, but it's easily clipped back each time you want to harvest the herb for cooking.

TIP: If your herbs grow faster than you can use them, either pick the excess and dry for your pantry or make a little bouquet of herbs for a friend or neighbour. Most people love to receive fresh herbs as a gift.

When you plant herbs, you can use smaller containers – regular pots will be fine. Herbs love the sun and it's easy to move them around to the best position all year round. Herbs will die if their roots sit in water, so plant them into free-draining potting mix that's been enriched with compost and don't use a saucer to catch the run-off water. During the growing season, apply weak liquid fertiliser every two weeks and water them when the soil in the pot is dry.

If you're like me and use a lot of green onions, try to find some Welsh onions, which are perennial. Two or three years after you plant them you'll have a thriving patch of green onions that will just keep growing and slowly multiplying – you'll never have to buy green onions again. If they're not pulled out when they're young, they'll grow quite a sizeable bulb, similar to a shallot, which is edible as well. They're a very handy plant.

Growing lettuce

It usually makes sense to plant lettuce as well, so you can have fresh leaves on hand. The best way to plant lettuce seeds is to scatter them over a tray full of potting mix, pat them down with the palm of your hand, then sit the tray in a larger tray of water for three hours to soak up the moisture. This gives the seeds the opportunity to fully hydrate and doesn't disturb them at all. Gently water the lettuce seeds every day, and when the green leaves appear, give them an application of liquid fertiliser to stimulate growth. When they've grown to about 10 cm and have four or five leaves, plant them out in larger containers. When you have no more space to plant out, use the leftovers as baby lettuce in your salads. When you start planting the lettuce in the larger pots, that is the time to start your next tray of seeds. If you plant them successively like this, you will be eating homegrown lettuce all through the season.

Growing pumpkins

If you love pumpkin but can't imagine growing it in a container, wait till the weather warms up and find some Golden Nugget seeds. They'll make a compact bush that produces delicious small pumpkins. Plant four to six seeds in a container full of potting mix, compost and manure. Add sulphate of potash to encourage flower growth, water frequently and stand back. When the seedlings have grown three or four leaves, transplant each of them to its own pot. Water them in with liquid seaweed made up to the directions on the bottle to help them overcome transplant shock. As they grow in the following weeks, apply weak liquid fertiliser every fortnight with a pinch of sulphate of potash around the roots. You'll need bees around to pollinate the flowers but you need bees for your tomatoes too, so let's grow a few flowers as well.

TIP: A small container of flowers will benefit the vegetables by bringing in the bees. Nasturtiums will grow well in a pot and the leaves are edible. You could also try any sort of daisy, while flowering salvias do very well in hot dry climates. If you don't have space for another container, sow a circle of alyssum/sweet Alice, pansies or violas under the pumpkin or one of your other vegetable plants.

Growing garlic

Do you long for your own homegrown garlic? Garlic is one of many vegetables that tastes better grown in the backyard. It's fairly easy to grow but does take a long time – however, I think that once you've tasted your first crop, you'll plant it again, year after year. Buy an organic garlic bulb, break it up and plant the largest cloves, which will grow the best – each will produce a full bulb. They grow well in one of those rubber tubs, filled with good potting mix and a small amount of manure and compost. The cloves should be planted 10 cm apart and with the pointed tip of the clove 2 cm below the surface.

Garlic takes about six to seven months to grow to maturity, so you'll have to be patient and look after it all that time, but it will be worth it. They'll be ready to harvest when you notice the green tops shrivel up and turn brown.

TIP: Don't forget fruit. Strawberries are easy to grow in containers, either hanging or standing on the ground. Blueberries grow well in large containers. We have four blueberry bushes in containers and they produce more fruit than they did when they were planted in the ground. You can also grow citrus from dwarf trees, or buy a regular tree and keep it pruned.

LOCATION, LOCATION, LOCATION

Most vegetables and herbs grow best in full sun. There are a few leafy green plants that enjoy life in partial shade, but most need sun. That's one of the advantages of container gardening: you can move the containers around to where the sun or shade is, and you can protect them under shelter if it's windy or raining heavily.

Before you put out your first pots, take notice of where the sun and shade falls in your outdoor area. You're looking for a place that has sun most of the day, with some periods of dappled or full shade. Don't forget that locating your containers against a brick wall will provide heat to the plants, which will be good in winter, but not so good during a hot summer. A paved courtyard will also provide heat.

Check for wind. There will be days when it's windy everywhere but some areas around flats and houses create tunnels that wind rushes through, even when it's not a windy day. Plants won't grow well in wind, so try to avoid windy spots or look for ways to block the wind at one end.

No matter where you decide to locate your small gardens, monitor them closely in the first couple of weeks to make sure your decision was a wise one. Be prepared to move your plants around if they need more or less sun or if they're just not growing well in their original position.

Be aware that these pots will be heavy, so if you want to set them up on a patio, deck or balcony, make sure the area is capable of holding the extra weight and remains safe. You can partially address the weight problem by adding perlite to the potting mix. Perlite is a natural siliceous rock that is treated to expand, making it extremely light; it can be bought in bags from the hardware store. Never use more than about 30 per cent perlite in the total mix, and make sure you mix it in thoroughly. If weight is an issue, you can also space your planters out rather than having them together in one spot.

CONTAINERS AND POTTING MIX

Choosing your containers

Look around your home, garden and garage to see what suitable containers you might have. They'll need to be big – if you restrict the root growth of what you're growing, it will also restrict your crops, so large containers are better than small ones. Of course, you can add a few herbs in small containers, or around the edge of a larger container. Look for old rubber tubs, an old wheelbarrow (it doesn't matter if it's slightly rusty), old boxes made from untreated wood, polystyrene troughs or metal containers. Most recycled containers won't last a long time because they'll be sitting in the sun all year long, but that doesn't matter. You can change containers whenever you change seasons and start planting again.

If you don't have enough containers on hand, you have two good options.

Plastic plant pots come in all sizes, right up to 510 mm, and are made to withstand sitting in the sun for months or years. Alternatively, you can buy coloured plastic or rubber flexi-tubs, which range in size from 15 to 60 litres, and drill a few drainage holes in the base. If you need something bigger than that, use grow bags. Don't forget that your containers all need to be filled with potting mix, so it can start getting expensive if you don't keep an eye on your costs.

TIP: You'll probably be able to recycle containers you already have at home, but the larger sizes may be a problem. Grow bags, which hold up to 75 litres of potting mix, can be bought at Green Harvest and Diggers. You could also make your own using weed mat. See the Resources for more details.

Filling your containers

Potting soil and garden soil are very different. Potting soil is a free-draining light mix that will support the growth of roots in a container while allowing water to drain away. Garden soil contains microbes and minerals that are good for your vegetables, but it doesn't drain well when used in pots. Plants will suffocate if there is always water around their roots. There's no doubt about it; you'll need to buy potting mix if you're going to plant your garden in containers.

TIP: Fill your containers where they'll grow. You can move the potting mix around in a wheelbarrow. And don't forget to add perlite if weight is an issue.

You can buy good potting mix in 25-litre or 65-litre bags, but if you're going to use a lot of mix, ask a local landscaper for a bulk potting mix quote. They'll usually supply loads of half or 1 cubic metre, which can work out cheaper than buying bags. There are two things to remember, though. The first is to go to the supplier's yard, look at the quality of the mix and ask if they mix it to the Australian standard or the standards set in your country. You don't want potting mix full of pine bark or too much sand. The second thing is that you'll have to be home when the delivery is made because you'll need to deal with it fairly promptly. It will wash away if there's rain when it's just sitting in the open, so either use it, store it in bins, or cover it with a tarp.

If you live in a dry or windy climate and your pots dry out quickly, it may be worthwhile adding water crystals to your potting mix. This has to be done before you plant, so consider your climate before planting and add the crystals if you think you'll need them. Look for organic water crystals or powder if you're growing organic vegetables.

Reusing potting mix

At the end of the season, your potting soil will probably hold a few roots and will have lost many of its nutrients. You can pull out the roots, replace the nutrients and use the mix again for the coming season. The only time I wouldn't reuse potting mix is if it's had tomatoes or potatoes in it, because it may be harbouring one of the wilt diseases. Put that soil into the compost heap. That way you will use it again, but after it's had enough time for any pathogens in the soil to die off.

Replacing the nutrients simply means adding more fertility and organic matter to the old soil. Additives include very old cow, stable or sheep manure, very good compost, worm castings, perlite and new potting mix.

TIP: Never use manure straight from a paddock because you'll surely introduce weeds you don't want. As manure ages, it kills off weed seeds, and what's left is the best kind of fertiliser. If you're using horse manure, make sure it's from a stable and not a paddock. Ask the horse owner if they've recently wormed the horse – if they have, don't buy it because it will kill off all your earthworms.

Setting up tripods and trellises

Many of your container plants will do very well indeed without any extra support, or with a single bamboo stake to anchor the plant. Other plants need more elaborate support structures. Vine vegetables such as cucumbers, climbing beans and tall tomatoes need a trellis or a tripod. If you can give the plant a good trellis to grow on, you'll be rewarded with abundant vegetables.

If you live close to bushland and can find long sticks, choose three fairly straight ones of the same length to make a good tripod. Push the ends right down into the soil at the edge of the pot, bring the top ends together and secure tightly with string, wire or thin rope. You'll need a sturdier structure and a wall if you're hoping to grow a tall tomato. Attach horizontal wires to the wall about 1 metre wide and 2 metres tall, and as the plant grows, attach it to the wires with string, clips or wire.

THE HOUSEKEEPING OF GARDENING

Watering

Watering effectively is one of the most important parts of container gardening. A plant in a garden bed can send its roots out, looking for water. In a container, that can't happen; the plant is dependent on you. There are no fixed watering rules; how and when you water will depend entirely on where you live. This is one of the skills you'll develop, and it won't be the same all through the year. Put your fingers into the soil and feel how dry it is – if you can still feel moisture, it doesn't have to be watered that day.

TIP: Never let potting mix dry out completely. The mix will become water-phobic and it will repel instead of absorb water.

It does matter when you water. Plants can develop a condition called powdery mildew if they're constantly damp. In cool or warmish climates, water in the morning, because that gives the leaves all day to dry out. In sub-tropical and tropical climates, water in the evening – this gives the plant about twelve hours to take up the moisture before the sun hits the leaves again. It will be fully hydrated in the morning and able to cope with a day of sun. Watch your plants: wind and sun will dry out the soil, so don't be afraid to add water when you see the plant is stressed and wilting, or if you notice the soil is very dry.

TIP: Don't sit your containers in a saucer or trough that catches water. That will stop the water draining away and could kill the plants.

Fertilising

All plants need nourishment to keep them healthy and productive. Plants will take up any nutrients they find in the soil, so you have to keep replacing them to keep your plants in top condition and producing the vegetables you'll be eating. There are three major ingredients in plant food: nitrogen, phosphorus and potassium. Nitrogen helps plants produce healthy leaf growth; phosphorus is essential for the development of healthy roots, flowers and fruit; and potassium helps the movement of water through the plants. Commercial fertilisers are a mix of these ingredients and are commonly known as NPK fertilisers. If you want to grow organic fruit and vegetables, look for organic fertilisers.

Of course you can buy fertiliser, but it's quite easy, and much cheaper, to make your own. You can make liquid fertiliser using many common garden leaves – if the leaves are green and either thick or plentiful (or both), they're suitable. Most homemade fertilisers are applied as a tea. That means the concentrate you make is watered down before you add it to the plants, and because it looks like tea, it's called tea.

TIP: Do not use tomato or potato leaves in your liquid fertiliser.

Most liquid fertilisers can be made in the same way. The steps are:

1. Harvest leaves, nettles, comfrey, yarrow, weeds or seaweed and place in a bucket with a lid. Put a brick on top of the leaves to keep them submerged.
2. Fill the bucket with water, put the lid on and wait two weeks.
3. Remove the leaves and add them to your compost.
4. Dilute the concentrate with water, about 1 part fertiliser to 10 parts water. It should look like weak tea before you use it.

You can also make compost tea and manure tea. Put a shovelful of compost or any aged animal or poultry manure, or a cupful of poultry manure pellets such as Dynamic Lifter, into a hessian bag or an old pillowcase. Tie up the top so it's like a big tea bag. Place the bag into a bucket with a lid, fill the bucket with water, put the top on and wait two weeks. Dilute 1:10 as above before using it.

Composting

Composting gives you very valuable organic matter to add to your garden. But even if you don't want to use the compost, having a compost heap or bin can be a part of your push towards self-reliance, because it will account for a large part of the waste you're producing in your home. If you can cut down on 'rubbish', you're doing a great service to yourself, your neighbours and your area.

Our compost heap is a very simple affair: just lawn clippings, green leaves, fruit and potato peels, old straw and paper from the chicken pen, chicken manure – anything at all that was once alive can be thrown together in a pile and kept moist. Cutting the bits you throw in as small as you can hastens decomposition but it's not absolutely necessary. Compost will also decompose faster if it's a hot heap, but we don't try to keep ours hot; we know it will decompose in a few months regardless.

To set up a compost heap, find a space on garden soil away from the house so you don't have to look at it all the time. It's ideal to have three sides holding the compost in, but it can be a free-standing heap if that's not possible. If you live in an extreme climate, it's best to shelter the heap up against a wall. If you have dogs or chickens, the compost heap will need to be fenced off, otherwise they'll eat what you put in there.

You need both brown matter – paper, cardboard, dry lawn clippings, old cotton or wool, and green matter – vegetable scraps, fresh lawn clippings and garden waste. The approximate brown-to-green ratio that will make up good compost is 30:1, but don't worry about the ratio too much; just add many more browns than greens. Don't add dairy, meat, bones or anything else that might attract rodents.

When you add food scraps to the heap, dig them in or cover them with fresh lawn clippings. That will stop any smells and keep the heap safe from visiting birds. When it's dry, water the heap. Comfrey will help activate and speed up the composting process, so if you have any, add a few dozen torn-up leaves every so often, or if you have any spare comfrey fertiliser, pour it into the compost heap.

Even though you add to the compost heap all the time, it should be decomposing and therefore shrinking in size. But if the heap does grow and you're making good compost, get a spade and distribute it on your lawn or ornamental plants to use it up. You can also barter with it – many people want good homemade compost.

Making compost is not rocket science. The truth is, if you threw all the pieces of paper, hair, manure and kitchen waste into a heap in your backyard, it would all eventually rot down, no matter what you did. If you watch your brown-to-green ratio, though, it will evolve into beautiful dark-brown, sweet-smelling compost that you can add to your potting mix for the next season, and in doing so, complete one of the most satisfying natural cycles in the backyard.

may

LAUNDRY LOVE

'Without ambition one starts nothing. Without work one finishes nothing.
The prize will not be sent to you. You have to win it.'
— RALPH WALDO EMERSON

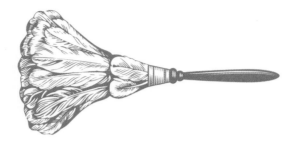

THE ELEGANCE OF CLEANLINESS

There is a kind of simple elegance in using and cleaning household linens. Clothes, sheets, towels, curtains and kitchen linens always look better when they're well cared for. When I see them in homes I visit, fresh and neatly stored away, especially when they have quite an age to them, I get the feeling there is a lot of love in that home. My aim is to have a clean house, clothes and linens, but I know that it can take a lot of time to achieve that consistently. The answer is to make the laundry room your cleaning headquarters. If your laundry room is organised to support your general cleaning tasks, it will go a long way to helping you keep a clean house and stay on top of the laundry.

There is no real reason to organise the laundry in May other than that I wanted it to be in the first half of the year, and this is the first vacant slot. I don't take laundry lightly, though; it's an important subject that can feel like an ongoing burden for some homemakers. If you organise your laundry and feel good about the products you use, if you understand your fabrics and have effective ways of dealing with cleaning problems, you'll not only get through the washing more efficiently, you'll be able to use the laundry room as the cleaning headquarters of your home. So let's throw open the laundry doors and make friends with what's in there.

Household washing used to be a riverside or community chore. When it moved into the home, there were no washing machines or electricity; washing was done by hand or soaked and heated in a boiler. In the 1930s, when the electricity grid expanded, washing machines started to be installed in homes. After the Second World War, washing machines became commonplace and most homes had a laundry room – but the laundry room back then was like another world. I clearly remember my mother boiling sheets, towels and shirts in a huge copper boiler in our outside laundry. When they were ready, she used a thick stick to lift the hot fabrics out of the boiler and into a very simple washing machine with an agitator inside and a mangle on the top for pressing the water out of the clothes. When the clothes were rinsed properly, it was my job to feed the fabric through the mangle. Then Mum would place them in a basket to be hung out to dry.

What's not to love about a laundry room? Most of us have a small room or area in the house set aside for laundry and cleaning. It's easy to shut the door on that room and go in only when you have to, but I encourage you to liberate yourself and the laundry room. You might not like it, but unless you pay to have it done for you, cleaning and washing are a part of life. All of us prefer wearing clean clothes and living in a clean home. So to help you do those cleaning tasks, accept laundry as a part of what you do, organise your workspace, set up your cleaners, buckets and brushes, and take control of your washing and cleaning. When you have an organised space to work in, with everything you need to carry out your cleaning, you'll probably spend less time doing so; you'll have a clean house and clean clothes and more time to do the things you love doing.

I also encourage you to use homemade cleaners. They're as effective as commercial cleaners, they're easy to make, they're much cheaper than anything you'll buy at the supermarket and there will be far fewer chemicals in your home. I have included recipes for commonly used household cleaners at the end of this chapter.

CLEANING AND ORGANISING
THE LAUNDRY ROOM

Organising everything to maximise efficiency will help you stay on top of your laundry and cleaning more than anything else. So let's start by cleaning the room out, purging all those old, unsafe products you'll never use and reintroducing the things you will keep in an organised manner. Most laundry rooms have a few things in common:

- Washing machine
- Tumble dryer
- Work bench
- Ironing board and iron
- Drying rack/s
- Dirty clothes hamper/s
- Shelf space or cupboard
- Rag bag
- Floor-cleaning equipment such as broom, mop, bucket, vacuum cleaner
- Large sink for cleaning and soaking

But even if you only have a washing machine and a shelf under the kitchen bench or in the bathroom, the area still needs to be clean and organised. In fact, smaller spaces must be better organised than larger spaces, as clutter will prevent you finding what you need. If your washing machine is in the kitchen, you'll have to be careful not to spill laundry products near food. Find a small basket or plastic tub and store all your laundry products in it, away from your food prep area.

A deep clean of your laundry can be done now to give you a fresh start, or whenever the room needs a good clean. Start by clearing everything out of the laundry. As you're removing the bits and pieces from the room, decide if they're in the right place and if they're needed at all. Have a couple of laundry baskets on hand – one to place items to be relocated and another for rubbish or recycling. Go through all of your cleaners, leaving only those you use for your washing, soaking and general household cleaning. Make sure you dispose of all chemicals in a responsible manner. If you have something toxic or a large amount of any chemical, check with your local council or on PlanetArk's website (see the Resources) about safe disposal methods.

When your laundry is cleared out, clean it thoroughly so you can start afresh. Spray the interior drum of the washing machine with vinegar and wipe it out. Rinse the rag out and pour some liquid soap or laundry liquid on the wet rag and wipe around the seal, inside and outside the door or lid, around the controls and over the outside of the machine. Remove the lint filter, if your machine has one, and wash it in warm, soapy water. Disconnect the drainage hose and make sure it's clean and the hose is not damaged. Reconnect the hose. Wipe the outside and the controls with a dry rag. Check the seal and make sure it's clean, and that the rubber isn't damaged or in need of replacement. When you're satisfied that the washing machine is clean, add ½ cup of bicarb soda to the detergent tray and a cup of white vinegar to the rinse dispenser and run a fast, hot-water cycle to clean out the machine and the hoses.

If you have a dryer, wipe the inside with vinegar, and the outside and the controls with soapy liquid on a wet rag before wiping dry. Remove all the lint from the lint filter, wash the filter with soapy water, then dry and put it back.

If you can move the washing machine and dryer, vacuum the backs of the machines and the area they sit in. Make sure you vacuum up all those little pieces of fly-away lint and dust bunnies – they're flammable and therefore a fire hazard. Half-fill a bucket with warm soapy water and a little eucalyptus, tea-tree or lemon myrtle oil and mop the area after unplugging the machines from the power point. Leave to dry before moving the machines back into place.

If your machines sit under a bench they'll need no protection, but if you can put objects on top of them, cover the machine tops with stick-on shelf liner vinyl or an old towel to prevent scratching and damage. Shelf liners come in several colours and patterns, and are a way of personalising the space and adding beauty to the room.

Check the ceiling and behind the door and vacuum everywhere you can reach. Wipe around the light switch, disconnect all appliances and wipe around the power points, then dry and replace power cords.

Using your cleaning paste (see page 123) or Gumption, thoroughly clean the sink, taps, soap containers, soap dishes and anything else in the vicinity of the sink. Rinse well and dry. Clean the outside of the sink as well, then dry with a clean rag.

CUSTOMISING THE LAUNDRY ROOM

Now that everything is spotless, it's time to customise the room to how you work and to help you get through your washing and cleaning. Have a good look at the space you have available, and reorganise it for maximum efficiency as you bring everything back into the laundry. But also make it a room you feel good in: don't be afraid to add some artwork, children's paintings or pretty shelf liners.

Organise your laundry liquids and powders and the ingredients you use to make them, keeping everything in the laundry. Have a look under all the sinks in your house to see what cleaning equipment is there, and move everything except your dishwashing gear and your cleaning kits into the laundry. Then you and those you live with know all your cleaners and cleaning chemicals are in the one place.

I organise my cleaning products in three zones on the laundry shelf:

- **Zone 1** is for the cleaners I use frequently: laundry liquid, lavender rinse, lavender ironing spray, vinegar spray, cleaning paste, floor cleaner (all homemade), plus vinegar and bicarb soda. I also keep my kit for general house-cleaning in this zone.
- **Zone 2** is for labelled containers of washing soda, borax, bicarb soda, essential oils and so on that are currently open and in use. These products are usually sold in flimsy packaging, so I decant them and store them in labelled jars.
- **Zone 3** contains a small stockpile of unopened Lux flakes, washing soda, borax, bicarb, vinegar, generic NapiSan, and soap-making ingredients like caustic soda and coconut oil.

In other parts of the room I have a soaking tub, clothes hamper, vacuum cleaner, rag bag, broom, mops, buckets and a supply of spray bottles and jars for storage.

Using rags

Over the course of your lifetime, you'll save hundreds of dollars by cutting up old towels, sheets, tea towels and T-shirts to make cleaning rags. Anything made from cotton or linen is suitable, and because they're old and well used, they'll be seasoned, absorbent and soft.

The wonderful thing about recycling household linens as rags is that you can use them for both wet and dry tasks, making your cleaning days easier, and you can just throw them in with the regular wash when you're done. If there is a particularly nasty spill or the dog throws up, you can use the rags to completely clean and dry the carpet, then throw all the rags out. Don't wash a rag that you've used for wiping up vomit or faeces – it will take too much of your time to deal with that rag properly, and it's unhygienic to put it in with the regular washing.

Cut the old towels and sheets into squares with pinking shears or scissors and pack them into your rag bag, or a small basket stored on the shelf. For step-by-step instructions for making your own rag bag, refer to the tutorial in the August chapter.

Let's throw open the laundry doors and make friends with what's in there.

DEALING WITH WASHING

I know it's difficult remaining upbeat when you're doing the fifth load of washing for the day and you're tired. I find that doing all the heavy chores like washing and ironing are easier in the morning, so if you can organise yourself to have the washing ready to go when you get up and your energy is at its highest, you'll get through it without having already worked a full day before you start. Maybe you can put a couple of loads through the machine in the evening and leave them in the washing basket overnight. Or just before you go to bed, fill the machine and soak a load to start in the morning.

It's also a good idea to use products you like. I love using the laundry liquid I make because I know it's safe on my skin. Recently I've added lavender and rose essential oils to my laundry product, and getting a whiff every so often of such a beautiful fragrance helps get me through the work – it reminds me of the gentle products I'm using.

Sorting

It's easy to become a bit obsessive about sorting, so I like to keep it simple. Rather than having separate hampers for different kinds of washing, I have one hamper where all dirty items go to wait for washing day. I hang damp dishcloths and tea towels over the rim of the hamper so they can dry out.

When I'm about to do a wash, I empty the hamper and sort the items into heaps. Most of our clothes are either cotton or linen and we have no permanent press to worry about. But you need to be familiar with your fabrics – every time you have something new to deal with, including secondhand items, read the care label. It will probably just confirm what you already know: that it can be washed along with the regular washing. But sometimes an item will require special care so that it doesn't get damaged or pulled out of shape.

As you pick up each item for sorting, empty pockets, do up zippers and turn your darks inside out if you want to reduce fading. It's a good idea to fasten the collar button on shirts and button long sleeves together to prevent tangling.

When you do your sorting, decide what needs pre-treatment, such as stained or dirty garments, and what has to be handwashed. Small items such as pantyhose, bras and hankies can go into a small mesh bag. If there are a lot of small items I sort the whites from the darks and wash as two separate lots. If you only have one wool jumper or one pair of jeans and no other dark clothes, it would be prudent to leave them both to be washed on the next washing day. It's not environmentally sound or economically efficient to run a wash for only one item.

This is a general guide for sorting:
- Whites and light colours
- Darks and jeans
- Towels, pillowcases and sheets
- Small items and pantyhose
- Stained or very dirty items
- Wool and alpaca
- Delicate fabrics – silk, cashmere, embroidery, lace, etc.

Care labels

Clothing care labels are added by the manufacturer to help you care for what you buy. I wouldn't buy anything that indicated I had to dry-clean the product, because the clothes are dipped in chemical solvents. However, I've bought secondhand clothes that were supposed to be dry-cleaned and have handwashed them instead, and they've turned out beautifully.

Get to know your fabrics. Most natural cottons and linens are cared for in the same way. They can be machine- or handwashed, and tumble-dried or line-dried. The main threat to fabrics comes from temperature in both the washing and drying phases. Hot water, hot air and hot sunshine can shrink and fade clothes. If you use cold or warm water, you lessen the chance of damage.

If you read the label and you're still not sure, cautiously handwash the article with a little liquid soap, then hang in the shade to dry. Wool should be laid flat in the shade.

Common laundry symbols

MACHINE WASH	MACHINE WASH, PERMANENT PRESS	MACHINE WASH, GENTLE OR DELICATE	HAND WASH	DO NOT WASH	WATER TEMPERATURE NOT TO EXCEED:				
					30°C	40°C	50°C	70°C	95°C

WATER TEMPERATURE NOT TO EXCEED:					DO NOT WRING	BLEACH IF NEEDED	DO NOT BLEACH	NON-CHLORINE BLEACH IF NEEDED	NON-CHLORINE BLEACH IF NEEDED
30°C	40°C	50°C	70°C	95°C					

TUMBLE DRY	DRY NORMAL, LOW HEAT	DRY NORMAL, MEDIUM HEAT	DRY NORMAL, HIGH HEAT	DRY NORMAL, NO HEAT	HANG TO DRY	DRIP DRY	DRY FLAT	DRY IN THE SHADE	DO NOT DRY

DO NOT TUMBLE DRY	DRY	IRON ANY TEMP, STEAM	DO NOT IRON	MAXIMUM IRON TEMP 110C	MAXIMUM IRON TEMP 150°C	MAXIMUM IRON TEMP 200°C	NO STEAM	DRYCLEAN	ANY SOLVENT

ANY SOLVENT EXCEPT TETRACHLOR-ETHLENE	PETROLEUM SOLVENT ONLY	WET CLEANING	DO NOT DRYCLEAN	SHORT CYCLE	REDUCED MOISTURE	LOW HEAT	NO STEAM FINISHING

TIP: Be particularly cautious with red fabric: red dyes are prone to running, so test for colourfastness with every new red item. To test, just wet an inside seam or underarm, wait two minutes then rub the fabric on a white cloth. If there is a red or pink stain left there, the item is not colourfast and will have to be washed separately.

Baby laundry

When the first baby clothes appear, there's a smile on everyone's face. Who doesn't love those tiny clothes? It's best to get into a good routine with your baby laundry, because it will create a backlog fast if the weather isn't right for drying or you're too tired to do the washing. You might be very fussy with

the baby's clothes to start with, but it's perfectly acceptable to wash them with the family's clothes to ease your workload. Wash nappies separately, but everything else will be fine. Use the same principles with baby clothes as with the rest of the things you wash: separate out the delicates for handwashing, and pretreat the stained and dirty items before adding them to the family wash.

Never use chlorine bleach or heavy chemicals on your baby's clothing or nappies. Homemade laundry liquid, vinegar rinse and drying in the sunlight is all that's needed to keep everything clean and fresh.

Wash all clothes and nappies before your baby wears them, whether new or secondhand. The new clothes may have some sort of dressing on the fabric that should be washed off, and the secondhand clothes need to be freshened up, even if they've been sitting in a cupboard for a year.

Some other tips for washing baby clothes:

- Use homemade laundry liquid, and ¼ cup of white vinegar instead of fabric softener.
- If you don't use homemade laundry liquid, buy a fragrance-free one formulated for sensitive skin.
- Buy or make a small mesh bag in which to place all the small items such as socks, mittens and hats.
- Wash nappies separately.

The manufacturers of modern cloth nappies suggest keeping dirty nappies in a dry bucket with the lid on until they're washed. You'll need to wash the nappies every second day or so using this method. The old soaker bucket is a drowning hazard for small children and no longer recommended.

TIP: To help mask odours in your nappy bucket, put a few drops of tea-tree, eucalyptus, citrus or lavender oil on a large terry towelling rag and place it in the bucket with the nappies. Wash and dry the rag with the nappies, and replenish the essential oil before putting the rag in the bucket again. Alternatively, place a cup of bicarb soda into a preserving jar and add a few drops of essential oil. Screw the lid on, shake the jar, and each time you add a nappy to the bucket, sprinkle in a small amount of the fragrant powder.

Treating stains

Generally, you can treat stains on baby clothes, nappies or any of the clothes you're washing by soaking the clothes in oxy-bleach and water overnight before you wash. Almost all stains will come out with this treatment if you use water as hot as the fabric can take. Check the care label to be sure.

For small stains, soak the spot with homemade laundry liquid and leave it to sit for fifteen minutes before machine-washing.

Wet items waiting to be washed

If you use hand-knitted dishcloths like I do, you can't throw them into the laundry hamper because they, and the other fabrics, would become mouldy and start to smell. The best way to handle these – and any other wet items waiting to be washed – is to hang them over the side of the hamper until your next laundry day.

Soaking

I think soaking is the gentlest way to get fabrics really clean. It's old-fashioned but the time is taken up by the fabrics soaking, not by actual work.

I use a generic brand of NapiSan. It's an oxy-bleach that uses peroxide as its cleaning agent, which is much less harmful to humans and the environment than chlorine bleach. Oxy-bleach has no smell at all, and it doesn't strip colours from the fabric. I usually use the Aldi brand, but every generic brand I've used over the years has worked. So make sure you use an Australian generic and not the branded market leader – it will save you money over the years.

The best container for soaking is one of those rubbery storage tubs, around 20 litres in capacity. Place the recommended amount of oxy-bleach powder in the tub and fill with enough hot water to cover the clothes you plan to treat. Stir with a large spoon and throw in the clothes, making sure the tub isn't too crowded. Leave it overnight or for at least twelve hours, pull out the most stained garment and check that the stain has gone. If it has, transfer all the clothing to the washing machine and do a normal wash, adding other clothing to fill the machine to its normal capacity.

This treatment will work on almost any stain if it's fresh and hasn't already been washed and placed in the sun to dry. Make sure the water is *hot*.

Handwashing

When the care label calls for handwashing, use either a small amount of dissolved Lux flakes, ½ cup of laundry liquid or a tablespoon of Dr Bronner's liquid castile soap in a sink half filled with warm water. When washing wool, or delicate fabric such as silk, make sure the water isn't too hot. Water that you can comfortably put your hand into is fine. Add the garment, allow it to soak for a few minutes, then, depending on what it is, wash around the neck, underarms and front, using a bar of laundry soap. When you've finished washing all the items, tip out the water, add clean warm water into the same tub and rinse everything. Finish off by laying out a towel on a bench or table, spreading out two garments at a time and rolling the towel up to remove as much of the water as possible.

If the garment is wool or alpaca, don't allow it to stretch as you pick it up, as this will damage the fibres. Delicates and cottons can be hung to dry; the alpaca and wool should be laid flat on a towel outside under cover. Never leave wool or alpaca to dry in the sun, because they'll shrink.

TIP: Don't soak wool or any other delicate fabric such as silk, cashmere or alpaca.

Machine-washing

Get the most environmentally sound machine you can afford – one that saves electricity and water. My preference now is for a front loader, but when I had small children I preferred a top loader. I used to fill the washing machine every evening, soak the load overnight and turn it on to wash first thing the next morning. It was a good way of dealing with clothes worn by two very adventurous, outdoor-loving boys.

Read the instruction manual and be guided by it. Avoid overloading your washing machine, because it won't wash properly. Check out the eco or fast settings for regular washing: you'll find that, especially with front loaders, these settings can cut the washing cycle by at least an hour. Of course you would use a longer wash for soiled items, but a fast wash should be sufficient for the clothes you wear to work and around the house.

DRYING

Line-drying

There are few things better than slipping between sheets that have just been dried in the sun. Some people aren't able to line-dry because they live in high-rise apartments, and I know there are places in the US where line-drying is banned. I'm amazed by that: not only that it happens but that people put up with it. Outside is where it's all happening. All that free air, a gentle breeze – just enough to dry the clothes well.

Always shake your clothes with a sharp snap to get the wrinkles out. That should also unwind hems and sleeves that may have been caught up in the washing process. A bit of extra care when you're hanging out your washing will reduce the amount of ironing that needs to be done. Sensible shaking, hanging on clothes hangers, straightening hems and collars, pegging by the seams and supporting large items with more pegs will all give you better results. Often there will be only a couple of items that need ironing if you've put in the time to smooth and shake the fabrics as you work.

When I take washing off the line, I fold as much as I can as I unpeg it to avoid double handling. Sometimes there will be a circular tablecloth or a garment that needs to be laid on a table to be folded properly, so I just loosely fold those things. When your basket is full, take everything inside and sort it out – I sort mine on the kitchen table. I put all the washing away because Hanno hangs it out; however, in a larger household I think everyone should put their own washing away, starting at about age five. So sort the clothes in a convenient place and remind everyone their clean clothes can be taken to their bedrooms.

TIP: It's a good habit to hang shirts, trousers and dresses on clothes hangers secured to the clothesline with a peg on each side to prevent slipping. All garments that will stretch if hung should be laid flat on a towel on the top shelf of a drying rack or on a table. We use plastic pegs here because wooden pegs go mouldy in our humid climate.

Undercover clothesline

It sometimes makes sense to have an undercover clothesline. Where we live, summer is our wet season and it will rain for days if there's a rain depression or cyclone about. Hanno made a very good undercover line that can be clipped up out of the way when it's not in use. We only use it a dozen times a year, but it keeps us in clean, dry clothes when we need it to.

You can also use a small clothesline that attaches to a brick wall and pulls out when needed. There are many retractable clotheslines on the market, but with a bit of clever thinking and some nylon rope, you may be able to rig up a good line in the garage or on the back porch. There's a link in the Resources for making a small undercover clothes rack that can be stored out of the way.

Drying on racks

I use drying racks for small garments and wool. These are often in use during winter when I'm washing a lot of woollen jumpers and cardigans. They also come in handy when you have a small child in the house, because they're ideal for a small load of washing or hanging all the tiny socks, bibs, hats and so on. Make sure when you buy one of these racks that it can be easily folded up and stored away.

Tumble-drying

I'm not sure I can give good advice on dryers, because I've only bought one, and that was over thirty years ago when I had cloth nappies to dry. I do know that dryers have come a long way since then and although they still use a lot of electricity it's only a fraction of what they used to. Some of you wouldn't think twice about using a dryer, while others try to get around it until the wet laundry is too much to bear. If you have to use the dryer when usually you don't, maybe because of the weather or illness, don't feel guilty. If you can honestly say that you hang your washing out on the line as often as you can, then don't worry about the times when you don't.

For best results get into the habit of cleaning the lint filter before you start drying. The main point to remember about dryers is that high temperatures can damage and shrink clothes. Read your dryer manual, because this is the only way you'll know what each setting is capable of. If you no longer have the manual, set it to a lower temperature. And if you can hang your washing on the line for a while and just finish it off in the dryer, that's even better.

IRONING

You don't have to iron anything if you don't want to. Many people simply fold their laundry straight from the line or dryer. If you don't want to iron at all, you'll get the best results if you smooth and shake clothes and fabrics before hanging them on the line, and if you fold and put them away as soon as they're dry. Leaving dry clothes sitting unfolded in a washing basket will wrinkle them.

Be guided by the settings on your iron for wool, silk and other delicates. If you're not sure, use a pressing cloth – a piece of lint-free cotton. Dampen the cloth and place it over what is to be ironed, adjust the setting on your iron according to the fabric and iron the fabric through the cloth.

So what should you iron? I don't iron clothes I wear around the house, but I iron those I wear when I go out. I don't iron tea towels, but I iron pillowcases because I like to spray them with lavender ironing spray (see the recipe later in this chapter). Just be guided by what you feel comfortable with. Don't be intimidated by anyone who says you must iron everything, or those who say not to iron at all. The only guidelines I will offer are these:

- Iron only clean clothes, not those that have been worn.
- Ironing a stain may set it forever.
- Don't iron velvet, terry towelling, nappies, underwear or nylon.
- Use your common sense. There's no point in adding work to your day when you don't have to. You decide.

CARING FOR OTHER HOUSEHOLD ITEMS

Leather

You'd think that caring for leather would be pretty straightforward; leather has been used for hundreds if not thousands of years. But no, everyone has their own method, and if you look on the internet, as many claims are made for one method as against it.

There are products that clean and condition at the same time but I prefer the two-stage method because leather usually just needs cleaning. To clean leather clothing, hats or couches, check the seams first and if they're dusty, put the upholstery head on the vacuum cleaner and go over them. Then add half a teaspoon of Dr Bronner's liquid castile soap or a mild liquid soap to one cup of warm water and moisten a soft cloth – don't make it too wet. Clean a small area at a time, and finish by rubbing the leather with a clean soft cloth, making sure everything is dry. Every three months or so you can apply a leather conditioner – the products available at car care or equestrian shops seem to be better than those from the supermarket.

For spot-cleaning, deal with the problem as soon as possible. Clean with liquid soap as above and then nourish the area with the leather conditioner.

Wicker baskets

All my wicker baskets are workhorses, used to store everything from potatoes to wool. If you have a dirty basket, brush the wicker with a little liquid soap, not detergent, on a soft wet brush. When you've given it a good clean, take the basket outside and hose it down. This sounds harsh, but it tightens up the wicker and pulls it back into shape. Dry the basket completely before using it again. If you have fragile baskets, simply brush them over with a dry bristle brush and rub a moist cloth over the wicker, then dry in the shade.

Straw hats

Straw hats can be maintained with a soft-bristle brush (I use a paintbrush), all over, as often as you feel like doing it. To clean a dirty hat, mix half a teaspoon of Dr Bronner's liquid castile soap with one cup of warm water. Dip a soft cloth into the warm soapy water and clean small areas of the hat at a time. Make sure you don't wet the hat too much, because it will weaken the straw.

For oily stains, sprinkle the area with cornflour or talcum powder and gently rub it into the straw. Leave it for a couple of hours, then either vacuum or brush off. Repeat if necessary. When not being worn, straw hats should be stored away from the sun, either in a box or on a hook resting on the sweatband, not the straw. Cover with a soft cloth to protect it from dust.

Stuffed toys

Read the care label and if the toy can be washed, wait for a dry, sunny day, place the toy in a pillowcase and close with a rubber band. Add laundry liquid or powder and a teaspoon of either lemon myrtle or tea-tree essential oil to the machine and wash in cold water on the eco or fast setting. Hang the toy on the line in the sun, using an ear or tag to peg it to the line.

If the toy can't be machine-washed, place it in a pillowcase and add 2 tablespoons of bicarb soda. Close the top of the pillowcase with a rubber band and shake it. Try to rub the toy all over through the fabric to make sure every part is covered with bicarb. Leave it for a few hours, then take it out of the pillowcase. Finish off by shaking it outside and then vacuuming the toy with the small upholstery head attached to your vacuum cleaner.

LAUNDRY CLEANING PRODUCTS TO MAKE AT HOME

This is an important part of cleaning, because if you learn how to make your products at home, then customise them to suit your own taste for scent, you'll do two important things: stop adding the phosphates and salt in commercial cleaners to our waterways, and save a lot of money over the years.

These homemade products work well, they don't take a lot of time to make and they won't make your skin itchy and red. Many of these products can be used for multiple purposes. For instance, the laundry liquid will clean your clothes and remove spot stains, but with a couple of simple additions, it can also be made into cleaning paste.

Most of all, you'll know what's in the products you're using. You'll buy only a few natural ingredients – borax, washing soda, vinegar and soap – to make cleaners yourself. If you bought the commercial cleaners and laundry products recommended for the modern home, you'd be using hundreds of chemicals. The incidence of cancer is rising and although we don't know what's caused this, I think living with fewer chemicals is better for our health.

Pure soap from four ingredients

MAKES ABOUT 18 BARS

If you've never made soap before, it's a great skill to have. It will give you excellent soap that everyone can use, from baby to grandpa, including anyone with sensitive skin. I've used it to wash my hair for the last few years, and my hair is healthy and shiny. Listed below are the ingredients I now use in my soap recipe. See *Down to Earth* or the tutorial on my blog (web address in the Resources) for the instructions for how to make it.

450 ml rainwater, or tap water that has been allowed to sit for 24 hours

172 g caustic soda/lye

1000 g olive oil

250 g copha or coconut oil

Laundry liquid

Add about ¼ cup of this liquid to your machine. It's fine in a cold-water wash and in front or top loaders. You can find borax and washing soda in the supermarket.

1 cup grated soap or
Lux soap flakes

½ cup washing soda

½ cup borax

1½ L of water

1. Add the ingredients to a saucepan and heat the mixture on the stove. Stir until all the ingredients are completely dissolved then remove from the heat.
2. Pour the hot soapy mixture into a bucket or tub that holds at least 10 L, add warm tap water until the bucket is about three-quarters full, and stir. When the mixture is thoroughly combined, fill the bucket to the 10 L mark and stir. You can add essential oils for fragrance at this point if you want to.
3. To store the laundry liquid, gather some containers (clean plastic milk bottles serve the purpose well) and pour the liquid in, leaving enough room in the containers to allow you to shake them well before use. As the mixture cools, you'll see two layers: a gel layer at the top and a liquid layer at the bottom. That is as it should be. The gel gets quite thick but combines well with a good shake.

Stain remover

The laundry liquid above makes an excellent stain remover. Just cover the stain with some laundry liquid and rub it in. Wait for 15 minutes before adding the items to the regular wash.

Cleaning paste

You can use the laundry liquid in other ways as well. Just add ½ cup of bicarb soda to ½ cup of laundry liquid and mix together to form a thick paste, adjusting the consistency by adding more liquid or more bicarb. This mix can be used for cleaning baths and stainless steel sinks, or for any difficult-to-remove grime on benchtops or around light switches. Store it in a small container with a lid. It will dry out within a couple of months, so make a smaller amount if you need to.

Fragrant ironing spray

MAKES 2 CUPS

To infuse your fabrics with a lovely smell, give this liquid a good shake then spray onto fabrics before ironing.

6 drops essential oil (such as lavender, rose or citrus, or a combination of your choice)

¼ cup vodka

500 ml purified or spring water

1. Combine the essential oil with the vodka in a jug. Mix with a fork or small whisk.
2. Add the water and mix again. Pour the mixture into a 1 L bottle and shake for at least a minute to fully mix the ingredients. Put it on a shelf to sit overnight to settle, then store it in a spray bottle so it's ready for use.

june

FOOD PRESERVING AND STORAGE

'A place for everything, and everything in its place.'
— MRS ISABELLA BEETON

In June our task is the preserving and storing of food. Whether you're living in a warm climate or a cold one, you'll be changing the type of food you cook now. You'll either be going from summer salads and lighter foods to hearty soups, roasts and stews, or you'll be going in the other direction. What better time to preserve the fresh fruit and vegetables available now to enjoy in the coming seasons? This month, we'll also do some stockpile and pantry maintenance, clean out cupboards, and reorganise provisions. With this, plus a small tidy-up in December, you'll be fully prepared for many new seasons of cooking. Of course, if you don't know how to put up jars of preserves, and if you haven't yet set up a stockpile or pantry, now is the ideal time to learn and create.

Food storage is one of those home chores that may not seem exciting, but as you get into it and think about how your pantry and stockpile support your cooking choices, you'll discover they are a vital part of a productive kitchen. Having those supplies in place can save your sanity on busy days, as well as time and money in the longer term.

THE IMPORTANCE OF FOOD STORAGE

Our great-grandparents knew how to cook wholesome food and also how to manage their time and provisions. They took full advantage of inexpensive but nutrient-dense dried and canned foods, and when there were abundant harvests or cheap local fruit and vegetables, they preserved as much as they could, again saving time and money while keeping that all-important stockpile full.

Cooking, grocery shopping and food storage still have a big impact on how we live. Kitchen management needs to be taught and practised by each generation. Just one break in the chain means that the following generation will not have the skills to pass on. Then those skills are at risk of being lost.

Many of us understand the good sense behind cooking our own meals from scratch. This has been part of the food revolution, and it has reduced our dependence on meat and encouraged us to rediscover old ways of cooking with legumes, pulses, flour, eggs, nuts, vegetables, fruit and preserves. But our lives are so busy that we need to find a way to cook and shop that cuts down on the stress of keeping everyone fed, rather than adding to it. In many homes, food is just parked in the fridge for a day or two between the supermarket and the plate. There may be just a packet of coffee, a few tins of soup or beans, salt and pepper, cereal, dry pasta and tomato sauce in the cupboard.

That is only a fraction of what could be there. We can build on our grandparents' example, transforming our stockpiles from a back-up food cupboard to a delicatessen by adding our own homemade goodies such as flavoured oils and vinegars, jams and marmalades, preserved fruits, dried fruits, spiced nuts and dried home-grown herbs, sauces, chutneys and relishes. Fresh, seasonal food, supplemented by the ingredients we have in our cupboards, gives us the makings of dinners through the week, memorable weekend feasts and long lazy lunches. And all with very few trips to the supermarket.

Properly managed food stores can reduce the cost of living while giving us a variety of delicious food. And if we plan our menus and keep those stockpiles full of what we want to cook, we'll have it right at our fingertips. Non-perishable food can save us time and time again: either cooked as a favourite pantry recipe such as macaroni and cheese, or teamed with fresh food, like adding white bean mash with a drizzle of flavoured oil to some fish and salad.

TIP: When the shopping is done and you're home again, take the time to pack everything away properly. Some food will go into the fridge and freezer, some in the pantry and some in the stockpile. Often the fridge and freezer food has to be divided up and repackaged in freezer bags, zip-lock bags or foil, so start with the cold and frozen foods, and when they're safely stored, move on to the non-perishables.

STOCKPILING

As I mentioned in the March chapter, stockpiling groceries will support your efforts to cook from scratch perhaps more than anything else. It's like having your own private supermarket, open 24/7, with the cheapest prices. Some of the other advantages of stockpiling include:

- You save all that time you currently spend grocery shopping. When your stockpile is fully operational, you'll only have to buy fresh foods such as milk, meat, fruit and vegetables every week. You can do a bigger shop to top up your stockpile when it's needed.
- You save money because you can stock up on the specials.
- You give yourself more cooking options because you have a much wider range of ingredients at your fingertips.
- If there's an unusual situation – if you or your partner are sick or out of work, your children need more of your time for school projects or sports, or friends ask if they can stay with you for a few days – you'll know you can still feed everyone with what's already in your home, sitting in the stockpile cupboard.
- If there's a national emergency – floods, cyclones, terrorist attacks, bushfires – you won't need to leave the safety of your home, because you'll have sufficient provisions.

How to start a stockpile

I started my stockpile by putting aside a certain amount of money each week to buy whatever we used that was on sale. It took three or four months to have my stockpile cupboard at the stage I keep it at now. We have enough non-perishable food, groceries and toiletries to last us about three months.

To start your own stockpile, write out a list of the meals and snacks you usually eat and the ingredients you need to make them. Mark with a highlighter any items that don't need to be stored in the fridge and freezer. This is the start of your stockpile: everything that can be stored for a period of time in a cupboard without deteriorating.

Include only what you know you'll eat and will use. There is absolutely no point in buying a great bargain for stockpiling if you don't eat it. If you bake your own bread, include bread flour, seeds and yeast; if you bake your own cakes and biscuits, include sultanas, dates, brown sugar, cocoa, choc chips, nuts and so on. But also make room for tinned salmon, sardines and tuna, olive oil, a variety of vinegars, spices and seasonings, pulses, grains and legumes, dried pasta, milk powder, sugar, flour, cornflour, canned tomatoes, tomato paste, honey and peanut butter.

TIP: In addition to food, look for soap, toilet paper, tissues, toothpaste, toothbrushes and cleaning products - or the ingredients for these if you make your own (bicarb soda, white vinegar, borax, washing soda and laundry soap).

Usually stockpile goods are bought on special or produced at home. However, if you shop at Aldi, where the prices are consistently lower than the other supermarkets, you may be able to add to your stockpile whenever you see something you need. If you shop at one of the other supermarkets, monitor the grocery flyers and read your supermarket webpages for specials and stock up on the items you need when they're on sale.

You'll find that most supermarkets have a large number of groceries and food they put on special regularly over a period of about three months. (Be aware that some things, such as vanilla extract, nuts and baking goods, are rarely reduced in price.) When you see a good price for something you need, buy enough to carry you through until it comes on special again, or as much as you can afford. Check the use-by or best-before dates and make sure the packaging isn't damaged – the items will need to last a while. Don't buy dented canned goods or jars with rust on the lid, but it's okay to buy something in a ripped paper, cellophane or plastic bag – it's easy enough to transfer it to a new bag for storage.

Don't forget that you can add homemade food to your stockpile as well, such as relishes, chutneys, sauces, jams, pickles and sweet fruit preserves. If you add home-preserved food, make sure you use proven preserving recipes because the acid and sugar ratios will be correct and the produce will therefore last for as long as the recipe indicates. All your jars must be labelled and dated too.

Freezer stockpiling

I encourage you to buy a deep freezer if you can afford one. Look around for a good price, or save up for the mid-year or end-of-year sales. I think chest freezers are excellent, but if you have a bad back or don't have time to keep it organised, an upright freezer may be the way to go for you.

Having a deep freezer will allow you to store a wide variety of raw and cooked foods for several months, depending on the food. You'll be able to take advantage of buying meat in bulk. You can also store harvests from your garden, or cheap buys at the markets, by blanching and freezing. Most bread, cakes, pikelets, scones and so on can be baked and then frozen. Pizza scrolls, cinnamon rolls and biscuits can be made up and then stored unbaked in the freezer; it's simply a matter of taking out the scrolls and rolls the night before you want to bake them. The biscuit dough should be frozen in a long log so you can slice off the amount you want to bake and put the rest of the log back in the freezer.

Freezing doesn't require special equipment apart from the freezer itself. If well wrapped and added to the freezer when it's fresh, food usually retains its nutrition, texture and colour. Most freezers have a guide to how long certain foods can be kept frozen. However, freezers do cost money to operate; you also run the risk of losing food to spoilage if your power is cut for a length of time.

For the best results, keep your freezer running according to the instructions in the freezer manual and away from a window that might cast sunlight on it. The Australian *Choice* magazine recommends that it be kept at -18°C. If you have an older freezer, or a freezer compartment within a fridge, check its temperature to make sure you can safely store food for a long period of time.

> TIP: A freezer, particularly a chest freezer, can be a difficult space to manage. A record of what goes in, with the date, and what comes out, will give you an accurate inventory at any time so you don't have to unpack the freezer to see what's at the bottom.

Where to store food

You can store non-perishable food anywhere: in a cupboard, under the bed, in the garage, or any sheltered place that suits you. I have mine in a few places. My main stockpile cupboard holds unopened food that is not needed yet. When I need it, I take it from the stockpile near the kitchen, transfer it into a sealed container and then store it in the pantry, which is in my kitchen. I also use two freezers: one attached to the fridge in the kitchen for vegetables, homemade cakes, bread and ice cream, and a chest freezer, located in the second bathroom, that holds my stores of meat, fish and homemade fruit juice. I also use that freezer to kill any bugs in the flour and dried foods I buy, such as rice, oats and grains. After placing them in the freezer for a couple of days, I can store all those things confidently in the stockpile, knowing I won't have weevils in the oats or a cupboard full of pantry moths ready to fly out into the kitchen.

We have a toiletries stockpile in a cupboard in the second bathroom and a cleaning ingredients stockpile in the laundry. So as you can see, a stockpile can go anywhere you have space – but try to keep the items as close as possible to where you'll eventually use them.

TIP: If you have no cupboard storage but you do have space under a bed, build a shallow box slightly smaller than the bed. Attach four castors, and a rope handle on the side so you can slide it out easily, and you'll have a good space for tins, jars, packets and boxes.

Keeping the cupboard clean and orderly

Group products that are the same or similar in one place. For instance, if you have tins of tomatoes, tomato paste and tomato puree, keep them together. This will help you when you're searching for something or checking your supplies before shopping. Always rotate your stock by adding new products to the back and taking from the front, and make sure you check your supplies every so often:

- Look at the home-preserved food to make sure there are no bubbles, which indicate fermenting.
- If a container leaks, clean it up straight away and replace the container.
- Check use-by dates and use any items that are close to expiring.
- If you see a split or ripped packet, take it out and place it in a zip-lock bag or a storage container.

Glass or plastic containers?

As soon as you open a packet, store its contents in a sealed container. If you're buying containers you hope to use for many years, I'd encourage you towards glass – it won't deteriorate over time or change colour. If you're careful not to drop them, glass containers will outlast you. I prefer glass containers for food, and most of my containers in the pantry are preserving jars with metal lids. I do use plastic bins for bread flour and rolled oats because I can't get glass containers large enough.

You'll need a few shallow storage baskets to keep dried herbs and spices and other small items in. If they're all together in a container, they won't get pushed to the back of the cupboard and lost.

HOME PRODUCTION

There are many food products that are easy to preserve at home. They are usually tastier, healthier and cheaper than those you can buy, and by adding them to your stockpile you'll be increasing your options when it's time to prepare a meal. The trick is to find a few hours when you can make some of your favourite preserves, pickles, spice blends or whatever you want to store.

TIP: Invite a friend around for a preserving afternoon and share the fruits of your labour.

Be inspired by the seasons: when your backyard lemon tree produces a good crop or there's a seasonal abundance of cheap lemons in the shops, pick or buy enough to make lemon butter, cordial, sweet preserved lemon slices, salted lemons, marmalade and lemon juice ice cubes. These will add such splendid variety to your cooking, you'll be looking around for your next preserving project in no time. You're never going to preserve everything you want in one afternoon, but make it an ongoing activity and explore the endless options.

Here's a list of dairy foods, baked goods, sauces, spreads, relishes and chutneys you can make and store at home:

DAIRY
Yoghurt
Ice cream
Cheese
Butter
Buttermilk
Sour cream

BAKING
Bread, bread rolls and fruit buns
Biscuits and crackers
Cakes
Slices
Scones
Pikelets
Pizza scrolls (premade, un-baked)
Cinnamon rolls (premade, unbaked)

CONDIMENTS
Tomato sauce
BBQ sauce
Mint sauce
Chutney
Relish
Chilli jam
Chocolate sauce
Butterscotch sauce

PICKLED FOOD
Bread and butter pickles
Gherkins
Pickled beetroot
Pickled eggs
Pickled onions
Sauerkraut
Kimchi

SPREADS AND PRESERVED LEMONS
Berry jams
Stone fruit jams
Citrus marmalades
Lemon and passionfruit curd
Salted preserved lemons
Sweet preserved lemons
Nut butters (I always store these in the fridge)

SALAD DRESSINGS AND VINAIGRETTES
French dressing
Italian dressing
Ranch dressing
Mayonnaise
Flavoured mayonnaise

SPICE BLENDS
Curry powder
Taco seasoning
Garam masala
Chilli seasoning
BBQ spice mix
Beef stew seasoning
Chicken seasoning
Gravy mix
Potato wedges mix
Spicy breadcrumbs

SNACKS
Spicy nuts
Potato crisps and straws
Popcorn
Dips

ODDS AND ENDS
Breadcrumbs
Cinnamon sugar
Vanilla sugar

Strawberry jam

MAKES ABOUT 1.4 LITRES

If you've never made jam, sauce or relish before, I encourage you to make this the first recipe you try. You don't need special equipment and, in season, strawberries are fairly cheap and easy to get for most of us. Commercial jams often taste like very sweet syrup; this jam tastes like sweet strawberries.

You have to be careful when changing recipes for preserves because the sugar and acid – be that lemon juice or vinegar – help with the preserving and setting process. If you plan to store the jams or sauces in the fridge rather than the cupboard, it doesn't matter how you change the recipe. It will last for at least 3 months in the fridge. However, if you're going to store it in the cupboard, be careful and avoid making adjustments to the ratio of ingredients. You can store it unopened in the cupboard for up to 12 months. And don't forget you can freeze jam too. It won't freeze solid so you can pack it in small containers and just bring out one when you need it.

1 kg strawberries

500 g white sugar

500 g jam sugar (widely available in supermarkets)

150 ml fresh lemon juice

YOU'LL ALSO NEED:

4 recycled jam jars or 4 preserving jars about 350 ml each in capacity

wide-top saucepan

saucer (placed in the freezer)

jug or funnel

1. Wash the strawberries and remove the stems and leaves.
2. Over low heat, place about a quarter of the strawberries into the saucepan with 1 cup of the white sugar. Mash well with a potato masher. This will release the juice and you won't have to add any water.
3. When the fruit heats up a little, add the rest of the strawberries. Stir while the fruit comes to the boil and make sure it doesn't burn. Turn the heat down and let the berries simmer. After 5 minutes, while the fruit is simmering, add the rest of the white sugar and jam sugar and stir until it has completely dissolved. Stir in the lemon juice.
4. Increase the heat and keep the jam at a rolling boil for 5–10 minutes. It will set when it reaches 104.5°C/220°F, so if you have a thermometer, test the temperature. If not, use the saucer method: drop a spoonful of jam onto a very cold saucer and allow it to cool, then push your finger into it. If the jam is thick and sticks to your finger, it's ready. If it's still liquid and thin, continue boiling for another 3 minutes. Then test again.

5. When the jam is set and still hot, pour into warm, sterilised jars and seal. Label the jars with name and date. As the jam cools, the pop-top on the metal lid will invert and you'll know a vacuum in the jar has formed a good seal. Don't put these jars on display in the light as it will darken the jam and it won't taste as good. If the pop-top doesn't invert, the jam is still good to eat but you should store it in the fridge.

    TIP: The strawberries should be bright red, and about half of them should be under-ripe. If you are given some ripe or overripe strawberries, you can still use them but use all jam sugar instead of a mix of white sugar and jam sugar.

If you're careful not to drop them, glass containers will outlast you

Lemon curd

MAKES ABOUT 1 LITRE

Lemon curd is the great Australian backyard preserve. In the past, many of us had chickens in the backyard, along with at least one lemon tree. Now that great backyard duo is making a return, so if you have eggs and lemons, you can make lemon curd till the cows come home. Having lemon curd in the fridge during the year will help you produce many desserts and cakes, as well as it taking pride of place on your morning toast, crumpets, pancakes or muffins. When you perfect your recipe, make extra – jars of lemon curd are always well received as gifts at Christmas and throughout the year.

Store in the fridge and use within two weeks. When a jar is open, use within four days.

360 g sugar

140 g unsalted butter

5 small eggs, lightly beaten

juice and fine zest of 4 large clean lemons

YOU'LL ALSO NEED:

saucepan

heat-proof bowl

4 x 250 ml recycled jars or preserving jars

1. Quarter-fill the saucepan with water so that when you place the bowl on top, it doesn't touch the water. Place the saucepan on the heat and bring to a simmer.
2. Put all the ingredients into the heat-proof bowl and mix with a whisk. As the mixture heats up, it will start to thicken. When the mixture coats the back of the spoon, it's ready.
3. Pour into warm, sterilised jars. Label the jars with name and date.

Dehydrated apple rings

Apple rings are a great addition to your stockpile cupboard because they can be used as snacks or, rehydrated, in baking and desserts. If you have an apple tree, use whatever variety you're growing. If you have to buy apples, buy Granny Smiths: they're available everywhere, they're fairly cheap and they hold their shape.

Drying fruit is simple. You need to place the apples in an area that will heat up enough to remove all liquid from the fruit without cooking it. When all the moisture has drained from the apples, they're ready to be eaten or stored away. You can dehydrate your apples in an oven that operates on a very low temperature (40–80°C/100–170°F), on a drying rack in the sun, or in your car if you have warm to hot weather.

There is a bit of flexibility in drying apple rings; it doesn't need the precision of preserving. I prefer peeled apples because the skin is quite tough when it's dried, but you can leave the peel on if you prefer. Many people recommend dipping the apple rings in acidulated water, but I have found they don't need it: there will be a small amount of browning either way. If you want to dip them, add one part fresh lemon juice to three parts water.

These slices can be stored in the cupboard in a sealed jar for up to six months.

apples

YOU'LL ALSO NEED:

knife or mandolin

oven tray or large cake rack

baking paper

1. Peel the apples and slice them thinly and evenly with a mandolin or knife, so that each slice dries at the same rate.
2. Cover an oven tray or cake rack with baking paper. Place the slices on the paper and put the tray in the oven, outside in the sun or in the car. Leave until the slices are completely dry. The drying time will depend on a few things such as thickness of the slices, the variety of apple, how crisp you want the slices to be and the humidity and temperature. It will take longer in high humidity and less time with high temperature.

TIP: Make sure the apple slices are completely dry, or they'll rot in the jar. You can test them by placing a few slices, still warm, in a jar with the lid on. If a lot of condensation forms inside the jar, they aren't dry enough. It's okay to leave the slices covered overnight and continue the drying process the following day.

july

SIMPLE HOME BAKES

'. . . he got out the luncheon-basket and packed
a simple meal, in which, remembering the stranger's
origin and preferences, he took care to include a yard
of long French bread, a sausage out of which the garlic
sang, some cheese which lay down and cried, and
a long-necked straw-covered flask wherein lay bottled
sunshine shed and garnered on far Southern slopes.'
— KENNETH GRAHAME

DID YOU MAKE THIS?

When visitors are expected, it always makes me feel good to set the kitchen table with a special cloth, fresh flowers, napkins, tea, coffee and just-baked cakes, slices or biscuits. Always, the first question I'm asked is: did you make this? I smile when I answer 'yes'. I think such a spread acknowledges the importance of our visitors and the significance of providing hospitality. I believe that offering visitors good food, drinks and a comfortable place to rest, especially visitors who have travelled a long way, is part of living a simple life.

In addition to baking for visitors, many of us see the good sense in providing our family with bread and simple baked goods every day. If you're a new baker, and even if you aren't, this chapter will guide you through baking, whether it's a daily or occasional task. If you eat bread or like to put snacks such as cakes, biscuits or slices in lunchboxes, then baking is a good skill to develop.

I've placed baking in July, which is in the middle of the Australian winter, but while it is a delight to bake in winter, and to fill our home with the aroma of hot bread and freshly baked biscuits, baking can be done any day of the year. In fact, for many years now I've baked several times a week, and still feel comforted and satisfied each time I serve what I bake to my family and friends.

There is no doubt that by making your baked goods at home you'll save money, but you'll also be healthier for it. Home baking doesn't rely on the preservatives and flavour enhancers that are commonly included in super-market-baked products such as bread, biscuits/cookies, cakes, flans and pies. You'll be able to offer your family a greater diversity of baked goodies, including the traditional baking of your own heritage, and you can modify favourite recipes exactly to your own liking or dietary needs. These are the main benefits for me. I'm glad that we're not eating the preservatives and additives that are so common in food nowadays. I enjoy adding what we like and making our food right in my own kitchen.

Storing ingredients

If you do a lot of baking and have the storage space, try to buy your baking ingredients in bulk. I often buy bread flour in a 12.5 kg bag with a few 5 kg bags of other flours such as rye, mixed grain, corn and barley or wholemeal. There is a shop in a nearby town that sells bulk flour and other dry goods such as dried fruits, coffee, tea, spices, sugar and cereal. If you have no local shop, you may find a similar store online that can deliver through the post or by courier. Make sure your potential purchases will be cost-effective before you order. Buying in bulk helps you bypass the wasteful packaging that more often than not surrounds purchased food. Supermarket cakes, biscuits and snacks are often over-packaged, with plastic and aluminium trays, small bags in larger bags, and a lot of cellophane or plastic wrapping.

Store your ingredients in sealed glass or plastic containers so you never waste any, and when you bring home new bags of flour, or any dry goods, if you have the space, put them in the freezer for a couple of days to kill off any larvae that might be in the packet. Once they've had that initial time in the freezer, you can take them out and store as normal on the shelf, confident that you won't be troubled by pantry moths or weevils.

TIP: A chest freezer with a very good energy rating is generally a sound investment in a simple home. It will allow you to kill off insects in dry goods such as bread flour, store bulk ingredients and meat as well as pre-prepared food. It doesn't have to be situated in the kitchen because you won't use it frequently. Any cool place out of sunlight will be fine.

Caring for your equipment

I don't have many fancy gadgets, just an electric mixer, food processor, baking trays and utensils such as a spatula, measuring spoons and cups, cookie cutters and a rolling pin. I have good-quality baking trays and pie tins and I look after them.

Some bakeware will be sold with specific instructions on how to bake in the tin or tray for the first time and how to care for it over the life of the item. Always follow those instructions.

Aluminum is an excellent conductor of heat and aluminium cake tins are the best value for money bakeware. If there are no instructions, wash the baking tin or tray by hand without using detergent or soap, then dry. The first time you use it for a butter cake, or any cake containing fat, either brush melted butter on the interior of the pan or line it with parchment paper. You can hold the parchment paper in place with a dab of butter in a few places. If you're cooking a sponge or other cake with no fat in it, don't butter or line the baking tin. Do not use olive oil to grease your aluminium bakeware because, over time, it will discolour it.

When you finish baking, wait till the tin has cooled and soak it in warm soapy water for about an hour. Then simply rub over the tin with a soft dish-cloth and make sure all the fat and any remnants of cake are removed. Dry completely before storing. If you're storing one cake tin inside another, it's a good idea to place a sheet of paper towel or a clean cotton rag inside the tins so they don't rub together.

Never cut a cake in the tin and don't use a pointed knife to help remove the cake from the tin.

I have a range of enamel cookware, including a cookie sheet and pie dishes. To clean them after baking, allow them to cool, soak in warm soapy water for an hour and wipe over. If there is a lingering stain, make a paste of bicarb soda and water and apply that to the stain. Let it sit for a couple of hours and then wash off. Dry completely before storing and be careful when storing one thing inside the other because enamel can chip.

RECIPES

As with any made-from-scratch recipe, the results you get will depend on the ingredients you use, as well as your techniques. I hope you don't substitute margarine for the butter because, frankly, if you do, you might as well buy commercial biscuits and cakes full of trans fats. Try to source local ingredients if you can; if not, buy the best quality you can afford. That doesn't mean buying the most expensive ingredients. You'll need to do a bit of test buying and tasting. Look for different butters, flours and milk and see which of them you prefer. From then on, buy them and not what's on special or the most expensive.

For the new bakers, I'll include some tips that I picked up from my mother, father (a baker) and grandmother, and from my own experience over the many decades I've been baking. I hope they'll help you develop your baking to the point where you can have homemade bread, cakes and biscuits for your family and visitors every day.

There is a link for a conversion calculator and a list of Australian measurements in the Resources section. See tables on page 294.

Offering visitors good food, drinks and a comfortable place to rest is part of living a simple life.

OUR DAILY BREAD

Bread is one of those foods that, when made with our own hands, gives a great deal of satisfaction and delight. It's only a mix of basic ingredients but it symbolises so much of what I hold close, such as home cooking, self-reliance and slow living. I have tried making sourdough breads but I've not been happy with any of them. I'll continue to experiment with it, though, because I like the idea of using wild yeasts and saving the starter over the years to develop flavour and become a part of the family.

I hope I can encourage you to make bread at home. If you find a good supplier of flour, homemade bread will probably be much cheaper than what you buy at the bakery or supermarket. The price will depend on the type of flour you use. Organic flour and spelt is more expensive than regular flour, but your bread made with organic or spelt flour will be less expensive than the organic or spelt bread you'll buy at a bakery.

Bread flour, also known as high-protein flour, strong flour or baker's flour, is high in a protein called gluten. Some people can't tolerate gluten and if they want to eat bread, they have to find bread that is either gluten-free or low in gluten. I have never baked low-gluten or gluten-free bread, but I have added a recipe for a gluten-free buckwheat loaf that looks easy and delicious to the Resources.

Bread flour can be wholemeal, wholegrain, light or dark rye, white, corn and barley or a blend of a couple of different flours. One of the benefits of making your own bread is that you can mix your flours and make it exactly to your taste.

There are many ways to make good bread. You can make it entirely by hand or use a bread machine or mixer. You can use a bread machine to knead the dough and finish it off in the oven, or you can use the overnight no-knead method. All work well; you need to try them and find which method suits you the best and which your family enjoys. I make bread three different ways: sometimes I hand-knead, sometimes I use the no-knead method, and I often use the bread machine to knead the dough and then finish the bread in the oven.

Here are some tips for bread baking:

- Once you've opened a packet of yeast, pour it into a jar and store it in the fridge. It should keep well for many months.
- The amount of water you use will depend on the type of flour you use, and your climate. The denser flours such as wholemeal and wholegrain will need more water than white flour. Flour is affected by humidity, so you'll use less water in humid weather.
- Baking is a multi-sensory skill. You see, touch, feel and smell it. Not-quite-cooked bread and cakes may look cooked because they're golden-brown on top. Generally you can be sure it's cooked if it's golden-brown *and* it smells like baked bread or cake.
- Use warm rather than hot water as hot water will kill the yeast. If you can comfortably put your finger in the cup of water, it's the right temperature. And remember that the water you dissolve the yeast in is counted as part of your water content for the loaf.

Sandwich loaf

This is my basic bread recipe – it's tried and true over many years. It is made in the bread machine but the same recipe can be made by hand. You can find the web address for the step-by-step tutorial on my blog in the Resources.

If you put the ingredients into the machine at night and set the timer, you'll have hot bread for breakfast and fresh bread for packed lunches the following day. Follow your bread machine's manual for details on how to pack the ingredients for an overnight bake. If you get it in the machine by 9 a.m., you'll have hot bread for lunch. With this one simple recipe and your bread machine, making additive-free fresh bread can be an easy part of your daily routine.

If you're new to bread baking, take some time to work on your bread, adjusting the quantity of salt, adding a tablespoon of soft butter or oil when you add the liquid, using milk instead of water, or half milk and half water. Experiment with different flours. Of course, you may just find that you, like me, enjoy the basic recipe, but experimenting is the only way you'll settle on the bread that suits you and your family, the bread you'll bake for years.

2 teaspoons dried yeast

1 teaspoon sugar or honey

¼ cup warm water

1 teaspoon salt

4 cups bread flour
(any variety – wholemeal, rye, white, grain or spelt)

350 ml warm water

1. Mix the first three ingredients together in a cup to check the freshness of the yeast. It should be frothy and bubbling after about 5 minutes. If nothing has happened after 10 minutes, the yeast is dead; you'll have to buy a fresh packet.

2. Add the salt to your bread machine bucket, then the flour, then the water and yeast mixture. (It doesn't really matter which order they go in, although you should keep the salt and yeast separate.) If you need more water, add it slowly, one tablespoon at a time.

3. When all the ingredients are in the bucket, if you only want the machine to knead and proof the dough, turn the machine on to the dough setting. If you want to bake the loaf in the machine, choose the setting appropriate to the flour you used.

Five-minute bread

This five-minute loaf was popular on the internet a few years ago. Although many people have forgotten it now, I'm still making it, and everyone I serve it to still enjoys it. You have to do some of the preparation the day before, but it takes only about five minutes of actual work and is the easiest of all bread varieties to make and to get consistently good loaves. It's similar to sourdough, with holes in the bread, a chewy crust and a great flavour. If you're having people around for lunch or dinner, this is the bread you'd bake, not the plain old sandwich loaf. I hope you try it.

The most effective container to use for baking this loaf is a cast-iron pot or Dutch oven, although you could try a stainless steel pot as long is it's all metal. Pyrex is not recommended. It must have a lid to give the loaf a steamy environment in which to cook in those first 30 minutes. It must be capable of getting really hot, because you want the dough to bake as a tight ball and not spread out over the bottom of the pan, and the high heat at the beginning will help that. I don't grease my Dutch oven, but I do put in a small disc of baking paper on the base that does not need to be changed every time I bake.

I'm sure there are many ways to make this bread, but this is how I do it, based on the old *New York Times* recipe (the web address of the original is in the Resources).

3 cups flour (*any variety – rye, wholemeal, white or wholegrain bread flour, or even plain white flour*)

1 teaspoon salt

¼ teaspoon dry yeast

1 ¾ cups warm water

1. Late in the afternoon before the day you want the bread, place the flour in a large bowl. Add the salt, and then the yeast (don't add them together as salt can kill yeast) and mix together. Add 1¾ cups water and mix with your hands until all the flour and water have mixed together completely. This mixing (not kneading) will take less than a minute. The dough should be moist and sticky, so if you have to add slightly more water to get the right consistency, do so now – a tablespoon at a time.

2. Cover the bowl with plastic wrap and leave it on the kitchen bench overnight. During the night it will puff up and expand.

3. The next day, turn the dough out onto a floured surface and knead it. You want it to look smooth and to all come together, but kneading will only take a minute or so. Form the dough into a tight ball, with a smooth top and a folded bottom, and place this ball on a floured tea towel and allow it to rise for an hour. About 45 minutes later, place a cast-iron Dutch oven, with lid, in the oven and preheat to about 260°C/500°F – or as high as your oven will go.

4. When the dough is risen and the oven is really hot, slide the oven shelf out slightly to give yourself a bit of room, then plop the dough into the Dutch oven, smooth side up. Snip the top of it with a pair of scissors or slice it with a very sharp knife. This helps the loaf rise and will give you that rustic look you want in a loaf like this.

5. Put the lid on, close the oven door and bake for 30 minutes. The loaf should have risen and be a pale golden colour. Turn down the heat to 200°C/390°F, remove the lid and bake for another 15–30 minutes, depending on your oven. When the loaf is a golden-brown colour and smells cooked, remove the Dutch oven and place the bread on a rack to cool.

Bread is one of those foods that, when made with our own hands, gives a great deal of satisfaction and delight

Flat bread

MAKES 6

Flat breads add variety to the lunchbox and they're easy to carry if they're wrapped firmly, or left flat to be filled at lunchtime. Those who like a hearty lunch will probably enjoy chicken, cheese and avocado with sweet chilli sauce, or leftover roast lamb and coleslaw – the lamb can be rolled in the flat bread at home and the coleslaw carried in a small, lidded container to be added just before eating. You can cut the flat bread into triangles and add them to the lunchbox with a thermos of hot soup in winter, or for dipping into a small container of homemade guacamole or cheese dip as part of a summer lunch.

I like to cook my flat bread in a cast-iron pan, but use any pan you have that you know won't stick.

250 g self-raising flour, plus a little extra for dusting

1 teaspoon sea salt

1 teaspoon baking powder

250 g natural yoghurt

1. Place all the ingredients into a food processor and pulse until a dough forms. If the dough is too wet, add a small amount of flour and pulse again. Remove the dough and place it on a floured board.
2. Roll into a long sausage shape and cut into 6 equal pieces. Roll each piece into a disc and then flatten it using a rolling pin. The discs need to be very thin and about the size of a bread-and-butter plate.
3. Place one disc at a time into a non-stick pan and cook each side for about 2 minutes on medium heat. When it's ready, it will have small charred spots on each side and will smell baked. Place on a cake rack to cool.

TIP: Flat breads freeze well. Store them in a freezer bag with a piece of baking paper between each of them.

CAKES AND PUDDINGS

I would like to share a few easy recipes with you so you have something tasty for morning tea and dessert. All these cakes and puddings are well tested – I've been making them for my own family for many years. Some are family recipes, and some were recipes I found that were so easy and delicious I kept making them.

Here are some tips to help with your cake and pudding baking:

- Creaming is mixing butter and sugar together with an electric mixer to create a light mixture that will help the cake rise. The butter should be fairly cold, but not hard. Using room-temperature butter will give you a flatter cake with a dense texture. Beat the butter without the sugar first and when it has formed a creamier texture, add the sugar and beat on a medium setting until pale and creamy.

- It is better to undercook a cake than overcook it. Even five extra minutes in the oven will dry out a cake when what you're looking for is a moist texture that will retain freshness for longer. As soon as you smell the cake baking, start checking with your toothpick. Remember, the cake will continue cooking for a short while after you remove it from the oven, so err on the side of moistness rather than dryness.

- If you run out of self-raising flour, make a batch by adding 1 teaspoon of baking powder to 1 cup of plain flour, then sifting together.

- While not absolutely necessary, using cake flour when making cakes will give a lighter and more tender crumb and a cake that will remain fresh for a day or two longer.

- To make a substitute for cake flour, remove 1 tablespoon of flour from a cup of plain flour and add 1 teaspoon of cornflour and 1 teaspoon of baking powder, then sift together.

Butter cake

The best recipe to start off with is the butter cake, because it can be used as the basis of so many other cakes. A butter cake is excellent as itself, but you can add almost any kind of flavouring or fruit to give variety – chocolate, coffee, apple, sultana or ginger, for example. A plain butter cake is perfect for a child's birthday: it's fairly solid and will hold its shape, even with a lot of icing and decorations (wait until it's completely cold before decorating it). The cake is also a good morning tea or lunchbox cake, served plain or with a scrape of butter.

This recipe is from Fiona at Buena Vista Farm, and I must have made it dozens of times since I found it. It's similar to my grandmother's butter cake recipe, but I think slightly better. It's a never-fail cake, and we all need those in our repertoire.

125 g chilled butter

1 cup white sugar

2 eggs, room temperature

2 cups self-raising flour

1 cup milk

1. Preheat the oven to 180°C/350°F and lightly grease a 20 cm round cake tin. Using electric beaters, beat the butter and sugar together until thick and creamy. Beat in 1 egg at a time.

2. Stir in 1 cup of flour. Add half the milk. Stir in the other cup of flour. Stir in the other half-cup of milk.

3. Pour the batter into the tin and bake for about 30 minutes. Check the cake with a toothpick as soon as you smell it baking. If the toothpick comes out clean, take the cake out of the oven and let it sit in the tin for 5 minutes, then turn it out carefully onto a rack to cool.

TIP: If you forget to get the eggs out of the fridge in time for them to come to room temperature, place them in a jug and fill the jug with warm, not hot, water. Leave the eggs in the warm water until you're ready to use them, or about 5 minutes.

Chocolate yoghurt cake

I love using yoghurt or sour cream in cakes. They make lovely cakes that can last in the fridge, moist and delicious, for four or five days. This recipe is for a chocolate cake, although the basic recipe can quite easily be modified to produce a coffee, lemon, orange or vanilla cake. It's made using natural ingredients and probiotics, but when you serve it to most people, all they'll see and taste is chocolate cake.

125 g chilled butter

1 cup brown sugar

3 eggs, room temperature

1½ cups self-raising flour

2 tablespoons cocoa

¾ cup natural yoghurt

1. Preheat the oven to 180°C/350°F and lightly grease and line a 20 cm round cake tin. Cream the butter and sugar together, then add the eggs, one at a time. When the mixture is fluffy, add the sifted flour and cocoa and fold in.
2. Fold in the yoghurt. The batter should be fairly thick, but this will depend on the thickness of the yoghurt. If it's too thick, add a little water or milk to thin it down a bit.
3. Bake for about 30 minutes or until a toothpick inserted in the middle comes out clean.

Basic icing

2 cups icing sugar

4 tablespoons milk, water or fresh fruit juice

1 teaspoon vanilla extract

1. Sift the icing sugar into a bowl and add the liquid. Stir until it comes together at a thick pouring consistency. Add the vanilla extract, mix well and use the icing straight away. The cake must be completely cool before you ice it.

Bread and fruit pudding

SERVES 6

It's a good idea to have a number of recipes in your collection to use up leftovers of all types and minimise food wastage. This baked pudding is a good one to make on a cold winter's evening when you need to use up some leftover bread. It's hearty and warming and you can use any kind of fruit you have on hand. Fresh, frozen or canned apples, cherries or blueberries are all excellent additions. You can even use dried fruit; just soak it for a few hours before using. Use what you have; don't buy anything specially for this. This pudding is best served straight from the oven.

½ loaf stale bread, thickly sliced

2 cups milk

40 g soft butter

½ cup sugar

3 eggs, separated

zest of 1 lemon

3 tablespoons plain flour

¼ teaspoon baking powder

500 g fruit

1 tablespoon breadcrumbs

5 small knobs of butter

1. Preheat the oven to 190°C/375°F and grease a small baking pan or lasagna tray. Place the bread slices in a bowl, pour the milk over them and allow to soak.
2. Place the butter, 5 tablespoons of the sugar and the egg yolks into a bowl and whisk until light and creamy. Add the lemon zest, flour, baking powder and milk-soaked bread and mix thoroughly.
3. In a separate bowl, whisk the egg whites until stiff and then gently fold them into the other ingredients.
4. Spoon a layer of the mixture into the tray, and then a layer of the fruit. Continue layering until all the mixture is in the baking tray. Sprinkle the breadcrumbs and the last tablespoon of sugar over the top and dot with the knobs of butter.
5. Bake for about 40 minutes and serve hot with cream, ice cream or custard.

Jam roly poly

This is an old favourite from my childhood, a classic dessert because almost everyone would have all the ingredients in their pantry. I hesitated to include this recipe because it's so simple; when I was young it was something everyone knew how to make. But times have changed and it's exactly this kind of old-fashioned cooking that many modern cooks want to learn.

If you don't have jam, you can use stewed fruit – stewed apples and sultanas would be ideal. You need a 23 cm pie dish with sides for this recipe because the roly poly will spread out if cooked on a flat tray.

2 cups self-raising flour

pinch of salt

2 tablespoons sugar

40 g butter, at room temperature

enough milk to make a firm dough

½ cup jam

1. Place the flour, salt and sugar into a mixing bowl and mix with a fork to combine. Using your fingertips, rub the butter into the flour. When it's combined, add the milk and mix to form a dough.
2. Place the dough on a plate, cover with a moist cotton tea towel and leave it in the fridge for about 30 minutes to firm up.
3. Preheat the oven to 180°C/350°F. On a lightly floured board or bench, roll out the dough into a rectangle. Cut off any bits that poke out so you have a neat shape. Cover the dough with jam and carefully roll it into a sausage shape. You might need the help of a palette knife or egg lifter. Brush with milk and place into an ovenproof baking dish. Curl it around to fit the dish.
4. Bake for about 30 minutes or until golden and bubbly. Serve with custard or cream.

Easy cheese crackers

MAKES 20–30

This is a modified version of the common recipe for cheese crackers. Although this can be made with almost any hard cheese, the crackers will be better if you use a sharp, strong-flavoured cheese. If you want a spicy cracker, add 1 teaspoon of chilli powder or paprika to the dough. Sprinkle with sesame seeds before baking if you'd like an extra level of flavour and crunch.

125 g grated cheddar cheese

125 g grated parmesan cheese

80 g butter, room temperature

1 cup plain flour

2 tablespoons iced water

1. Preheat the oven to 180°C/350°F. Place the cheese, butter and flour in a food processor and mix. (Or you could rub the butter and cheese into the flour with your fingertips instead.)
2. Add enough iced water to bring together as a stiff dough, similar to a pastry dough. Let it rest in the fridge for about 30 minutes.
3. Roll out thinly and cut into squares or rounds with a cookie cutter or knife. Make holes in each cracker with a fork and add preferred topping.
4. Place on a baking tray and bake for about 15 minutes, or until the biscuits are golden-brown. Cool on a rack and store in an airtight jar.

TIP: These crackers will go from golden-brown to overcooked very quickly, so check them after 10 minutes and every minute after that until they're cooked.

Chocolate crinkle biscuits

MAKES 50

This biscuit dough is suitable for freezing, so you can make the dough up and cut off the portion you want to bake. Store the other portion well wrapped in baking paper in a freezer bag in the freezer until needed.

1 cup cocoa

1 cup white sugar

½ cup vegetable oil

4 eggs

1 cup choc chips

2 teaspoons vanilla extract

2 cups self-raising flour

icing sugar for dipping

1. Preheat the oven to 180°C/350°F and line a biscuit tray with baking paper. Into a large bowl, add the cocoa, sugar and vegetable oil and mix with a wooden spoon. Beat in the eggs one at a time, then add the vanilla.
2. Add the flour and choc chips and mix into the cocoa mixture. Cover the bowl with plastic wrap and chill in the fridge for at least 4 hours, or overnight.
3. Roll the dough into walnut-size balls and dip in icing sugar before adding them to the tray. Space the balls apart, because they will spread a small amount. Bake for 10–12 minutes, then let them stand on the tray for a minute before transferring to wire racks to cool.

TIP: You'll get better results with all biscuits if you chill your dough before placing it in the oven to bake. If the dough is room temperature, the biscuits will spread and join up on the tray.

Lunchbox food needs to be transportable and tempting. It helps if you have a container that separates the courses and stops lunches breaking up. Following are some recipes for savoury and sweet food; be sure to add vegetable sticks and cheese or a dip and some fresh or dried fruit and a drink.

If you're packing a lunchbox that will go to an office, it might sit in a fridge, but be mindful of the outdoor workers' and schoolkids' lunches – they'll have to be packed in a small esky or an insulated lunchbox.

Easy ham and egg pies

MAKES 12 SMALL PIES

These little pies are easy to make and kids love them. If you're finding uneaten sandwiches in the lunchbox after school, try these pies – I'm sure they'll soon become a once-a-week favourite. They are delicious served hot or cold.

2 sheets of puff pastry

4 eggs

100 ml sour cream

1 clove garlic, crushed

a sprinkling of chives or parsley

salt and pepper to taste

4 slices good-quality ham, chopped

1 cup grated cheese

1. Preheat the oven to 180°C/350°F and grease a 12-cup muffin tray. Cut each sheet of puff pastry in two equal portions, place one on top of the other and leave for a few minutes.
2. Place the eggs, sour cream, garlic, chives and salt and pepper in a bowl, and mix well until everything is combined. Drop the ham and cheese into the egg mix.
3. Roll up the long sides of pastry into tight logs and then cut each log into 6 discs. Lay each disc on a lightly floured board and roll out with a rolling pin.
4. Press the discs into the muffin tray, one per cup, then pour the egg mixture into the cups. Bake for about 20 minutes or until the pies smell cooked and are golden on top. Turn out onto a cake rack to cool.

Harvest turnovers

MAKES 12

2 tablespoons olive oil

1 onion, diced

1 potato, diced

1 carrot, diced

1 turnip, diced

100 g pumpkin, diced

½ teaspoon curry powder or paste *(to add seasoning, not heat)*

salt and pepper to taste

½ cup vegetable stock or water

1 tablespoon chopped spring onions

3 sheets puff pastry

1 beaten egg

1 tablespoon sesame seeds

1. Heat the oil in a frying pan and add the onion. Fry for 2 minutes, then add the other vegetables. Fry for a further 2 minutes and add the curry powder, and salt and pepper. Mix thoroughly and cook for 1 minute.
2. Pour in the stock and mix through, then turn down the heat and simmer until the vegetables are soft and the stock has completely evaporated. Add the spring onions and mix in.
3. Turn off the heat, and place the vegetables on a plate to allow them to cool for a few minutes.
4. Preheat the oven to 210°C/410°F – puff pastry must go into a hot oven to allow the pastry to puff up. Using a saucer or small plate as a guide, cut four rounds of about 12 cm/5 inches from each puff pastry sheet. Place a tablespoon of vegetables on each round, brush the edges of the pastry with the beaten egg and fold over the pastry so the two edges meet, enclosing the filling. Use a fork to press the edges together to make sure the vegetables don't seep out.
5. Brush each turnover with beaten egg, sprinkle with sesame seeds and place on a baking sheet. Bake for about 25 minutes or until the turnovers are golden and puffy.

Pizza scrolls

This snack travels well and it's delicious. The base is pizza dough or bread dough with a dash of olive oil added. If you make your own bread, make a bit of extra dough and before it rises, put it in the freezer until it's needed. Or, if you have some time on the weekend, make up a batch of pizza dough, divide it up in batches and freeze until you need it for pizza or these scrolls. This dough can be made in the bread machine, but this is how you make it by hand.

½ cup warm water

2 teaspoons dried yeast

½ teaspoon sugar

4 cups bread flour

1 teaspoon salt

2 tablespoons olive oil

1 cup warm water

MAKING THE DOUGH

1. Mix the water, yeast and sugar well and leave to sit for 5 minutes.
2. Add the flour and salt to a large bowl and make a well in the centre. Pour in the oil and yeast water and start mixing the liquid with the flour with your clean hands. Add half the remaining cup of warm water and mix it in, then add the rest of the water a tablespoon at a time until you have moist dough. If you need a little more water, add it, but be careful not to make the dough too wet.
3. When all the ingredients are combined, knead the dough in the bowl until it is holding together, then place it on a floured surface and continue kneading for 10 minutes.
4. When the dough is smooth, and springy when touched, cut off about a quarter for the scrolls, roll it into a tight ball, put it back into the bowl with a cover over it and allow it to sit for at least an hour, until it has doubled in size. The remaining dough can be stored in three portions in the freezer.

PREPARING THE SCROLLS

1. When the dough has doubled in size, preheat the oven to 180°C/350°F and place the dough on a floured surface. It's probably going to be springy and a bit hard to manage at first, but soon it will roll. Roll it into a rectangle about 1 cm thick. Then you can start adding your filling.

2. Start with some homemade tomato sauce, relish or passata. Add a layer of thinly shaved salami or ham, then top with a sprinkling of cooked onion, mushrooms and capsicum, or whatever your family prefers. Make sure you don't overload the dough, because you have to roll it up.
3. Starting with the edge closest to you, roll the dough and filling into a long tube shape. With a sharp serrated knife, cut into pieces about 4 cm wide. Lay the scrolls flat, side by side on a baking tray and allow to rise for 30 minutes. When risen, grate a layer of cheese over the top and bake for 15–20 minutes.

Date and walnut loaf

1 cup brown sugar

1 cup chopped and pitted dates

1 cup chopped walnuts

80 g butter

a drizzle of vanilla extract

1 teaspoon bicarb soda

1 cup boiling water

1½ cups self-raising flour

1. Preheat the oven to 180°C/350°F, grease a loaf tin and line with baking paper. Add the sugar, dates, walnuts, butter, vanilla and bicarb soda to a large bowl, and pour the boiling water over the ingredients – the mixture will fizz a bit. Mix thoroughly with a wooden spoon, making sure the butter has melted. Add the flour and mix thoroughly.
2. Pour the batter into the tin and bake for about 45 minutes, or until you can smell the aroma and a toothpick inserted in the middle comes out clean.

Coconut and raspberry slice

The base of this slice is a good all-rounder that can carry a variety of fruit toppings.

2 cups plain flour

¾ cup sugar

125 g butter, chilled and diced

3 eggs

1 cup raspberry jam

2 cups coconut (*either desiccated or flaked*)

1. Preheat oven to 180°C/350°F, grease a Swiss roll tin or a 20 x 30 cm tray with sides and line with baking paper. Place the flour, ¼ cup sugar and the butter into a food processor and pulse until the mixture resembles breadcrumbs. Add 1 egg and pulse again until the dough comes together.
2. Remove the dough and press it evenly into the baking tray so that the base of the slice is completely flat and held together. Bake for 15 minutes, or until the base smells cooked and is golden brown. Leave the slice in the tray and spread with raspberry jam.
3. Whisk the 2 remaining eggs with the remaining sugar and, when creamy, fold in the coconut. Spread the coconut mixture over the jam and bake for about 20 minutes or until the top layer is set and golden-brown. Cool in the tray, then slice into serving portions and store in an airtight container.

august

DOMESTIC CRAFTS, SEWING AND HOUSEHOLD LINENS

*'Have nothing in your house that you do not know
to be useful or believe to be beautiful.'*
— WILLIAM MORRIS

NESTING

There are few things better than settling down on a winter's day or evening to do some craft work or mending. As the cold weather swirls around the house, it's cosy inside with plenty of flannel, wool and fleece to keep you warm. Like all of our simple life activities and tasks, handiwork, making and mending continue all year, but it's useful to allow a specific time to plan projects, organise your materials and learn new skills. This is it: welcome to domestic crafts and household linens month.

I am certain that many of you are very skilled in various domestic crafts, some will have made a few things, and others nothing at all. So for those of you who are experienced, this chapter will serve as a reminder of the importance of the skills you possess. I encourage you to share your knowledge and abilities with your family and friends so that more people are able to do this kind of work in their homes. If you're less skilled, you'll find inspiration and ideas here. There are many projects within the scope of a beginner that will add to the beauty, productivity and comfort of your home. So let's use this month to organise materials and working spaces, and make a list of projects.

Crafts, sewing, knitting and crochet are wonderful ways of connecting with your community. If you've never done any craft work before and you're not sure where to start, have a look at the noticeboards in your neighbourhood and at the local library to see if there are any beginner classes. Working on individual or group projects is a great way to socialise with your friends too.

Meeting up to work, talk and drink tea and coffee gives a warm feeling of productivity as it strengthens those friendly ties. When I had small children, I was part of a small craft circle that met on a Tuesday morning. Every week we talked and laughed our way through macramé, knitting and embroidery as we looked after our babies and toddlers. Right now, my sister, Tricia, who is seventy, meets monthly with her friends in a sewing circle they formed over thirty years ago. Craft brings people together, and if we take Tricia's experience as an example, it helps them stay happily together over the years.

Craft work, sewing and mending used to be a regular part of a home-maker's daily tasks. Nowadays, with more couples working full-time, and the availability of cheap goods from China, a lot of what used to be crafted, sewn and mended is just bought or replaced by something new and mass-produced. Homes have become carbon copies of the ones they stand beside, and the people in those houses work far longer than they should to pay for all those purchases. Along the way, the desire and ability to create a unique style using domestic crafts has almost been lost.

With the resurgence of needle and fabric crafts, brought to our attention by blogs and the ability to see what is happening in homes around the world, has come the inspiration to hand-make a lot of what we have been buying for the past forty years. We are nesting again! Now people are creating homes that feature homemade embroidery, leatherwork, wire and cane baskets, clothes, hats and soft furnishings that come from vivid and wild imaginations rather than from an overseas crate. It's an enriching creative renaissance, and we can all be part of it.

If you feel guilty about taking time out to do craft work, don't. It's the creative part of housework; embrace and celebrate it. Sewing kitchen curtains, cushion covers and aprons and mending clothes adds to your worth as a home-maker, so don't feel guilty for doing something you enjoy. Imagine all the gifts you can make, the unique touches you can add to your home: the tea-cosies, jug covers, scarves, slip covers, baby clothes, woodworked breadboards and coasters, leather pouches, belts and bags. Most of these aren't for sale in shops the way you'd make them. Creating these bits and pieces can also help you recycle various things that will get a second life rather than ending up with all the rotting rubbish at the local landfill.

Of course, you are not restricted to fabric crafts by any means. They are the ones I have experienced, but I encourage you to do a wide range of craft work. Learn to make whatever you like the look of. I particularly love wire work, basket-making, pottery and painted furniture; I plan on teaching myself how to make a wire basket and a wisteria cane basket soon. I hope to use materials we have here at home so I don't have to buy too many extras. There's also leather work, calligraphy, scrapbooking, spinning, weaving, woodwork, whittling and paper-making; you'll find good how-to instructions and video tutorials on YouTube for all these, and many more. Learning to do any craft will help you add a wonderful array of items to your home. Don't limit yourself. Others will try to do that; don't do it to yourself. If you want to make something, learn how.

GETTING STARTED

Finding space

Find a place where you'll store your materials as you recycle or buy them. This could be a box, basket or even a room. Just make sure you keep your fabrics and supplies away from dust and moths.

If you do have a spare room, I encourage you to set up a table or desk next to the window, find a good table lamp or craft lamp, and make that your craft room. You'll be able to close the door and let your creativity take over.

Craft, sewing and knitting supplies make wonderful decorations in a craft room and having them on display may give you the inspiration to take on a few new projects. Find an old glass jar with a lid and start your own button jar. Use all those old biscuit tins you've saved to house newly prized ribbons and lace. Tins, jars, embroidery hoops, wool in a basket and colourful embroidery cottons will all make fine additions to the look of your craft room. If you don't have a spare room, a box or basket will keep a collection of materials together and provide a focal point for your fabric crafts.

Finding time

Decide on a regular time for your craft work. I tend to put aside an hour or two in the afternoons now that I'm retired, but a weeknight or weekend afternoon might suit you best if you're working. You might sit with your work in the evening while the family is watching television or doing homework. If your partner goes out to play sport on the weekend, that might be your ideal time. Or maybe you'll want a regular time to join a craft class or sewing circle with a housemate.

> TIP: Don't forget to take your portable projects out with you, particularly if you spend time on public transport. All that time looking at Facebook and Twitter could be better spent on interesting handicrafts.

Gathering materials

Part of the benefit of making things for your home is the recycling aspect – it gives you a way to reuse fabrics that have outlived their usefulness in their current form. If you haven't decluttered, or if there are still a lot of old clothes in your home, you may be able to use that excess to make some of your items. It will be easier for you to create all those wonderful projects if you prepare a little stockpile of materials first, so go through the clothes with an eye to using the fabric in a project. Make sure the clothing is washed and clean, then fold it and place it in your new fabric stockpile. Store your fabric according to size, colour and type. Also gather buttons, old zippers, lace, ribbons and anything that you like the look of. Most craftspeople have similar weirdly wonderful collections.

Tell your family and friends that you want to learn how to sew/mend/crochet/knit, and that you're building up a stockpile of fabric, yarn, sewing and embroidery cotton. With that information out there, you'll probably soon get calls saying that something is available, and you'll be on your way to building up your supplies. I've been the very grateful recipient of a large collection of vintage knitting needles, given to me by an older lady who no longer knitted, and quite a bit of fabric from my daughter-in-law, Cathy, who teaches patchwork and quilting. She had ends of pieces and fabric she no longer liked, and they were clogging up her cupboards. I've used pieces from that gift for many years.

My preference is for cotton and linen fabric, and those natural fibres can be used for a large number of projects. If you've never sewn before, learn a little about fabrics – it will help you to select the right materials for the job (see the Resources for more information). Cotton and linen are soft and easy to cut, so they're suitable for clothing and quilts. If you need something more durable, you might choose duck cloth for older children's clothes, or twill, canvas or denim for teenagers' and men's clothes or tote bags. Lawn is a good fabric for baby. If you're choosing scraps of fabric for a patchwork project, choose fabric of the same type and weight and you'll have a better end product.

RECYCLING WOOL

Old jumpers and cardigans can be reused too, so if you have a few knitted items you no longer need, do the same – make sure they're clean, take off the embellishments, fold and store for a future project. If you find a good-quality hand-knitted item at the op shop, the yarn can be unravelled and you'll probably have enough to make up a similar-sized project. Just make sure the yarn is in good condition and it's pure wool. If it looks new, that's ideal but you might also consider buying it if it's a pure-wool handknit that is in perfect condition. When you get it home, wash it and dry it in the shade. When it's completely dry, unwind the garment.

Most jumpers are knitted from the waist to the neck and sleeves are done from the wrist to the shoulder. Unwind sleeves from the shoulder to the wrist, and the body of the garment from the neck to the waist, and wind the wool into balls. Once you have the balls, wind the balls onto your wool winder if you have one, or around the back of a chair if you don't. You want to wash the wool when it's wound into a skein. A skein of wool is when the wool is wound into a loose O shape, and tied to hold it in place. If you hold your arms beside your body and extend your arms out from your bent elbows, winding your wool around those two extended hands in an O would give you a skein. Tie it in four places to secure.

When you have the skeins wound, soak the wool in hot water with ¼ teaspoon of liquid soap added. Let the wool soak till the water is cold, then

squeeze the water out by laying the skeins on a towel and rolling it up. Don't wring the wool and don't agitate it when it's in the water. Handle with care while it's wet. Hang the wool on hangers over the sink to drip-dry and when it's completely dry, put it back on the wool winder or get someone to hold the skeins for you while you rewind them into balls. Don't stretch the wool. Even if you have kinks in it when you're knitting, they'll come out when you block the garment.

Preparing fabric for use

NEW FABRIC

Many people wash new fabric before they use it, many people don't. Most fabrics are pre-shrunk and it's wise to ask if it's been treated before you buy new fabric.

One good reason to wash new fabric before use is to see if it's colourfast. Red in particular can run in the wash, so pre-wash red fabric if you're combining red and white in one project. If you find the colour does run, you can pre-treat it before it causes any problems.

To set the colour in cotton fabric before using it for sewing, add ½ cup of white vinegar and a tablespoon of Epsom salts to 1 litre of cold water in a large bowl. Place the fabric in the liquid and squeeze it a few times with your hands to make sure it's saturated. Swirl the fabric around the bowl for a few seconds, squeeze it again and then remove it from the liquid. Rinse it in fresh water to make sure the colour is set and stable. When you're satisfied the fabric is colourfast, wash, dry and iron it and store it with your fabrics.

PRE-USED FABRIC

This could be fabric sourced from the op shop, friends and family, or from your own wardrobe. All fabrics should be washed, dried then ironed. If you're collecting fabric for patchwork quilts, most of the cotton you have will be suitable for patching small pieces of fabric together. If you want fabric for children's clothes, soft furnishings or bags you'll need larger pieces. For all the pre-used fabric, strip the buttons, zippers and trims off and save them for future projects. Cut the sleeves off and cut the front from the back. The back sections will usually be the largest pieces. Fold all the pieces and store according to size, colour and type of fabric.

You can test fabric you're not sure of to see if it's cotton, poly-cotton or synthetic. Cut a small square from the edge of the fabric and take it outside with a flameproof container. Place the fabric in the container and set it alight. Cotton and linen will burn fast and smell like paper. Poly-cotton and synthetic fabrics will send up dark grey or black smoke and smell of chemicals. When you examine the ash, the cotton will be a fine ash that collapses, while the poly-cotton may be stiff or have melted into a solid piece.

There are two ways to test if yarn is 100 per cent pure wool. Wool will dissolve in bleach, so drop a short piece of wool into ¼ cup bleach and check it in the morning. If it's dissolved, it's pure wool. The second way is similar to the burn test for cotton and linen. Take a couple of strands outside and light the end. If it's pure wool it will smoulder and smell of hair or feathers. If it's acrylic it will burn quickly and smell of plastic.

Setting up a sewing kit

When you have a bit of spare money, buy a pair of good-quality dressmaking scissors, a pair of snips for cutting thread as you sew, a pair of pinking shears, and cotton or poly-cotton thread – first in white, black, beige and dark grey, because those colours will cover most mending jobs when you're starting out. When you're more established and are well into craft work, buy embroidery threads in the colours you like or those you need for a project you're planning. As you build up your collection of embroidery threads, you'll need thread organisers too – boxes that store the rewound threads on spools and keep them safe.

You'll also need:
- A set of sewing needles in all sizes, suitable for general sewing, darning and embroidery
- Tape measure
- Straight pins
- Seam ripper
- Embroidery hoops if you want to do any fancy work

If you'll be mending, you'll need a darning mushroom or egg. I bought my darning mushroom on eBay for five dollars. If you can buy a self-healing cutting mat and a rotary cutter you'll be able to cut straight lines very easily. If you can't afford those straight away, make do with a ruler, fabric marking pen or tailor's chalk and scissors.

There is no reason to buy everything at once. Just add pieces as you can afford them, but always buy the best quality scissors you can so they will last a long time.

Do I need a sewing machine?

If you'll only do basic mending and a few projects that use straight hand-sewing, you don't need a sewing machine. I love hand-sewing: it's quiet, repetitive and relaxing, very much like knitting. A sewing machine will allow you to create more extravagant pieces but it's by no means a definite requirement when you start sewing.

If you do want to start dressmaking or make a lot of household linens, you may be able to borrow a sewing machine. Ask family and friends if you can borrow theirs. If you're really lucky, someone might tell you they never use their machine and you can have it. If no one you know has a sewing machine, ask your local community or neighbourhood centre, as they sometimes have sewing machines available for use. I bought my sewing machine secondhand on eBay, and while it is a leap of faith if you don't know much about sewing machines, mine hasn't given me any problems in the seven years I've had it. If you do buy a new machine, sometimes they come with basic sewing classes attached. It's always wise to take up the offer. Sometimes TAFE or adult education centres offer basic sewing classes too, but if you can get a friend to teach you, that's the best solution.

SEWING 101

Two of the most common tasks you will undertake when starting to sew are seams and hems. Seams are where two pieces of fabric are sewn together. Hems are the ends of the fabric that are folded, pressed and sewn in place to create a neat edge. Over the page is some more basic terminology that will help you along the way.

Basic stitches

Most sewing and mending can be done by hand-stitching or on the sewing machine. Until the invention of the sewing machine, all fabric was sewn by hand, and very successfully too. Even when you have a sewing machine, some stitching, such as hemming and darning, is better done by hand. But the sewing machine does allow more durable and neat stitching, and it's much faster. Whether you have a sewing machine or not, start learning some hand-stitches. They always come in handy for a quick repair, and you'll gain a useful craft that was used by our ancestors but still has a place in our modern world.

Most hand stitches are sewn with a single thread, although buttons, hooks and eyes are sewn with double thread. When you thread your needle, don't make the thread too long – a length of 45–60 cm is sufficient. A longer thread will get tangled. Hand-stitching and machine-stitching can be done with either cotton or poly-cotton thread unless you're following a pattern that advises a different thread. Make sure you anchor your stitches at the beginning and the end and try to hide thread ends, if there are any, in a hem or seam.

Hand-sewing is slow because you need to keep your stitches straight, the same size and evenly spaced. When you are more experienced you'll go faster, but in the beginning, take it slow and steady. This is a gentle art, and it has the potential to slow you down and introduce a calm and peaceful rhythm to your day.

HAND STITCHES

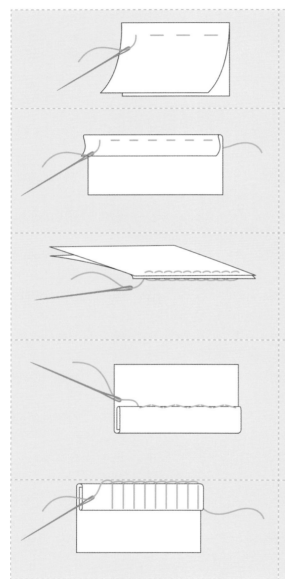

Basting or **tacking stitch** is a long loose stitch that temporarily holds two pieces of fabric together. Use a contrasting colour so the stitches are easy to remove when the fabric has been sewn permanently.

Straight stitch is the most commonly used stitch. It is 10–12 stitches per 2.5 cm. **Running stitch** is the same principle, and used for seams and hems, and for gathering. The spaces and stitches are the same size and the length should be between 5–8 mm depending on the weight of the fabric. It's also an embroidery stitch.

Backstitch is used when you want a stronger seam than straight stich will give you. Follow the seam line from right to left, bringing the needle out a stitch-length ahead of the previous stitch, then working each stitch backwards from left to right. Keep all stitches the same length.

Hemming stitch should be barely visible on the right side, so use a thread that closely matches the fabric. Only the smallest amount is picked up by the needle on the main fabric. Bring the needle up through the folded hem, and then back into the main fabric, moving forward about 5 mm at a time. Take care not to pull the thread too hard as the hem will pucker.

Blanket stitch is an edging stitch as well as an embroidery stitch. The edge is formed by working the needle front to back, bringing it under the stitch to form a loop. Vary the space between stitches for different effects.

Basic skills

ANCHORING STITCHES

It's important to anchor your stitches at the start and finish of a row so the line of stitching doesn't come undone. You should do it for both machine- and hand-stitching. To anchor a line of stitches when using a machine, sew a short line of straight stitches about 1 cm in length, stop, reverse back over the stitches for 1 cm, then go forward to continue your sewing.

To anchor a line of stitches by hand, make a knot near the end of the thread, leaving a short tail. Sew your first stitch from below the fabric and bring your needle out where you're going to sew. Thread the needle through the fabric again, turn the fabric over and thread the needle through the knot. Then bring the needle back up through the fabric and continue sewing.

TURNING CORNERS

When sewing by hand, use a dressmaker's pencil or tailor's chalk to mark the line of your hand stitching, and simply follow that line with your stitches.

If you're using a machine, when you come to a corner and you need to continue the line of stitches at an angle to the row you're on, stop the machine with the needle still embedded in the fabric. Lift the presser foot on the machine, then turn the fabric, release the foot and continue sewing. Leaving the needle in the fabric will ensure it doesn't slip while you're turning the fabric.

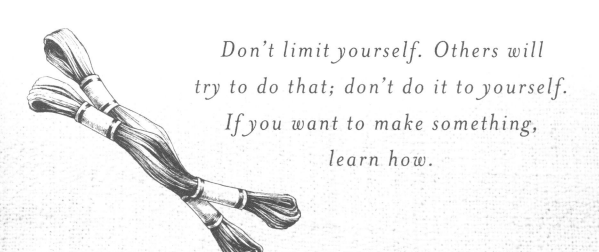

Don't limit yourself. Others will try to do that; don't do it to yourself. If you want to make something, learn how.

MENDING 101

Clothing and linens are a substantial investment, so if you can extend their usefulness with mending, patching and darning, you'll be living true to your frugal values. These repairs require a few basic mending techniques, but they're easy to learn and most can be done by machine or hand. The real skill is to make your repairs blend in as much as you can.

Fixing a hem by hand

1. Work with the garment inside out. To secure the hem that's still attached, unravel the thread that was holding the hem up, thread a needle with that thread and anchor the end of the machine-stitching that's just unravelled. Cut the thread.
2. Pin the unattached hem in place. Working right to left (if you're right-handed) with matching colour thread in your needle, anchor the first stitch close to where you just anchored the last stitch.
3. Pick up a few threads of fabric with the needle on the inside of the garment, level with the hem. Be careful not to make a big stitch that shows on the right side of the fabric.
4. Put the needle though the edge of the hem and pull the needle and cotton right through. Make sure you don't make the stitches too tight or too loose, because it will make the finished repair look untidy. All your stitches should be just tight enough so that when the fabric is laid flat, there are no loose loops and no pulling on the fabric. Don't make the stitches too long: they should be about 5 mm/¼ inch long at the most. Try to pick up only a few threads, because your stitch will show on the outside of the garment. Check the outside of the garment as you go and undo your stitches if it looks untidy.
5. Repeat steps 3 and 4 until you reach the edge of the original stitching. Anchor your stitch and cut the thread. Iron the hem flat.

Fixing a seam

This can be done by hand using backstitch, or on the sewing machine.

BY HAND

1. Pin the seam together where it has come apart. Using matching thread, tie a knot in the end to help you anchor the stitch and insert the needle into the seam line of the fabric from the underside, above the line of stitches that have come apart.
2. From the top side of the fabric, put the needle back into the fabric close to where your thread came through from below, then pull the needle down and through the knot. That will anchor the stitches.
3. The next stitch is the backstitch. Insert the needle into the entry point of the first stitch, going back to do so, then bring the stitch under, completing the stitch by coming up under the fabric 1 cm from the entry point of the first stitch. Pull the cotton through again.
4. Repeat this backstitch along the line of the seam as straight and even as you can make it. The stitches will be 0.5 cm long from top to bottom. Anchor your stitch and cut the thread when you pass the end of the old stitches. Iron the seam flat.

WITH A SEWING MACHINE

1. With matching thread, anchor your stitch.
2. Use a medium-length straight stitch and sew along the line of the seam from about 2 cm before the seam came apart to 2 cm after.
3. Anchor your stitch, cut the thread and iron the seam flat.

Mending a cut or rip in fabric

BY HAND

1. On the wrong side of the fabric, pull the two cut edges together and pin. Trim away any threads or untidy fabric along the rip line.
2. Using backstitch, anchor your stitch just outside the cut area, then backstitch parallel to the cut edge about 0.5 cm in. Stitch as straight as you can to the other side of the cut. Anchor your stitch and cut the thread.
3. Cut away any hanging threads and tidy the repaired edge, removing as much of the cut fabric as you can without compromising the repair.
4. Separate the seam on the wrong side of the fabric and press the edges open and flat. Turn the fabric over and press the repair flat on the right side.

WITH A SEWING MACHINE

This is very similar to the hand repair above.

1. On the wrong side of the fabric, pull the two cut edges together and pin. Trim away any threads or untidy fabric along the rip line.
2. Anchor your stitch just outside the cut area, then sew parallel to the cut edge about 0.5 cm in from the edge. When the edges are sewn together, anchor your stitch and cut the thread.
3. Cut away any hanging threads and tidy the repaired edge, removing as much of the cut fabric as you can without compromising the repair.
4. Separate the seam on the wrong side of the fabric and press the edges open and flat. Turn the fabric over and press the repair flat on the right side.

Darning

Darning is an old technique used to repair small holes and worn areas that are not on a seam. Instead of using a patch to cover a worn hole, darning stitch is used to weave in and out of the remnants of the old fabric or wool, anchoring the repair to the edges of the damaged area. In effect, it rebuilds the worn area with thread or wool without the need of a patch. It's used in places where a patch would be uncomfortable, such as the heel of socks or elbows.

BY HAND

Traditional darning is done by hand, using a darning stitch. This is a long running stitch that is woven in and out of the remaining fabric or wool in one direction, then reversed at the end of the row and continued a short distance over. When the hole is darned in one direction, the process is started again at a 90-degree angle and the hole is completely closed.

A) STITCHING WITH WARP OR FILLING

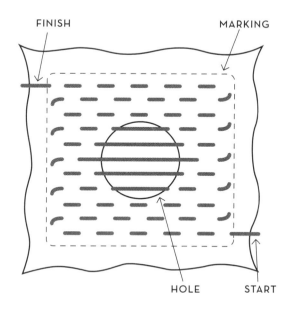

FINISH

MARKING

HOLE   START

B) HAND DARNING COMPLETE

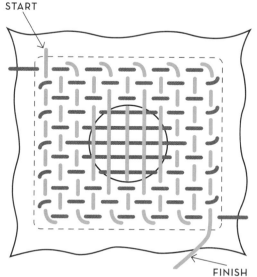

START

FINISH

1. Start by anchoring your stitch. Work with a medium-length straight or zigzag stitch in a matching colour, and neatly stitch back and forth widthways across the hole, making sure you sew right up to and over the edges of the repair.
2. When there is good coverage, turn the fabric 90 degrees and repeat the process over the stiches already made. Keep the stitch lines straight and evenly placed.
3. When you've finished, cut off the frayed edges of the original hole and press the repair flat.

Darning a knitted garment by hand

1. Choose a strand of wool that matches the colour and ply of the original, or close enough to it. Using a darning mushroom, cover the mushroom with the part of the garment that needs the repair.
2. Make a knot in the wool and do several medium-length horizontal running stitches in one direction, weaving in and out of the remaining wool. When you overlap the repair area, turn your stitch around and repeat in the other direction. Repeat until you cover the area with horizontal stitches woven in and out of the old stitches, then anchor the stitch and cut the thread.
3. Repeat the process vertically, weaving in and out of the stitches. Cover the repair area, stitching right to the edges of the hole. When you've covered the hole with vertical stitches, anchor the stitch and cut the thread.
4. Cut any frayed threads to leave a tidy repair.

Applying a patch

Patches are hard to hide, so don't expect an invisible mend with them. You can go two ways: use a decorative patch that will stand out, or match the fabric so it will be less obvious. Either way you'll save the garment, and that's a useful thing to do. Throwing away a shirt, dress or pair of jeans that still have a lot of life left in them is wasteful and unnecessary. Even if you prefer not to wear the garment when you go out, it will still give you several years of wear at home.

1. Using small scissors, tidy up the edges of the hole and make it a square, rectangle or circle.
2. Iron the edges of the patch under 0.5 cm to form a neat patch when viewed from the top.
3. Pin the patch to the hole and look underneath the garment to make sure the hole is completely covered and the patch is pinned to every edge. Adjust if necessary.
4. Turn the fabric over again and, with a short zigzag stitch on the sewing machine or a short running stitch by hand, run a border of stitches around the edge of the patch as neatly as possible, making sure you sew the patch to the fabric. Don't forget to anchor your stitches at the beginning and the end. Snip the thread and press the patch.

Hand-sewing has the potential to slow you down and introduce a calm and peaceful rhythm to your day.

PROJECTS FOR THE WAY YOU LIVE

'Measure twice, cut once.'

When deciding on what projects you'll try, the first thing to do is to look around your home to see what you need. I've found that many things I want to use in my home aren't sold in shops, or the quality isn't nearly as good as what I can make myself. Think about the gifts you have to give as well. A lot will depend on what fabrics and yarn you have stashed away. When you have one, two or ten things to start with, check you have all the materials you need. If you have to buy supplies, do some research beforehand so you get the right material for the job, and try to do this when the sales are on in January and June.

Here are some projects you might like to try.

Cloth napkins

This is the ideal first project for beginners – it only requires cutting and sewing straight lines. Cloth napkins will last a few years, can be washed with the regular washing, and you'll never have to buy disposable napkins again. The fabric should be either cotton or linen, and you can use matching or contrasting thread. The napkins don't have to match one another; they are the ideal project for using ends left over from larger jobs. Make at least six, or one for each person in your home and a few extra for guests.

Materials:
- Cotton fabric
- Thread

You'll also need: a tape measure, straight pins, snips and, if you have them, a cutting board and rotary cutter. If you don't, use a tape measure, fabric marker or tailor's chalk and scissors. The only sewing on these napkins are the hems, which can be machine-stitched or hand-stitched.

1. Measure out and cut six squares about 30 cm – they can be larger or smaller if you prefer. If you have a cutting board, cut out the squares with a rotary cutter by lining up the correct measurements

on the board. Alternatively, make a square template from cardboard and use a marker or chalk to mark the cutting edge of the squares.

2. Lay the fabric on a table wrong side up, then turn over the edges 5 mm to form the hems and press with a hot iron. Turn the hems in another 10 mm and press. Neatly square off the hem on each corner and stitch it. When you're a little more experienced you'll know how to mitre a corner, but a squared corner is fine for now.

3. Either hand-stitch or machine-stitch along the inner edge of the hem, right around the square.

Rag bag

Having a rag bag will remind you to recycle all the worn-out cotton, towelling and linen fabric you come across during the year. This project makes a bag that hangs on a coat hanger and is ideal for storing rags, but it can be used to store other things too. Hang your rag bag in the laundry, inside the back door or where you store your cleaning supplies.

Materials:
- About 1.5 m of fabric, preferably cotton
- Matching thread
- Wooden (or very sturdy plastic) coat hanger
- Plain brown paper for template

You will also need: a sewing machine, tape measure, straight pins, thread, snips, a marker and, if you have them, a cutting board and rotary cutter. If you don't, use a tape measure and scissors.

MAKING THE TEMPLATE

1. Lay the coat hanger on the top edge of the brown paper and with a marker, trace around the shape of the hanger. This will give you the shape of the top as well as the width of the bag. Allow about 1.25 cm for the seam on all sides.

2. Fold the template in half to find the centre and mark it, then mark the template 1.25 cm out from the centre on both sides for the hook opening.

3. Allow a drop of 65 cm and use a ruler to mark that on your template.
4. The bottom edge is 46 cm wide, so using the ruler again, make a horizontal line as the base of the bag.
5. Bring the line back up to the top, using the ruler as your guide.
6. To mark the opening, draw a horizontal line with a ruler, about 25 cm down from the top point of the template. Don't forget to add a seam allowance of 1.25 cm to the opening.

CUTTING OUT

1. Place the fabric on a flat surface and lay the template on it. If you can, position the template so you're left with a generous piece of scrap material to use in another project. Leave a seam allowance on all sides and when you're happy with the placement of the template, pin it to the fabric.
2. Cut out around the template. You'll need two identical sides, so do this twice, or if you're confident, double the fabric layers and cut once.
3. When both pieces are cut, take one piece and measure down 12.5 cm from the shoulder curve. On the wrong side of the fabric, draw a horizontal line across from side to side for the bag opening. Cut along that line.
4. You'll now have three fabric pieces: a top and bottom for the front and one for the back.

SEWING THE BAG TOGETHER

1. Take the front pieces and turn both hems under twice to form a hem on the edge of the opening. Iron both hems and sew them.
2. Now you're ready to pin and sew the sides together. With right sides facing in, pin around the edge of the bag. Be careful at the opening to line up the edges properly. Then at the top of the bag where the coat hanger hook will sit, pin two marker pins vertically and facing downwards at your template marks so you don't sew over the hook opening. The pins should be about 2.5 cm apart.
3. Leave a 1.25 cm seam allowance and start stitching on one side of the vertical pins at the top. Stitch around the perimeter of the

bag, finishing off at the second vertical pin. Take extra care when you sew over the opening, and reverse-stitch over it to reinforce the stitching.

4. Iron the bag again and, using the front opening, fit the coat hanger in position.

Crossover apron

Aprons used to be in every home, and most homemakers wouldn't have even thought about doing housework without putting on an apron to protect their clothes. I still wear an apron daily, although these days you'll usually find a digital camera in my apron pocket along with some pegs, a few Lego blocks and an egg. Over the years, aprons disappeared, but I'm happy to say they've recently made a comeback. This linen crossover apron, suitable for women, men and children, has become quite popular.

This is an intermediate project but if you're a keen beginner, it's basically just cutting and sewing straight lines. If you make a mistake, you can always carefully unpick and start again. We've all done that. Mistakes are the gifts that help you learn and remember.

TIP: This is the ideal project to do with a friend. You can take each others' measurements, help with the accurate fitting of the straps and crossovers, have cups of tea together and spend time with someone you love while producing something beautiful.

These aprons are made using linen or hemp that is easy to wash and will look good and last for many years. It's fine to use a homespun fabric, a heavy cotton or cotton-linen blend if linen or hemp is too expensive. You'll need about 1.5–2 metres of fabric. I think the natural colours of camel, clay and sand suit this apron well, and I've also seen them looking beautiful in black and pastels. Linen is usually sold in widths of 135 cm or 150 cm. You'll need extra fabric for the straps and pockets, so if you buy the wide linen you'll be able to cut the two straps in strips from the side of the fabric. I've added an Australian online shop that has a range of good-quality linen to the Resources section. If you're in another country, look on eBay – you can usually find a range of linen there.

You'll need a rectangle of fabric cut according to the chest and length measurements you take. Measure the person you're making it for from the middle of the back between the shoulder blades, over the bust/chest and around to the middle of the back again. Across the bust/chest, you want the apron to just touch at the back where the straps attach. The apron will then conform to the shape of the person wearing it, which is generally an A shape, wider at the bottom than the top. Whatever the measurement is, add 12.5 cm to the width and the same to the length for the 1.25 cm seam allowance and 5 cm hems. We're going to sew hems to match the line of the 5 cm straps.

CUTTING OUT

1. Cut the linen to fit your measurements, making sure you add the extra 12.5 cm for the seam allowance and hems. It can be any length. I've seen them short, long and all sizes in between.
2. Cut two large squares the size you want for the pockets, adding 1 cm to three sides for a narrow hem and 2.5 cm for the top hem.
3. Cut 2 shoulder straps 7 cm wide (5 cm with a 1 cm seam allowance on both sides). The length of the straps will depend on where you want the apron to sit on the bust/chest, but the length will be somewhere between 38 cm and 50 cm on an adult apron.
4. To calculate the length of the straps, pin them onto the body of the apron, making sure the end of the shoulder straps line up with the hem along the top of the apron. Cross the straps over at the back, making sure they're not twisted, and pin to the back corners at the top of the apron.

For the body of the apron:

1. Using a ruler and pins, go around the perimeter and turn over the edge of the fabric 1 cm and pin as you go.
2. Go around the perimeter again and turn over the hem 5 cm. Remove the pins you used for the first fold to pin the hem down. Then iron and sew, making sure your lines are straight.

For the pockets:

1. On three sides of both pockets, turn over 0.5 cm then pin and press the hem down.
2. Form the top hem by turning the fabric over 0.5 cm, pinning, then turning the fabric again 2.5 cm. Pin and press. Then sew along in a straight line at the edge of the hem.
3. Pin the pockets to the body of the apron, perfectly level with each other, then sew the three sides to attach the pocket, leaving the top edge free; make sure you're sewing in a straight line all the way.

For the shoulder straps:

1. Pin a strap to the corner of the body before sewing to hold it in place, then sew a 5 cm square on the corner to attach the strap. This must be exact because it is one of the features at the back. If you don't think you'll do it properly, pin the strap on, then do a temporary basting stitch on the inside of the square to secure the corners and the straps, then remove the pins. When you finish sewing the square on the machine, remove the basting stitch.
2. To finish it off, sew a cross in the middle of the square, both front and back, for extra strength.

Jug cover

There was a time when jug covers were in most Australian homes. Now you rarely see them, but they can still play a valuable part in home life, especially if you live in a warm climate or you eat and entertain outside a lot. You can make a few of these at a time and add them to your gift stash if you don't need all of them. These covers are ideal for a milk or cordial jug, as well as for your glass of water beside the bed at night. They are also the ideal cover for fermenting because they allow air in and keep insects out.

Materials:
- Cotton tulle
- Small crochet hook
- Fine crochet cotton
- Beads

1. Cut a circle of cotton tulle big enough to cover the top of the jug, adding an extra 5–7 cm to fall over the sides.
2. Crochet the outside of the tulle circle in whatever crochet stitch you fancy, dropping a loop every 3 cm to fit a bead on.

Net bag

Making yourself a set of net bags will help you cut down on the amount of packaging and plastic you bring home from the farmers' market and super-market. You can see through them, and their weight is so miniscule it makes almost no difference to the weight of your produce. If you buy flour and dried food in bulk, a set of calico bags will serve the same purpose. All bags can be made using the same instructions – just change the fabric. I don't think the net bags need a drawstring – I use a rubber band to secure the top for the trip home – but add one if you prefer it that way. These bags are easy to wash and dry in the sun with the regular washing.

Materials:
- Tulle is best, either cotton or acrylic (the acrylic lasts longer)
- Thread

You'll also need: scissors, a tape measure and a sewing machine. If you're add-ing a drawstring, either make a drawstring with a strip of fabric or recycled ribbon, or buy cotton tape.

1. Cut out two rectangles in whatever size you want your bag to be. With the two long sides facing, and starting at the top of the long edge, stitch along the perimeter of the bag on three sides, giving yourself a 1.5 cm seam allowance.
2. Turn the unstitched top of the bag over 0.7 cm and iron flat, then fold it over another 1.25 cm, pin and press. Then stitch along the line of the hem. Anchor the stitches at both ends.
3. Turn the bag right side out and run a knitting needle along the seam from the inside to give it a neat, crisp edge. Press.

TIP: If you often have to replace the same button on a pair of pants or shirt, use three strands of embroidery cotton for the repair instead of cotton on a reel. It will last much longer.

CHANGING YOUR WORLD WITH
NEEDLE AND THREAD

If you've never done anything like this before, I hope you try a couple of these projects to see what you're capable of. Don't be worried about making mistakes; everyone does at the beginning. This is not like cooking in that if you burn the food, it's wasted. If you make a mistake here, you can usually rectify it. Many crafts involve putting something together, then undoing it to make minor adjustments. It's not set in stone on the first try.

I encourage you to investigate other crafts as well. I've focused on particular projects here that are difficult to find or expensive, but there are many items we can make for our homes. You'll probably settle on a couple of favourite crafts in the end, but open up your horizons and see what's happening out there in the craft world. It's amazing.

If you've been following the monthly themes of the book, you'll already have your year's gift list and a basket or box full of mending to do. That's as good a place as any to start, so work your way through the mending first; make sure your sewing kit in the mending basket is doing the job and add the extras if it isn't. You may have to add more buttons, thread, embroidery cotton or pins.

Be patient, learn the skills, and, as you put the time in and do a few projects, you'll become better at it. Don't limit yourself to what you see others do. Look around your home and see what you need. Even if you've never made anything before, there are ways to get started. Ask your crafty friends if they can help you with the parts of a project you're not sure of. Why not organise a little 'crafternoon', with you and your friends each bringing along what they're working on? You might make it a regular event if you add some hot tea and scones or some homemade jam drops, and take it in turns to meet at each other's homes. If you don't have friends who are crafting, there are plenty of websites with tutorials for knitting, sewing, mending and upcycling – I've added a few of them to the Resources. Starting a project is often the hardest part of it, but if you get hooked on this creative side of homemaking, you'll soon be looking around for a follow-up project.

Just make sure you measure twice and cut once.

september

THE HOME DAIRY

'The friendly cow, all red and white,
I love with all my heart;
She gives me cream with all her might,
To eat with apple-tart.'
— ROBERT LOUIS STEVENSON

LEARNING TO LOVE MILK
AND CREAM

One of my lasting childhood memories is being lovingly cared for by my mother when I had chickenpox. She covered me in calamine lotion and flannelette pyjamas, and propped me up on a cane lounge she'd dragged into the kitchen. We talked, I had books and girls' magazines to read, I slept on and off in the sunshine spilling in through the kitchen window, and every few hours she'd bring me a small bowl of junket. In those days, when you were sick, you were fed 'invalid food'. Junket was in that category because it was so easy to digest. That junket was cold and creamy; it restored my health and energy, and helped build my love of family life. Even to this day, junket is one of my favourite foods. Thanks, Mum.

Spring is a good time to make dairy food because milk is at its best then. We don't think of milk as a seasonal food, but when pastured cows start grazing on spring grasses, they produce the best milk of the year.

In past years, it was fairly common to see a dairy, butter factory or creamery in country towns, surrounded by lush pastures and rolling hills. It was also fairly common to make dairy products in the home kitchen. Nothing was wasted then, and even small amounts of cream were made up into butter, while excess milk was transformed into all sorts of warm, milky puddings, custards or junket. Times have changed and many of us don't have a dairy nearby; most of us buy milk from the supermarket and we don't know much about it, or the other dairy foods we buy.

I hope this chapter will help give you a better understanding of milk and cream, and how they can be not just what they are but also transformed into all sorts of delicious and healthy dairy foods. Butter, buttermilk, sour cream, yoghurt, ice cream and a range of cheeses are all easy to make from scratch in the home kitchen. I'm not going into the specialty cheeses – there are many other books that explain it much better than I can – but there are recipes and instructions for making easy cheddar, ricotta and a soft, mild, spreadable cheese suitable for children that contains no preservatives or artificial flavourings. With a couple of exceptions you can make these foods with equipment and ingredients you probably already have in your kitchen. If you need to buy starters and rennet, information about online sellers is provided in the Resources section.

There are several benefits to be had if you take the time to make these dairy foods:

- You will know exactly what's in your dairy foods, and you'll leave out all the artificial flavourings and preservatives that are in most supermarket brands.
- You can modify what you make to suit your family's tastes and health requirements.
- What you make will probably taste better.
- Homemade dairy products generally cost less than those bought at the supermarket.
- You will keep these life skills in your family.

I am a self-taught dairy-woman, although I have never owned or milked a cow. I have read a number of books and researched the few sites on the internet that were worth reading. In the end, though, while being guided by books and my favourite Dr Fankhauser's cheese site, most of my experience and eventual success came by trial and error – by trying the recipes and adjusting them to suit our taste. I made mistakes, learned from them and tried to improve each time. I hope you're adventurous enough to do the same – mistakes are life's best teachers.

MILK, CREAM AND THEIR BY-PRODUCTS

It's easy to think of milk as just milk, but it's actually quite complex. Nowadays we know there are different proteins in milk, so the milk you buy could be A1 or A2 milk. The milk you buy in most shops is A1, generally from the black-and-white cows you'll see if you pass through dairy country. A2 milk comes from Jersey and Guernsey cows and goats. From all reports, and certainly from our family experience, A2 milk is easier to digest and doesn't cause the bloating or stomach upset that A1 milk can.

Usually the milk at the supermarket is pasteurised and homogenised. Pasteurisation is the process of heating milk to kill any pathogens, and is done for safety. Homogenisation is more of a cosmetic procedure – the milk is put through a mechanical process that blends the milk and cream together permanently. Leaving non-homogenised milk to sit for a while allows the cream to separate and rise to the top of the milk. Many older folk like this; younger people, however, having grown up with the culture of 'low fat', often prefer not to see the cream – or fat – in their milk.

Cream is the fat component of milk. Natural, unprocessed cream is usually under 50 per cent milk fat. Different types of cows produce cream with differing fat contents. Jersey cows produce the creamiest milk and therefore the milk with the most fat. The fat content also varies from season to season, reaching its height in spring.

Butter is made by churning or mixing cream until the fat separates from the buttermilk.

Traditional buttermilk is the liquid removed from cream during butter making. It's low in fat, high in nutrients and is a very healthy drink. You can also use it in baking: cakes, scones and muffins generally have a lighter texture when made using buttermilk.

Cultured buttermilk is a watery-looking liquid made by adding either streptococcus lactis or lactobacillus bulgaricus to milk. This is the buttermilk you find in the dairy fridge at the supermarket. It is also a nourishing drink and can be used in baking and fermenting.

Whipped cream is made by mixing air into cream.

Sour cream is plain cream to which cultures have been added to produce an acidic, slightly sour taste.

Crème fraîche is a lighter and not so sour cream that has also been soured with a culture.

Clotted cream is high-fat cream that is boiled and dried slightly to produce a thick cream with a unique taste.

Whey is the liquid left when milk is made into cheese or yoghurt. Whey is a healthy drink that can also be used in baking and fermenting. Cultured milk whey, the liquid left after making yoghurt, contains lactobacillus, which is the key ingredient in lacto-fermented vegetable recipes. If stored in a sterile container, whey will last in the fridge for a long time. I've stored whey for three months in the fridge, but I think your risk of contamination is lower if you freeze your leftover whey in 1- or 2-cup containers. Frozen whey will last up to six months. You can also feed whey to chickens, goats or pigs – they love it and will benefit from drinking it.

Milk will vary in quality and taste depending on where it is produced, the type of cow it's from and the land the cow has grazed on. If you're lucky enough to be able to barter or buy milk from a single cow or herd, then you'll have very good milk and you'll probably also notice changes in taste and creaminess throughout the year.

The largest proportion of milk sold in Australia, and possibly most other countries, is a pasteurised, homogenised mix of milk from many different breeds of cows. It is nutritious and safe to drink, but it won't taste like the milk from a single breed. Milk from jersey or guernsey cows will be creamy and sweet, and I believe that fresh milk from these cows is the best you can get. But life often doesn't give us the best, and we have to work with what we've got. I hope you search for the best-quality milk you can get, because it will make a difference to the taste, and possibly the nutrition, of everything you make with it. I buy local milk from Maleny Dairies. I use their pasteurised, non-homogenised milk, so the cream rises to the top just like it did when I was growing up.

If you don't live near a dairy and need to buy your milk from a huge selection at your local supermarket, the best advice I can give you is to buy milk when you're ready to use it, and to choose a good-quality milk from the place closest to where you live. The most important thing about the milk you'll use in the recipes in this book is its freshness, so check the use-by dates and buy the best-quality, freshest milk you can find. Please, unless you absolutely have to, don't buy the cheapest generic milk. Dairy farmers should get a fair return on their products, and you'll get what you pay for. If you want good-quality milk from cows that are treated well, you have to pay for it.

I expect you want to make as much as you can from scratch. I'm the same, and I don't want to buy anything new unless it's essential. When you make dairy foods at home you need to think ahead for a few supplies, such as rennet and cultures, but most of these recipes use equipment and utensils you've probably already got in your kitchen.

The main point to keep in mind when you're making diary foods is that everything that touches the milk – spoons, funnels, jars, lids, saucepans, pouring jugs and your hands – must be scrupulously clean, and some things need to be sterile. You only want to introduce the beneficial bacteria to your milk. Contamination caused by equipment that isn't completely clean will introduce bacteria and yeasts that will ruin what you're making. In each recipe I'll indicate what needs to be sterile, so there will be no doubt about what has to be very clean and what has to be sterilised. Making dairy products like yoghurt and cheese takes a bit of time, and you don't want to come to the end of it expecting to eat something delicious and finding instead some inedible contaminated mess.

Equipment and utensils

- **Large stainless steel saucepan:** a heavy-bottomed, stainless steel pot with lid is essential. The size of the pot will depend on the size of the cheese or yoghurt batches you intend to make but I find a 6 L pot is fine for most of what I do here. If I want to make a larger quantity, I do it in two pots. Make sure your saucepans have lids, because the milk must be covered during the ripening times.
- **Measuring cups, jugs and spoons:** I use a pyrex 1 cup jug and a pyrex 1 litre jug. I also use a ¼ teaspoon for measuring rennet.
- **Mixing bowls and food processor:** when mixing flavours into yoghurt you'll need a bowl; if you make the spreadable cheese, and I hope you do, you'll need a food processor or a blender.
- **Thermometer:** if you're going to make dairy foods, you'll need a thermometer with a clip on the side. I use the same candy

thermometer I use for making soap. Of course, it's thoroughly washed and scrubbed in the crevices between jobs. You can buy milk or candy thermometers at most kitchen shops.

- **Slotted spoon:** this is a good all-round spoon for stirring cheese and yoghurt. It can be stainless steel or plastic.
- **Whisk:** rennet needs to be thoroughly mixed through the milk. The best way to do this is with a whisk.
- **Homemade cheese press:** if you start making cheese, love making it and want to incorporate it into your weekly or monthly tasks, go ahead and buy a cheese press. But if you're a more casual cheese maker, Dr Fankhauser's makeshift cheese press is perfect. Details are in the Resources section. I use a plate and bricks covered in plastic as my cheese press.
- **Cheesecloth and muslin:** traditional cheesecloth is used to cover cheese before you wax it. To drain curds you'll need cotton muslin or a new Chux cloth that will freely drain the cheese without losing any of the curds that make the cheese.

    Before using the cloth for the first time, handwash it in warm water with dish liquid or pure soap. Rinse well and dry the cloth. Before cheese-making sessions, wash your cloths. If they need to be sterile, you can boil them in a saucepan.
- **Cheese wax:** if you're going to store your cheeses for a while – and most hard cheeses need time to ripen and develop their flavour – they need to be waxed. The wax helps prevent the cheese from drying out and keeps mould spores off the surface of the cheese.

Special ingredients

Starter cultures: many dairy cultures can be bought online in powder or granule form. You can buy enough for six months because most of them keep well in the freezer. Yoghurt, buttermilk, sour cream and some cheeses can also be made using dairy products containing live cultures, bought fresh from the supermarket.

When buying your dairy products, particularly those you'll use as starters, check the labels and make sure you're buying fresh, natural, live cultures, with no gelatine, sugar or flavourings in the mix. If you see 'live cultures' on the label, you'll know that it's suitable as a starter for several of the dairy foods you can make in your own kitchen.

The main cultures for making yoghurt are lactobacillus acidophilus, lactobacillus bulgaricus and streptococcus thermophilus. Streptococcus thermophilus is the bacteria that makes yoghurt thick and creamy, so if that's the kind of yoghurt you like, look for this bacteria on the label or when you're buying starters online. Overall, any fresh yoghurt, buttermilk or sour cream containing live cultures is capable of starting off another batch of the same product.

When you start making your own dairy products at home, it's wise to put aside some from each fresh batch to use as a starter for the next batch. Like sourdough, these cultures can live for decades if stored correctly. However, let's be realistic about this – not all cultures are strong and robust. There may be something in the air in your kitchen one day that weakens your previously very healthy starter culture. We're dealing with living organisms here, and they don't always do what we expect. I use a combination of powdered starter cultures and my own starters from a previous batch. Starters from my own batches save me money but they sometimes fail; powdered cultures are reliable and can be easily stored in the freezer.

Rennet: this is used to coagulate milk, which allows it to separate into curds and whey. I use vegetarian rennet but you can also use animal rennet or plain junket tablets. I haven't used junket tablets, but Dr Fankhauser does, and that's a good enough recommendation for me. He says one junket tablet will coagulate 5 gallons of inoculated milk (milk that has had a starter added). You can sometimes find junket tablets in the dessert section of the supermarket.

Cheese salt: salt is used to help draw the whey from the curds, to improve flavour and to help preserve the cheese. You can buy cheese salt, but you can substitute cooking salt or kosher salt. *Do not use* iodised salt. It will kill the lactic acid and spoil the cheese.

Cheese moulds: of course you can buy cheese moulds, but bear with me and try to make do with what you have in your kitchen. You can use the cheesecloth to contain and set soft cheese, or if you're making hard cheese and you need to apply pressure, you can punch holes in the sides and bottom of a plastic food container.

TIP: If you prefer to buy starter cultures, there are some reputable online companies listed in the Resources. The business you buy your culture from will probably also sell rennet, cheese salt, moulds, cheesecloth and all the other requirements for making various dairy products. Check out their online catalogue to make sure you can buy everything you need in one parcel so you don't spend too much on postage.

RECIPES

The recipes here are a mix of those I've used for years and fairly new (to me) recipes that I've modified to suit my family. Some of the processes may be unfamiliar at first, but there's nothing fancy here; it's all within the reach of the home cook in the average kitchen.

Yoghurt

There are many ways to make yoghurt, but this is how I do it. You probably already have everything you need in your home. If you start making yoghurt in the afternoon, it will be ready to eat the next morning. You can enjoy it straight from the jar, or add some jam or honey.

I believe that homemade yoghurt is equal in quality to the yoghurt I buy to use as a starter, but it's cheaper. So if you've been thinking about buying a yoghurt maker, try this method first. You'll save yourself some money and increase your self-reliance at the same time.

You should make yoghurt in a very clean kitchen and store it in a sterile container. Even if it's already pasteurised, the milk might have bacteria in it, so I scald it to kill off any pathogens. When the milk has cooled, I introduce the probiotic bacteria in the form of yoghurt or yoghurt starter, then pour it into a sterile container. Beneficial bacteria produce lactic acid during the process of fermentation. The acid conditions in the milk help preserve yoghurt because harmful bacteria find it difficult to grow in acidic conditions.

2 L milk

½ cup good-quality natural yoghurt

2 tablespoons powdered milk

YOU WILL ALSO NEED:

2 L preserving/canning jar

whisk or fork

spoon

large saucepan, an oven or dishwasher (to sterilise the jar)

small heavy-bottomed saucepan (to scald the milk)

1. To sterilise the equipment: fill a large saucepan with water, place the jar, lid, whisk and spoon in the pan and bring to the boil, then keep it boiling for 10 minutes. Turn off the heat and leave everything in the saucepan until you're ready for it.
or
1. Place the jar, lid and utensils on an oven tray, place in a low oven 160°C/320°F for 15 minutes, then turn it off and leave in the oven till you need the jar.
or
1. Run the jar, lids and utensils through the dishwasher on a normal wash.
2. Pour the milk into a small saucepan. Add the powdered milk and whisk it in, making sure it's completely dissolved in the milk. This will result in a thicker yoghurt.
3. To scald the milk, heat it to 90°C/195°F, then take the milk off the heat and let the saucepan sit in a sink half filled with cold water. This will help cool down the milk quickly.

4. When the milk has cooled to about 45°C/113°F, add ½ cup yoghurt or the recommended amount of starter granules and whisk in thoroughly. Make sure it's at the correct temperature. The milk must be warm enough to activate the bacteria, but adding the yoghurt to the milk when it's too hot will kill the beneficial bacteria.
5. Place the sterilised jar on the bench to cool down slightly. While the yoghurt is still hot, at around 40°C/104°F and the jar is still warm, add the yoghurt to the jar and seal with the lid. Don't touch the inside of the jar or lid.
6. Now the jar must sit in a warm place for about 12 hours to ferment. You want the jar to retain the heat for as long as possible. Don't open the jar, don't stir it, don't shake it. Just leave it to sit in a warm location: that, and time, is all it needs. The next morning, the milk will have thickened and you'll have a good batch of delicious and nutritious yoghurt. Store it in the fridge, but freeze about half a cup in a container to start off the next batch.

IMPORTANT POINTS

- You can use full cream, skim, UHT, powdered – any milk you have on hand will do but whole milk will give you a smoother and creamier yoghurt than skim milk.
- In summer and most of spring here, I put the jar on the verandah table. In winter, I wrap the jar in towels and leave it on the bench in the laundry, sitting on, and covered by, a woollen blanket. Of course, if you're lucky enough to have a wood stove, an open fire or combustion stove, place the yoghurt jar in a warm area nearby.
- Use good-quality yoghurt as your starter. It needs to contain live bacteria but no gelatine. Check the use-by date on the container and choose the freshest one. Alternatively, you can use a sprinkling, according to the instructions, of yoghurt starter granules.
- Make sure you whisk in the powered milk and the yoghurt properly, as this will give you a smooth yoghurt.
- Pour the warm yoghurt milk into a warm, sterile jar – do this step quickly so you don't lose too much heat.

Cultured buttermilk

Cultured buttermilk is slightly different to traditional buttermilk. It is thick, like light cream, but it's low in fat and high in protein. You can make cultured buttermilk at home and use it in baking, cooking and for drinking.

To start off your first cultured buttermilk, you'll need to buy fresh buttermilk with live cultures in it. Then, like with yoghurt, you can use a portion from the previous batch to continue. Cultured buttermilk will store well for a couple of weeks but if you make a large batch or want to keep it longer than that, it freezes well. The bacteria will go dormant, so freezing won't kill them.

1. Add ½ cup fresh buttermilk to 1 L of fresh milk. Mix well.
2. Cover the container and leave out on the kitchen bench for about 12 hours. If you like the taste of it, bottle it and store it in the fridge. If you'd prefer a more developed taste, leave it for another 12 hours.

TIP: To make cultured buttermilk using a bought culture, simply follow the instructions on the pack regarding the amount to use. The rest should be the same as above.

Butter

It's not cheaper to make butter like this, but it tastes *much* better and you know what's in it. Using good-quality cream will give you good-quality butter. I always use Jersey or Guernsey cream; they have a higher fat content so they turn into butter easily, and the taste is second to none. Whatever cream you use, it should not contain any gelatine or stabilisers – you need pure cream. About 6 cups of cream will give you about 500 g of butter. If you want to add salt to your butter, you'll need about ½ teaspoon of salt for 6 cups of cream.

1. Place the cream into a food processor, or into a bowl if you're using electric beaters. If you want to make salted butter, add the salt now. Start processing or beating. If you start off with very thick cream with a high fat content, it will form butter faster than if you use thinner cream. Thick cream will start to form thick yellow granules within 20–30 seconds of processing.
2. After about 45 seconds, you'll notice the cream separate into butter and buttermilk. Stop the processor and pour off the buttermilk. Don't throw it away; it's valuable in baking and will give you the lightest scones, pancakes and cakes.
3. Get some ice-cold water from the fridge and pour about ½ cup into the butter and continue processing. This will wash the butter. It's important to wash it properly – if you leave buttermilk in butter, it will go off fairly quickly. Make sure the water you use is ice-cold, as room temperature water might mix in with the butter.
4. Pour the milky water off, then remove the butter from the processor and place on a clean muslin cloth. Twist the cloth to tighten around the butter and wring out as much liquid as possible. This liquid is not pure buttermilk like the first lot – you could use it in your cooking in the same way as you use buttermilk, but I usually give it to the chickens. Remove the butter from the cloth and shape it. This butter can be stored in the fridge for up to 2 weeks.

TIP: Despite its name, the buttermilk produced in the process of making butter has no butter in it. It can be enjoyed as a healthy drink or used in baking because it is high in protein and low in fat.

Sour cream

Good sour cream starts with good fresh cream. It must be pure cream, not cream thickened with gelatine. There is absolutely no secret to making it – it's just a mixture of cream, heat and the right bacteria. You will find these cultures either in commercial cultured sour cream or buttermilk, or in a starter that you can buy online. I do both. I generally make the new batch with some of the old batch, but when I want a break, or there is no old batch, I use a starter that I've bought and kept in the freezer. You can use the same starter to make cultured buttermilk. There are details on where to buy all these dairy cultures in the Resources section. Have a look at the yoghurt recipe for how to sterilise your jar.

1. Put 500 ml pure fresh cream in a saucepan and heat to 30°C/86°F. (If the cream is very thin, mix in ½ cup powdered milk to make thicker sour cream.) Take the cream off the heat and stir in half a starter pack (or whatever the instructions for your starter say). Usually it's one sachet to make 1 L but I only make up half that amount at a time; the leftover half-sachet can be wrapped in foil and frozen. If your starter is fresh sour cream, use ½ cup.
2. Heat the oven for 5 minutes on low. Pour the warm cream into a sterilised warm preserving/canning jar and put the lid on, then wrap the jar in a towel and put it in the oven. Turn off the oven and leave the jar in there overnight. The next day it will be ready. The cream will continue to develop in flavour while it is stored in the fridge, and will keep for 2 weeks.

TIP: If you beat this sour cream, it will make cultured butter. You can make cream sour by adding lemon juice or white vinegar to it, but cultured sour cream is either made this way – with a starter – or by using raw milk and cream that is left unrefrigerated until it goes sour naturally.

Vanilla ice cream

You don't need an ice cream maker to make good ice cream; you need quality ingredients and a good recipe. Unless you buy very expensive ice cream, it will be one of the processed foods full of additives and ingredients you don't want to eat or give to a child. This is one of those handy recipes that you can make with ingredients found in most pantries and fridges. You can even make the condensed milk at home – that recipe was in *Down to Earth* and you can also find it on my blog (the web address is in the Resources section).

2 cups milk *(can be any milk you have: no-fat, soy, powdered, full-cream)*

1 cup cream

2 teaspoons vanilla extract *(please don't use vanilla essence; it is fake vanilla and will not do the ice cream justice)*

1 can *(approx. 400 ml)* **condensed milk** *(homemade or purchased)*

1. Add the milk, cream and vanilla to a bowl and mix together. Add the condensed milk (and glucose if you're using it – see tip) and stir.
2. Pour the mixture into a plastic container with lid and put it in the freezer. After the mixture has been in the freezer for at least an hour and formed ice crystals, take it out every 45 minutes and give it a good stir, until it's almost frozen. When it reaches that state, put the lid on and store it in the freezer.

TIP: Adding 2 teaspoons of glucose syrup will give you a creamier ice cream with fewer ice crystals. Glucose syrup is available in supermarkets near the cake icing and sprinkles. It's an optional additive.

Pouring custard

You can keep this delicious custard in the fridge, covered, for 2 days. Homemade custard is a good food for someone who is sick and can't face a meal. It contains eggs and milk, so it's nutritious without being too filling. Custard is also a good accompaniment to stewed fruit and will make iceblocks, with no colourings or preservatives, that children love. Simply make up the custard, pour into iceblock moulds and freeze.

2 eggs

2 heaped tablespoons cornflour (cornstarch)

2 heaped tablespoons sugar

2 teaspoons vanilla extract

3 cups milk

1. In a saucepan, whisk together the eggs, cornflour, sugar, vanilla and ½ cup milk until thoroughly combined and smooth. Add the rest of the milk.
2. Gently bring to the boil while stirring – it will burn if you don't stir it. Turn the heat down when it's getting hotter, and once it's boiled, stir for another minute and it's done. It will thicken up as it cools.

When pastured cows start grazing on spring grasses, they produce the best milk of the year.

Easy cheddar cheese

This is my modified version of the recipe in *Making Your Own Cheese* by Paul Peacock. It is a good-quality hard cheese that's easy to make at home and doesn't need too long to mature. At first glance, making cheddar might seem a bit complicated, but even though there are a lot of steps, most of the time will be spent waiting. The end result is well worth the effort, so I hope you try it. If you have a good supply of fresh milk, you'll be set to discover the wonders of making cheese in your own kitchen.

Before you start making cheese you should work out where you'll mature it. It will need a clean room that is a cool 9°C/48°F and humid. You might have a kitchen or bathroom perfect for that, or if not, I've added a link in the Resources to good instructions on how to make a cheese cave using an old fridge. I use a wine fridge bought from Aldi many years ago for about $70.

The water in this recipe needs to be unchlorinated. Allowing tap water to stand for 24 hours will let the chlorine evaporate, leaving water suitable for making cheese.

9 L full-cream fresh milk

1 sachet mesophilic starter

10 drops rennet

3 tablespoons rainwater or tap water that has been allowed to stand for 24 hours

3–4 tablespoons sea salt

cheese wax

YOU WILL ALSO NEED:

milk thermometer, a 10 L stockpot, cheese mould, cheesecloth or muslin, cheese press, large water bath or the kitchen sink and boiling water

1. Pour the milk into a large saucepan and warm to 32°C/90°F, then take the saucepan off the heat. Add the starter and combine thoroughly with a whisk or a slotted spoon. Keep the milk warm by covering the pan with a lid, then a clean tea towel, and placing it in an oven pre-heated to about 150°C/300°F for 5 minutes and then turned off. Allow the milk to sit in the pre-heated oven and ripen for an hour.

2. Add the rennet to a cup containing the water, mix, then pour into the milk. Whisk for 2 minutes so you know the rennet is incorporated. Don't let the milk lose heat – keep it at 32°C/90°F. If you have to put it back on the stove, do so.

3. After the rennet is added, the milk will set: these are the curds. Keep the pot at 32°C/90°F for 45 minutes. With the mixture still in the pot, cut the curds with a long, sharp knife in slow downward strokes 1 cm apart. Then cut the curds in a similar way across. You'll end up with small cubes of curd that should hold their shape and will release liquid (whey). Allow them to sit for 15–20 minutes.

4. If you have a water bath the stockpot will fit into, half fill it with water on the stove and place the pot containing the curds in it. Very slowly, raise the temperature of the curds to 38°C/102°F. If you don't have a water bath, use your kitchen sink: place the pot with the curds in the sink and surround with warm water a quarter of the way up the pot. Boil the kettle and slowly add the hot water to the sink water to gently increase the temperature of the curds to 38°C/102°F. Whichever method you use, the increase in heat needs to be slow – it should take about 45 minutes to reach 38°C/102°F. While you're raising the temperature, stir the curds gently with a large slotted spoon. When you reach the required temperature, cook for another 45 minutes, keeping the temperature steady. Stir gently on and off during that time.

5. Gently pour the curds and whey into a cheesecloth- or muslin-lined colander. To save the whey, place the colander over a large bowl or saucepan first. Gather up the ends of the cloth and hang the curds until they stop dripping. You can hang them on a doorhandle with a bowl underneath to collect the whey. Make sure the curds don't get too cold – close doors to stop any draughts.

6. When the drips stop, pour the curds into a clean bowl, break them up with your hands and add the salt. Keep mixing with your fingers to incorporate the salt.

7. You're almost finished. Line the cheese mould with cheesecloth or muslin and place the curd in the mould. You now need to apply pressure to extract the last of the whey. Remember, the success of the cheese depends on removing as much of the whey as you possibly can. Start with low pressure, then increase it. The suggested weights and times are:
   - 5 kg of pressure for 15 minutes.
   - Turn the cheese over and apply 10 kg pressure for 15 minutes.
   - Turn the cheese over and apply 15 kg pressure for 6 hours.
   - Turn the cheese over and apply 15 kg pressure for another 6 hours.
8. You can fashion a makeshift cheese press with house bricks and a slab of wood – the average house brick weighs about 2.3 kg. If you enjoy cheese making and decide to do more, you might make or buy a cheese press (see the Resources).
9. When the pressing is finished, remove the cheese from the mould and set it on a cheese mat to air-dry for 2–4 days and develop a rind (the hard, dry outer covering of the cheese). Cover it with a cloth or wire cover so the air can get in but the flies can't. When the cheese has a rind, apply the melted cheese wax and leave it to age in a cool humid place for at least 6 weeks. The cheese will develop in flavour as it ages, and the longer you leave it the sharper the flavour will be.

Spreadable cheese

This is the recipe that resulted from my search for a cheese good enough to give to my grandchildren. Often mature cheese is too sharp for a child and I didn't want to give them any of those processed slices or spreads, so I decided to make my own spread using a melt-and-pour recipe. What I came up with is a mild soft cheese that is very thrifty – you start off with 500 g of cheese and end up with 750 g of cheese.

If you remember the taste of the old Velveeta, the colby version of this spread tastes just like it – with no nasty additives. It is actually set in a block, but it's so soft it can be cut and spread. As well as using the cheese on bread with salad, it's good on crumpets and crackers. Hanno has it on his lunchtime sandwich. You can customise the cheese to suit – start off with colby cheese to make a mild spreadable for young kids, or with cheddar for a sharper cheese. You can add herbs or chilli if it's for adults.

1½ tablespoons water

2 teaspoons powdered gelatine

500 g colby or cheddar cheese, grated

2 tablespoons whole milk powder

¼ teaspoon cream of tartar

1 cup whole milk

1. Line a small loaf tin with plastic wrap, with excess over the sides to use for wrapping. Place the water in a small bowl, sprinkle the gelatine over the top, stir, and let the mixture sit.
2. Place the grated cheese, milk powder and cream of tartar in a food processor and pulse about 6 times until combined.
3. Pour the milk into a small saucepan and bring to the boil. Take it off the heat and stir in the softened gelatine until it's completely dissolved. Transfer the mixture to a small jug.
4. With the food processor running, slowly add the hot milk to the cheese mixture and process until smooth. Scrape down the bowl, particularly the bottom and sides, and process again for 30 seconds or until the cheese is completely smooth.
5. Pour the cheese into the prepared loaf tin. Pull the plastic wrap over the top and press down gently, making sure there are no air bubbles. Put in the fridge to chill for a few hours, or overnight. Remove the cheese from the tin, wrap it in plastic wrap or place in a lidded container, and store in the fridge.

Farmhouse hard cheese

This cheese doesn't need a special culture; you can use yoghurt.

5 L full-cream milk

200 g milk powder

1 cup plain yoghurt
*(containing live cultures
and no gelatine)*

1 cup cream

5 drops vegetarian rennet

2 teaspoons sea salt

1. Pour the milk, milk powder, yoghurt and cream into a saucepan and bring up to 30°C/85°F. Turn off the heat, cover the pan with the lid and a couple of tea towels and allow to sit for 3 hours.

2. Add the rennet, stir in with a whisk for a few minutes and let it sit in the pot and ripen for 1 hour. During this time the milk mixture will solidify. You'll know it's ready when the curds cut cleanly with a sharp knife.

3. With the mixture still in the pot, cut the curds into 1 cm strips. Then cut the same across to produce 1 cm cubes that should hold their shape. Whey will be released and you'll see a lot of liquid in with the curds. Put the pan back on the heat and slowly bring the temperature of the curds and whey up to 40°C/104°F over about 30 minutes, stirring gently. Make sure you increase the temperature slowly, because fast heat will make the cheese rubbery. When it reaches 40°C/104°F, keep at this temperature for 30 minutes and stir every few minutes.

4. Gently ladle the curds into a large square of cheesecloth laid out on a colander. Bring the top corners together and hang over a bowl for the whey to drain out completely. This should take about an hour. Pour the salt over the curds and, with your clean hands, gently mix it through. Ladle the curds into a mould and press down. Then, in a cheese press or with your arrangement of covered bricks, apply moderate pressure for 12 hours (see the easy cheddar cheese recipe).

5. Turn out of the mould and place the cheese on a cheese mat to dry out at room temperature, turning it twice a day for 3 days. The cheese does not have to be waxed, but should be wrapped in plastic and stored in the fridge, and eaten within 2 weeks.

Ricotta

Ricotta is one of the easiest cheeses to make at home. It's made using the whey collected when making cheddar and other cheeses, so don't waste this valuable ingredient. If you don't have enough whey, make up the amount with milk. Ricotta cheese can be made with either whey or milk or a combination of the two.

2 L whey (*or whey and milk*)

1 cup cream

½ teaspoon sea salt

¼ cup white vinegar or lemon juice

1. Heat the whey and/or milk to 95°C/200°F. Add the salt and vinegar or lemon juice, stir in and let it sit for 15 minutes. During that time the ricotta curds will develop and you'll have curds and whey.
2. Using cheesecloth in a colander and a slotted spoon, scoop the whey into the cheesecloth to drain, then place the ricotta in a bowl and fluff up with a fork. Store in the fridge.

TIP: There will still be a small amount of protein left in the whey, so catch it for your baking, or give it to your pets or chickens. They will love it.

october

SPRING CLEANING

*'Opportunity is missed by most people because it is
dressed in overalls and looks like work.'*
– Thomas Edison

A BREATH OF FRESH AIR

Spring in Australia starts in September, so by choosing October as our spring cleaning month, we're opening up our homes after winter, letting fresh air in and giving ourselves the gift of cleanliness, order, progress and regeneration. I think the cleaning and organising we do in spring is symbolic as well. It represents a fresh start, showing that we are in control of our lives. And by making the effort to clean and declutter we give ourselves the best chance to make our homes warm, comfortable and inviting.

Cleaning may not be high on your list of preferred home tasks, but it can make a real difference to the pleasure and comfort you get out of your home. When the work is done, you'll be going back to survey each room, pleased you did what it took to get your house in order. I hope you can look back in the months that follow and see the significant changes that came from your efforts.

DECLUTTERING YOUR HOME

Spring cleaning isn't only about cleaning – it also involves decluttering, which is just as important. Everyone understands cleaning, even if we don't all like doing it: cleaning gives you a healthy space to live in. Decluttering is more complex. All those excess things in your home cheat you of your time because they have to be looked after. Decluttering allows you to remove the excess so you have enough to live comfortably without being weighed down by what you own. Many of us live with wardrobes hiding clothes that we keep 'just in case'. We have too many possessions that we bought just because we could, and even though we try to hide a lot of it, we know it's there. It still affects our lives.

I don't think of myself as a minimalist, but I do like living with just enough, which is a level defined by me and not by the commercial world or anyone else. Almost every time I decluttered in the past I believed it would be the last one I'd need to do, but now I know that decluttering is an ongoing process that continues all through life. Although I try to maintain the knife edge of 'just enough', almost every year I'm there again, paring back so my life and psyche remain open, accessible and honest. And it's not that we keep buying too much; it's more that the older we get, the less we need.

Before you start spring cleaning, declutter your house and sort out everything you feel you can give away, sell or send to landfill. The first time you do this you might find it quite difficult. You'll make excuses to keep certain things you don't need; you'll feel sad that some of it is going. You might feel anger that you bought it all in the first place, or keep some things just in case you need them and wonder why you're doing it. But keep going: when you finish that first purge, you'll have less junk to care for and you'll feel that consumerism has loosened its grip on you. Hopefully, you'll sense a kind of gentle liberation that will grow when you declutter a second time.

Eventually, that constant letting go of things will begin to change how you live. You'll be much more mindful when buying new products and you'll probably question every one of your purchases. That doesn't mean you'll stop buying what you need, but you'll think about the difference between needs and wants and really be sure of what you buy.

Letting go of items you once valued isn't easy, but as the months go by and you give away more of your possessions, you'll realise you're being enriched by it. When you pare back the paraphernalia of life and live more simply, you stop being a curator of your own possessions. You won't have to find space for all that excess and you'll feel as though you've opened up the windows and let fresh air in.

When you're ready to declutter, find four medium-to-large cardboard boxes and mark them 'put away', 'give away', 'sell' and 'rubbish'. Now go through each room, searching for things you no longer need or want, or that should be in a different room (these go in the put-away box).

TIP: Supermarkets and fruit shops often have boxes you can take home.

When you sort through your items there will be some that you can't get into the give-away box fast enough and others that you're not sure about. Maybe it was a gift or an inheritance, and you feel disloyal getting rid of it. Maybe you paid a lot of money for it. When you come across one of those items, ask yourself: 'Do I really need this? Do I love this? Do I use this, or is it in the cupboard most of the time?'

You can often make a bit of money by selling your unwanted items. There are plenty of places to sell online, such as eBay, Gumtree and local Facebook groups set up to buy and sell. Alternatively, local notice boards and garage sales are still popular, or you could rent a stall at your local market – ask family and friends if they're interested in joining you to share the stall-hire costs.

TIP: If you sell a few things, use the money as an extra debt repayment, or put it in the bank towards a holiday or this year's festive season.

If you have items to give to charity, make sure what you donate is clean, undamaged and not too old to be of use. There are also websites such as freecycle.org and streetbank.com where you can offer items to your neighbours for free.

Don't fall into the trap of leaving the boxes you've filled sitting in the garage. Get rid of them in the week following your declutter; otherwise you'll have just moved the problem to another spot and achieved nothing.

Don't expect to finish decluttering quickly, or to do it once and never again. It's an ongoing process that you'll return to many times over the years. It's worth it, though, so start sorting and be ruthless.

STARTING YOUR SPRING CLEAN

Spring cleaning might sound like a big effort, but keep in mind that you're in control: you decide what has to be done, and either allocate the work to some helpers or do it yourself. Not every room will need deep cleaning; some will merely need a quick freshen-up. You know the standard you're comfortable with and what it takes to reach that standard, so your spring-cleaning lists are entirely up to you.

The first decision to make is how you'll go about your spring clean. Will you clean a room or zone, then go on to the next? This method gives you a sense of satisfaction as you tick off each room. Or will you clean all the walls first, then all the windows and doors, then all the cupboards and drawers? This method allows you to get all your cleaning equipment ready for one big job. The choice is yours. I prefer to tackle spring cleaning with the room-by-room method. I can clean, repair and rearrange while focusing on one space.

Don't expect to get through it in one day. Set out a timetable that also allows enough time for the other household tasks you need to do. It's complicated, hard work, so plan your attack as well as your meals on the very busy days. Let's say you can identify eight zones in your home – that's two zones per week over the month. If you tackle it like that, you'll be able to do a very thorough job without impacting too much on your other work. Let everyone in the household know what you're doing, and allocate jobs to others. Unless you live alone, this is not solely your job: everyone will benefit from it and everyone should help.

When you're ready, put on an apron, roll up your sleeves, and dive in.

General cleaning tips

- Open the windows and doors in every room you clean. Even if you use gentle cleaning products, you still need a lot of fresh air when cleaning. Inhaling stirred-up dust isn't good for anyone, so vacuum the dust when you can and keep those windows open.
- Most things can be cleaned with warm soapy water in a small bucket you carry with you, or in the laundry sink if it's a larger item

or a lot of them. Washing in the laundry will also give you a place to lay a towel to air dry everything.

- Unplug all appliances and electrical goods before you clean them.
- Don't spray cleaner onto appliances. Use a microfibre cloth dipped in vinegar, vinegar and water, or liquid soap; wring the cloth out well so that it's moist rather than wet.
- Screens of any kind – TV, computer, phone, iPad and others – are fragile and need special care. Never wipe a screen with paper products, because over time it will create fine scratches. Use a microfibre cloth or a lint-free cloth. If you need to remove fingerprints from the screen, use a microfibre cloth moistened with a 50/50 solution of water and vinegar.
- As you clean, check to see what needs repairing. If the repairs are minor, such as mending a hem on a curtain or replacing a light bulb, do those things straight away. Do larger repairs such as filling in scratches in a wall or painting after you finish cleaning the room and before you start the next.

Cleaning gear

You'll probably be able to get through the entire house with a well-stocked cleaning kit. If you need something extra in the kit, add it before you start work.

CLEANING KIT

- A small bucket to store cleaning products in and also to hold water
- General declutter box
- Rubber gloves
- Broom or vacuum cleaner with upholstery and crevice brushes
- Mop and bucket
- Long-handled duster or a small stepladder
- Clean cotton or terry-towelling rags
- Microfibre cloth
- Small scrubbing brush

- Old clean toothbrush
- Cotton buds
- Spray bottle of vinegar
- Container of bicarb soda
- Cream cleanser (homemade or commercial)
- Oil of cloves and a spray bottle

CLEANING ROOM BY ROOM

Of course, you can clean your rooms in any order you wish, but I find it's easier to break up the difficult rooms with those that aren't so difficult. For me, the wet rooms are harder, so I've alternated them with the dry rooms in this chapter. In all of the rooms we clean, we will do a quick declutter first if something belongs in another room, then clean from top to bottom.

Each home has its own footprint, its own range of zones. Yours may have a playroom, craft room, study, attic or hallway. I've identified seven zones in my house, and those are the ones I cover in this chapter: Living room, kitchen, dining room, laundry, bedrooms, bathrooms and verandahs/patios.

There's also the windows – I clean the outside when I tackle the verandahs and patios, but I like to get all my gear ready and go through the house doing all the windows on the inside in one go. For this you'll need:
- 50/50 solution of vinegar and water in a spray bottle
- microfibre cloth
- cotton cloths

Start at the top of the window. Just spray on the vinegar solution, wipe the glass with the cotton cloth and dry with the microfibre cloth.

It would be impossible to give you a guide on cleaning every particular thing in your home, but if you follow these general guides and your own common sense, you can't go wrong.

Living room

First, open up the windows.

If you find items in this room that shouldn't be there, put them in your declutter box. Don't leave the room to put them away, because that can take some time and you might get distracted from the main task.

Remove any soft furnishings that need washing, such as cushion covers, slipcovers, curtains, runners, doilies and throws. Light cotton floor rugs can be washed too. Take all the washing to the laundry and start the washing machine – or you could do this washing on another day if you prefer. Just cover the couch and chairs with towels and sheets until you can replace the covers.

Remove floor rugs and hang them, underside up, over the clothesline. Make sure it's not about to rain when you do this. Using a tennis racket or broom, whack the rug to remove dust in the pile. Leave the rug outside to air for a while. When you bring it back inside, vacuum it thoroughly.

Vacuuming is the easiest way of cleaning floors and upholstery, and you won't be moving the dust and dirt around only to settle in another place. Attach the crevice tool or brush tool to your vacuum cleaner and go around the ceiling dealing with spider webs and dust. Vacuum around the windows and along the windowsills. Pull out all the furniture and vacuum behind and under it. Go over all the furniture with the vacuum, making sure you remove all the dust from the crevices, under the seats and along any piping or decoration. Put each piece of furniture back as you clean.

Fabric couches and dining furniture usually have either care labels or an instruction booklet. Always be guided by that. It's a good idea to read the care labels or booklet as soon as you bring the furniture home, to understand what kind of cleaning is required. If a particular cleaner is recommended for spot-cleaning, buy it to have on hand when needed. Generally, fabric couches should be vacuumed about once a month to prevent a buildup of dust and pet hair. For couches that need a thorough cleaning, wash the removable covers according to the care instructions or use a professional steam-cleaner.

If you have leather furniture, you'll need to clean and then condition the leather every six months. Be guided by any care instructions that came with the furniture, but if you don't have them, find an inconspicuous part of the furniture and do a test clean before you apply the cleaner to the rest of the furniture. The back of a seat cushion or behind the couch should be fine.

Check it over to see if there are any areas that need spot-cleaning; if so, clean them first.

You'll need:
- Dr Bronner's liquid soap or mild baby shampoo
- Bowl of warm water
- Microfibre cloth

Add ¼ teaspoon of soap to the water, dip the microfibre cloth into the soapy water and wring out the cloth so it's moist, not dripping wet. Rub the spot with the moist cloth to see if you can remove it. If the spot is dirt, it will probably come off immediately, but if it's something like ink or blood and has been on there a long time, it will much more difficult to remove.

Using a circular motion and a couple of fingers inside the cloth for pressure, wipe over the spot for a minute or so to see if it makes any difference. If it does, wipe the spot dry and go on to the rest of the furniture, then apply the leather conditioner. If the spot doesn't change at all, you may need to get a professional leather cleaner in if the damage is noticeable, or place a cushion or rug over a smaller spot.

TIP: If your child has written on leather upholstery with permanent marker, spray the spot as soon as possible with a small amount of hairspray or nail-polish remover and wipe it with a dry rag. Apply again if the stain is still there. Once it's gone, wipe the area with a cotton cloth and some warm, soapy water, dry, then condition the area with your leather conditioner.

Treat the stain as soon as possible after the spill. Fill the water chamber of your iron with water and switch it on. Moisten a terry-towelling cloth with white vinegar and rub it over the stain, removing as much of the stain as possible.

Lay a clean terry-towelling cloth over the stain, and when the iron is hot and steaming, carefully place it on top of the cloth and allow the steam to penetrate the pile. Move the iron around over the cloth for about thirty seconds, then lift the cloth to check the stain. Usually it will be gone. If not, repeat the vinegar and steam treatment.

CLEANING BLINDS AND CURTAINS

If you remember to run the vacuum over the blinds every two months to prevent a buildup of dust and grime, a yearly deep clean will be much easier. For venetians, start at the top and work downwards. Using warm water and ¼ teaspoon of dishwashing liquid, rub each slat with a moist microfibre cloth, then dry with a soft cotton cloth. Wash every slat on both sides.

For roller blinds, pull the blind so it's all the way down, then starting at the top, wash using a microfibre cloth dipped in warm water with ¼ teaspoon of dishwashing liquid added. Wash one side and dry it, then do the other side and dry it. Leave the blind down for at least twelve hours, rolling the blind up before it's completely dry might encourage mould to grow.

Curtains should be washed according to their care instructions. Be very careful with them, because if they're ruined the replacement cost is usually high. If they're handmade or the care label is missing, wash in your machine with a mild laundry liquid on the wool/gentle setting. If the curtains are too big to fit in your washing machine, take them to your local laundromat then fold them and bring them home to dry. Don't overload the washing machine, and hang each load out as soon as it's washed to prevent creases. If you have enough line space, hang the curtains over two lines so they dry faster.

Wash delicate sheer or lace curtains by hand in warm water and dry in the sun. For rubber-backed curtains, especially if they're old, handwash in warm water with liquid soap or Lux flakes added. When drying these outside, keep the rubber out of the sun, and hang them fabric-side up over two lines.

Attach the upholstery tool to the vacuum cleaner and run it over the top of all the books to remove the dust. Then remove the books and vacuum the shelves. If your bookcase is timber, wipe the shelves with some homemade wood polish or your conditioning cloth (recipe and instructions can be found on page 254).

Television screens need to be cleaned carefully. They often have anti-glare coatings and can be damaged by harsh chemicals, abrasive cleaners or too much pressure. Often TVs come with their own cleaning cloth, which is similar to the small cloths used to clean spectacles. If you don't have one of these you should be able to buy one at the supermarket. Don't use paper towel, as over time it will scratch the screen.

Turn off the TV before you start cleaning. Look at the screen when it's dark and identify any fingermarks or dirty patches. Using the microfibre cloth, wipe the screen to remove dust and fingerprints. Don't apply too much pressure. If there are still marks, dip the microfibre cloth into a 50/50 solution of water and vinegar and clean the marks off with the moist cloth. Again, no pressure. When the screen is clean, go over the frame with the cloth.

Remote controls become very dirty over time and should be cleaned regularly. Rubbing alcohol is ideal for cleaning remotes as it will disinfect the surfaces and then dry quickly.

Start by removing the batteries. With a clean toothbrush, gently brush the front of the remote around the buttons and crevices to loosen any dirt. Dip a cotton bud in rubbing alcohol and clean around every button.

Dab some alcohol onto a clean rag and use it to wipe the entire remote. If you find a particularly dirty part, add more alcohol to the cloth and rub until it's clean. When you're satisfied you've cleaned it properly, sit the remote control on a flat surface to dry completely. When dry, replace the batteries.

TIP: Never spray any sort of cleaner onto a remote control because it might seep into the batteries or the circuit around one of the buttons. Dab your cleaner onto a cloth instead.

CLEANING STEREOS AND HI-FI EQUIPMENT

You'll need:
- Small hand-held vacuum or larger vacuum cleaner
- Pantyhose attached to vacuum cleaner with rubber band
- Cotton buds
- Microfibre cloth
- Rubbing alcohol

Turn off the stereo at the wall. Using the vacuum cleaner with pantyhose over the brush attachment, remove the dust from every side of the unit and where the unit is sitting. When vacuuming the front of the speakers, start at the top and take special care not to apply pressure to the fabric. Dab a microfibre cloth in rubbing alcohol and clean all the glass surfaces. Dip a cotton bud in alcohol and clean all the small areas and around the buttons and dials. Turn the unit back on at the wall. Don't sit anything on top of the unit, because it could muffle the sound.

CLEANING SMOKE DETECTORS

Generally there's more than one smoke detector in a home, so make sure you check and clean each of them when you're spring cleaning. Use the brush attachment to vacuum around the outside of the smoke detector and over the vents. Test the detector after cleaning. Smoke detectors, both battery-operated and hard-wired, should be cleaned and checked every six months.

If your detector is battery-operated, the batteries will need replacing every twelve months, or whenever the unit emits a low-battery warning signal. Either replace the battery when you do your spring cleaning, or pick another day and mark it on your calendar and in your home journal.

Kitchen

Before you start, open the windows and doors, make sure the kitchen is tidy and all the washing-up is done. Turn every kitchen appliance off at the wall before you clean it. Never spray liquid cleaner onto your electrical appliances – pour a small amount onto a clean rag instead.

Remove all the tea towels, tablecloths and any other fabrics that need washing, including curtains if there are any. The main part of cleaning a kitchen is to degrease everything that over the year will have gathered a film of cooking grease, such as cupboard doors and drawer fronts, handles and knobs, the sink splashback, tiles, the fridge door, microwave door, oven door and stove.

Attach the crevice or brush tool to your vacuum cleaner, then vacuum the room from the ceiling to the floor. Pay particular attention to the corners, and remove any spider webs you find. When you reach the floor, make sure you vacuum along the skirting boards to remove all the dust.

To degrease kitchen surfaces, use warm soapy water with ½ cup of vinegar added. Wipe all the surfaces to remove grease, marks and spots, then dry with a cotton cloth. You'll need to replace the water a few times when you do the entire kitchen.

Wash the walls down with warm soapy water with half a cup of vinegar added. Dip a clean rag into the water, wring it out and spot-clean the walls, especially around the light switches and the stove. If there are dirty marks around the switches, dip a soft scrubbing brush into the water, shake off excess water and scrub around the switch. After brushing, dry the area to check if it's clean. If not, redo with the soft scrubbing brush.

Remove the vent screens in your rangehood. If there are any other vents in the kitchen, remove them too and place them in the bucket. Take the vents to the laundry and fill the sink with hot water, a squirt of liquid soap and a cup of vinegar. Put the vents in to soak for two hours. When the time is up, scrub the vents with a brush to remove all traces of grease. Rinse and lay on an old tea towel to dry. Clean inside the rangehood with a solution of warm water, liquid soap and vinegar. The dirtier it is, the more vinegar you'll need in the water – start with half a cup, but be prepared to add another half cup to get the job done right.

Cleaning a fridge is a simple and straightforward job. The main thing to remember is to do it thoroughly but quickly. You don't want to have the fridge door open too long or the food to warm up too much while it's out on the bench. Remove everything from the fridge, including the shelves and fruit bins at the bottom. Wipe out the fridge using a clean, moist cloth and the general cleaner listed at the end of this chapter. When every surface is wiped thoroughly, dip a clean cloth in warm water and wipe off any residue.

Check the fridge seals, and clean them with a toothbrush dipped in water and then bicarb. Wipe with a clean, moist cloth. If you have anything stuck to the fridge door, remove it all and wipe the outside of the fridge with a cloth moistened with a 50/50 water and vinegar solution, then dry the surfaces with another clean cloth. Wash and dry the shelves and fruit bins and place them back in the fridge, then close the door so the fridge can cool down again.

Go through the food that was in the fridge and try to organise a meal for that night using up whatever is on its last legs. Check all the use-by dates, wipe the tops and bottoms of jars and bottles, make sure everything is wrapped or in a sealed container, and replace all the food in the fridge.

CLEANING FOOD CUPBOARDS

Empty everything out of your pantry and stockpile cupboards, making sure you place items in the same order they were in when inside the cupboard so you don't lose track of what needs to be used first. Vacuum the shelves, spray them with homemade spray-and-wipe solution (see recipe on page 253), then wipe them over with a moist rag. Dry the shelves before replacing everything in the same order it was in before.

Don't forget to clean out and organise all the drawers, including the cutlery and junk drawers; clean out your wraps, foil and freezer-bag drawer, and clean and reorganise the area under the sink. Use homemade spray-and-wipe for all these areas.

Dining room

The dining room should be fairly quick and easy. Strip off the tablecloth if you use one, and if you have chair cushions with removable covers, take them off and add them to the laundry hamper.

Vacuum around the ceiling, looking for any spider webs. Attach the crevice tool or brush tool to your vacuum cleaner, then work along the skirting boards with the brush tool. Check the walls – if they need a clean, wipe them over with warm water and homemade laundry liquid or a 50/50 vinegar and water solution in a spray bottle, spot-cleaning any areas that need it, and wipe dry with a clean rag. Clean around light switches with your homemade cream cleanser, as they tend to collect a lot of grime.

If you use cloth napkins, take them all from their container, wash the container, check the napkins and if they're okay, put them back into the container. If you're running low, make a note of it and add it to your sewing tasks. Any napkin rings can be cleaned and replaced.

Last but not least, set the table with a fresh cloth if you use one, place fresh flowers or a candle on the table and vacuum the floor.

Laundry

We covered deep-cleaning this room in May, so it may just need some light cleaning and organising now. The main points to remember are to keep appliances clean and maintained, and to store all your cleaning products and ingredients in one place out of the reach of children and pets. The laundry room is your cleaning headquarters, so it's worth the extra care in that room to help you do all your cleaning jobs during the year.

Bedrooms

Open all windows and doors, strip the bed and take the bed linen to the laundry for washing. Take all the pillows, doonas, quilts and floor rugs outside for airing in the sunshine. Pillows need to be replaced every three to five years unless otherwise stated on the care instructions. If your pillow doesn't give your head and neck the support it once did, it should be replaced. Those that are stained or going brown, or developing a smell, should be washed if washable and dried to see if it can have an extended life. Check the pillow again when it's dry and if you're happy with it, keep it; if not, replace it.

Modern mattresses are very heavy and can be a struggle to turn over, but you should do it at least twice a year. They should be flipped from top to bottom and from side to side. Vacuum the mattress with the upholstery nozzle before and after you flip it.

Move all the furniture out from the wall, attach the crevice tool or brush tool to your vacuum cleaner, then vacuum the walls from the ceiling down and remove any spider webs. Vacuum along the skirting boards.

Wipe the walls with a cloth moistened with a small amount of liquid soap, and clean around the light switches.

If there's a TV or phone in the bedroom, clean it according to the instructions earlier in this chapter, dry everything and plug back in.

With a moist rag or microfibre cloth, dust all the furniture, clean any ornaments that can be cleaned, dry, then replace them. Clean the bedside lamps by switching them off and removing any dust with a moist cloth. Clean the base and the switch, dry the lamp, then plug back in.

Dust and wipe over any pictures on the walls. Clean the ceiling fan if you have one with either a fan duster or a moist cloth.

When all the cleaning has been done, vacuum the floor.

Spring cleaning might sound like a big effort, but keep in mind that you're in control: you decide what has to be done.

Bathrooms

Open up the windows. Pick up all the items that shouldn't be in the room and put them into the declutter box.

Take everything that needs washing, such as towels, face cloths, bath mats and dirty clothes, to the laundry. Attach the crevice tool or brush tool to your vacuum cleaner and go around the ceiling looking for spider webs. Vacuum around the windows, along the windowsills and skirting boards. Wipe down the walls, paying particular attention to the light switches.

Remove everything from the vanity unit, drawers and cupboards. Go through all the toiletries and make-up and put any unwanted or out-of-date make-up in the declutter box. If you have any expired medications, seal them in a plastic bag and the next time you go shopping, take them to your local pharmacy to be disposed of properly. Organise all the make-up, toiletries, medicines and clips into small containers.

Wipe out the drawers and cupboards with homemade spray and replace the things you'll keep. Clean the shower and bath, using homemade cream cleanser on the tiles and other surfaces and vinegar on the glass. Check the grout and silicone sealers as you work. If there is a build-up of mould on the grout, you'll need to treat it with oil of cloves, which can be bought online at biome.com.au and in some chemists.

Make up a spray bottle of 1 litre of warm water and ¼ teaspoon of oil of cloves, and spray all the areas of mould. This is Shannon Lush's recipe and it works really well. Allow the spray to sit for twenty-four hours, and in that time it will kill the mould. Bleach doesn't kill mould, it just whitens it.

If there is mould growing on the silicone sealer, treat that with an old toothbrush dipped in vinegar and then dipped in bicarb soda. Scrub gently: you don't want to break or loosen the silicone. There may come a time when no amount of cleaning will improve the mould situation in a dark and wet bathroom, and in that case you'll have to remove all the grout and silicone and regrout the tiles.

Wipe down thoroughly with a dry microfibre cloth.

Plastic hairbrushes can be soaked, but those with wooden handles or a rubber base need to be hand-cleaned.

Remove any hair from the hairbrushes before you wet them. Place plastic hairbrushes in a shallow bowl of warm water containing 1 tablespoon of bicarb soda. Swish the brushes around and let them soak for an hour. With a toothbrush, gently scrub the bristles until they're clean.

Take any wooden-handled and rubber-based brushes and wet them under the warm water tap. Sprinkle on a teaspoon of bicarb soda, and gently scrub the bristles with the toothbrush to loosen all traces of hair spray or gel. When the brushes are clean, rinse them under the warm water tap and lay them on a towel to air-dry.

CLEANING MAKE-UP BRUSHES

Pour a small amount of warm water into a mug and add ½ teaspoon of vinegar. Allow the brushes to soak for thirty minutes, then remove them and pat dry with a clean cloth. Lay on a towel to air-dry.

Verandahs/patios

Remove any cushion covers, seat covers, tablecloths and mats and put them in the laundry for washing. Move the outdoor furniture to make the cleaning easier and remove everything that shouldn't get wet.

The easiest way to do the outdoor areas is to use a pressure cleaner. If you have one, blast the walls, ceiling and finally the floor. Go over the windows, screens, screen door, and any wicker, glass or metal furniture and allow it all to air-dry.

If you don't have a pressure cleaner, use a broom to brush over the window screens, screen door and furniture and hose it with a strong jet. Again, allow it all to air-dry.

If you have air-conditioner units on the verandah, turn them off at the switch before you start cleaning and make sure you don't get them wet. Wipe them over and vacuum out the vents on the side.

Citrus fabric softener

Use ¼ cup per wash

1 L white vinegar

¾ teaspoon citrus or lemon essential oil

2 crushed lemon leaves or lemon myrtle leaves

1. Mix all the ingredients in a large jug, then pour into a glass bottle and seal. Shake before using.

Spray-and-wipe solution

This is a good disinfectant spray for wiping cupboard doors and benchtops. It can be stored in a spray bottle.

1 teaspoon lavender, tea tree or lemon myrtle essential oil

1 L water

1. Shake before using, spray on and then wipe over with a microfibre cloth.

All-purpose cleaner for walls and fridges

To clean pencil, ink or crayon marks off walls or to clean and deodorise the fridge, simply pour this solution onto a microfibre cloth and wipe over.

½ cup bicarb soda

1 L warm water

1. Mix in a large jug, then pour into a sealable bottle.

Creamy scrubber

This is the perfect recipe for cleaning the bath and shower because it rinses easily and doesn't leave grit. If you plan to store the mixture, add 1 teaspoon of vegetable glycerine and store in a sealed glass jar; it will keep for about 1 month.

½ cup bicarb soda

liquid soap or laundry liquid

1. Simply pour the bicarb soda into a bowl, and add enough liquid soap or laundry liquid to make a texture like very thick cream. Scoop the mixture onto a sponge, and start scrubbing.

Wood polish

This polish doesn't keep, so make just enough for your current cleaning jobs.

juice of 1 lemon

1 tablespoon olive oil

½ tablespoon water

1. Add all the ingredients to a jar, put the lid on and shake it well. Dab a cloth into the mixture, taking up only a small amount of the cleaner, and rub it in a circular motion all over the wood. Make sure there isn't too much cleaner on the rag, because a film of oil on the furniture will attract dust and might eventually build up and become rancid.

Leather and wood conditioning cloth

After cleaning leather furniture, you can rub it with this conditioning cloth. It can also be used to polish wooden furniture.

1 teaspoon beeswax

1 teaspoon citrus essential oil

1 teaspoon lavender essential oil

soft lint-free cloth

1. Grate 1 teaspoon of beeswax over the cloth. Sprinkle the essential oils over the cloth and place it on a china plate in the microwave. Microwave on high for 15-second periods for 1 minute, or until the beeswax melts. The cloth will be ready when the wax and oils have seeped into the cloth.
2. Store it in a zip-lock bag in the freezer between uses. It should last about a year.

When you pare back the paraphernalia of life and live more simply, you stop being a curator of your own possessions.

november

HEALTH AND WELLBEING

'*Health is the greatest gift, contentment the greatest wealth,
faithfulness the best relationship.*'
— BUDDHA

A HEALTHY ADJUSTMENT

In my early days of simple living, the changes I made were financial and culinary ones. It didn't take long for me to realise that these were broad changes: the financial side of life is lightly woven through almost everything, and food isn't only about satisfying hunger but also about nutrition, health, animal welfare, value for money, planning, awareness and skill-building. Learning how to manage money helped me relax and enjoy life more, and the culinary changes saved us money and made us healthier. I started thinking about the possibilities of this new life and realised Hanno and I had the opportunity to reinvent not only what we ate and how we dealt with money, but most of what we did. All we had to do was to identify problem areas, decide what we wanted to change, then do the work to bring about the changes.

The single idea of saving money by buying ingredients instead of convenience food was opening up into the best kind of storybook, where I got to write the story.

One of the most significant things I noticed soon after we started changing was that I felt different. I was becoming more reflective and mindful. I started slowing down too; instead of wanting to race through my housework, I took my time and had breaks, and I started looking after myself.

Simple life isn't just about the practical aspects like gardening, organisation, decluttering, mending, cooking from scratch and budgeting; it's also about doing things that enrich and nurture us, and feeling secure and content because of that. So let's take the time in November to examine the more personal concepts of simple life: health and wellbeing.

There's no doubt you'll be healthier if you eat food that contains no preservatives or artificial additives, if you exercise and remain active, if you manage your money well so there is less anxiety, if you ensure there are fewer harsh chemicals in your personal hygiene, laundry and cleaning products, and if you get enough sleep and time to relax. All those things, which most of us accept as the common consequences of living a simple life, will keep you healthier than you were before. Like our finances, our health weaves its way through our lives, and affects most of what we do. Physical and mental health are greatly influenced by how we live.

BEING WELL

What is wellbeing?

We all know what health is, but what is your understanding of wellbeing? It's a more difficult concept because, like health, it incorporates both mind and body, but also relates to feeling connected to your family and community, your life's purpose, how successful you feel you are, your expectations, career and financial situation, and your overall satisfaction level. For me, wellbeing results from me feeling healthy, being mindful, filling my days with meaningful work, slowing down, appreciating what I have, being surrounded by a loving family, and having a group of friends I trust and can rely on. It's probably a whole lot more too. To simplify it, if you generally feel good about what you're doing and life seems to be bubbling along nicely, then your sense of wellbeing will be good too. When things don't go so well, when you feel defeated and pessimistic, usually your wellbeing will take a dive. So keeping all that in mind, like with our health, there are ways to influence wellbeing.

How to improve your wellbeing

I think one of the best ways to improve your wellbeing is to establish what your beliefs and values are and to live by them. Writing down your values will give you a map to follow when you're not quite sure of what to do, what choices to make or how to stay true to your decision to change how you live. Long ago I thought about my own future and how I wanted it to be. It took a while, but I came up with a list of things I wanted in my life. I still have that list and I still live by what I wrote. But everyone's list will be different – even your partner's will be different to yours, although I hope not too different. If you've not yet thought about what you want in your future life, start thinking and then make a list of your goals and core values. If any of your personal goals are health and wellbeing-related, single them out for close attention this month and work out a step-by-step method of how you'll achieve those goals.

Here are some other steps you can take towards improving your wellbeing.

DEVELOP AN ATTITUDE OF RESPECT AND CARE FOR YOURSELF

If you overwork yourself, if you don't take breaks, and if you fail to look after your own health and wellbeing, you won't be able to work or take care of your family and home. Care for yourself as much as you care for others. And remember, if you have children, showing them that you respect yourself teaches them the valuable lesson of self-respect too.

DON'T AIM FOR PERFECTION

Perfection is overrated and usually unnecessary. The problem with perfection is that if you aim for it and miss, you think you're not good enough or you've done something wrong. Aim instead to do your best – I promise you, that is good enough.

If you're working outside the home, look for a good balance between work and home life. Your work is vital because it funds your lifestyle and allows you to build your assets, but what good is a healthy bank balance and a fine home if you sacrifice your health or quality time with your family to get it? Think about what your ideal life would be and how family and work fit into that, and then be flexible and strong enough to make some healthy adjustments.

ESTABLISH THE HABIT OF QUIET TIME FOR YOURSELF AND YOUR SMALL CHILDREN

When you first start taking time out for yourself it may surprise your family and friends. But if you keep going and make it something you do every day, it will soon become a normal part of your day and everyone will accept it. This will give you time to relax between jobs, to think about what's going on in your life, or to just look at your surroundings and breathe deeply.

Quiet time is important for children too – they all need the ability to settle down and focus on sleeping, reading or talking quietly. This is particularly important when they start school, but the ability to be quiet needs to be there beforehand. Some children develop this ability naturally because it's part of their nature; others have to be taught. And you can do that by showing them, while they're very young, when you have your own quiet time.

If your toddler isn't one of the quiet ones, talk about your own quiet time and establish a quiet-time routine to help them slow down. Tell your child there will be quiet time soon, turn off the phone and any other source of noise in the house, and get a book, their blanket or sleeping teddy ready. They don't have to go to another room – it's better if they're near you so they can see what you're doing. Then sit with your book or tea and be quiet. There will be questions (*Why are we being quiet?*) and there will be distractions (*I have to go to the toilet*). I hope you can deal with it all quietly and know that, despite what it might look like, your child is learning from your gentle and relaxed manner.

GET ENOUGH SLEEP

I think sleep is the most underestimated element of health and wellbeing. I know if I don't have enough sleep, I don't function very well. But when I do sleep soundly, I'm eager to get up in the morning and do my work, no matter what it is. Sleep reduces tension, helps your mind process and store memories and gives you the energy to do what you have to do. Never underestimate the power of an early night.

EXERCISE

You don't have to go to a gym to exercise. Being active in your work and doing a bit of walking or gardening might be enough exercise for you. Swimming, walking the dog and tai chi are good gentle workouts; if you want to join a cricket or soccer team, or play tennis, contact your local sports clubs for information. There are so many sports and special interest groups in our communities now; I'm sure you'll find something that suits you.

SLOW DOWN, APPRECIATE WHAT YOU HAVE AND LIVE IN THE MOMENT

If you live and work at full speed, your body and mind won't have a chance to slow down. Build slowness into your routines, accept that you might not get through all your work and be okay with that. Housework never ends; it will still be there tomorrow and the day after that. Focus on what you're doing, stop thinking about what you'll be doing after work or tomorrow, and give whatever you're doing your full attention.

I always try to give my best to whatever I spend time on. To do otherwise is a waste. So when I write my blog or a book, when I look after grandchildren, when I clean the kitchen sink or mop floors, I do the best I can on that day. It's not the activity that determines how I work, it's that I'm spending my life hours on it and to do it poorly or without thought is to waste those hours.

Spending a lot of time online can waste hours you'll never get back and prevent you from focusing on your own life. If you're spending many hours online or watching television, why are you? Are you avoiding work or unsure of what work you should be doing? Make a list of what you want to do each day and tick off each item as you do it. If you can't seem to start a project or do the work you should, break it down into steps and make yourself do it for fifteen minutes.

IF YOU FEEL ANXIOUS, DO SOMETHING ABOUT IT

Talk to someone you trust about why you're anxious and see if you can work out what to do about it. If the problem is long-term or you've tried to shift the feeling and you can't, see your doctor about visiting a professional counsellor. Feeling that you have some control of your life will help increase your wellbeing.

EMBRACE AGEING

I don't wear much make-up now, and what I do wear is organic. I stopped dyeing my hair as soon as I started going grey. I enjoy my grey hair; I think I've earned it and I wear it with pride. Now that I look back on it, I'm pretty sure I did that to identify myself as an older woman. It's amazing how many people tell me I don't look old, or say that I shouldn't put myself down when I describe myself as 'an older woman'. I see it as a term of endearment and pride; they see it as disgusting, or something close to it.

The fact is that all of us will grow older. The only way to escape it is to die earlier than you should. I hold a warm place in my heart for the affection and respect our Aboriginal communities and many Asian cultures have for their elders. I wish we had that kind of appreciation here. Instead, we have an adoration of youth that I don't understand. I look back on my own youth with a kind of benign amusement. I know that all those wrong decisions, mistakes and insecurities paved the way for me to be the older woman I've become. And I wouldn't want it any other way; nor do I want to go back there, because maturity, acceptance and contentment is better than longing for what has already been and cannot be again.

A challenge for you

I have no delusions about living simply: it often means more housework to do in addition to child-rearing and paid employment. Sometimes you might feel that if you don't keep going, that work will never get done. Or worse, you might feel like giving up and going back to your old life. So this month I challenge you to establish small parcels of time when you stop whatever you're doing to relax and spend a moment with yourself.

I want you to take some time to make yourself a cup of tea or coffee, go and sit somewhere and just do nothing. Catch your breath, stare into space, clear your mind. Think about your day and what you've completed so far. If you go out to work, plan to have some quiet time when you have lunch. If you're a crafty person, take some knitting or quilting to work with you and do some after you've eaten; if not, read a book. Don't fall into the trap of going online to check social media or emails. Stay in your own space and collect your thoughts. That thirty minutes, spent alone and without talking, can keep you going through the afternoon and help you to be cheerful when you arrive home.

If you're working at home – decluttering, sewing, writing menu plans or whatever – it's okay to feel pride in what you've done. Know that it's part of the life you're building, one small step of many, and recognise the value in what you've achieved.

I know what some of you are thinking: *how can I do that when I have a baby or children to look after?* Or, *I can't take a break because I won't finish everything I have to do today.* For those parents with babies and small children, your time is when your children sleep; take a break then. Of course there will be household tasks that are easier to do when the children are tucked up in bed, but your wellbeing is more important than making a batch of soap or washing up. If you think you can't take a break because you have a lot of work to get through, take a break anyway. You'll return to your work fresher and more capable than you were before. It doesn't matter if you don't finish all your work in a given day; it will wait for you. I promise.

The importance of family, friends and community

I didn't know when I started living a more simple life that it would encompass so many other concepts as well. Health, wellbeing, strong community ties, gratitude, generosity and a strong sense of sharing and passing on what I knew were all there, right from the start. I was surprised by some of these things but they have become constant companions. I also developed an undeniable need for familial closeness. I'd always had that, but I thought that as I grew older and my sons made their own lives with their partners and children, we'd all become more independent. In fact, the reverse happened: we became closer.

Initially my friends thought I was a bit crazy for changing how I lived, but they soon saw the difference in me and loved being fed on good home cooking and leaving my place with eggs and vegetables. I have a handful of friends I've known for many years, but when I engaged with my community I started making new friends. The door that I thought had been closed by already having long-term friends reopened when I started volunteering and meeting new people.

Good relationships with family and friends are crucial for your wellbeing and self-confidence. Everyone wants to feel they belong, and being part of a family or included in a strong group of friends develops that feeling of connection like nothing else. Don't expect your relationships with either family or friends to survive without time and effort on your part, and on theirs. Spend time with the people you love and feel close to; talk to them about your life and ask about theirs. Include your family in your social life; invite your mother and father or your siblings to a barbecue or Sunday lunch with friends. Develop the confidence to allow your family and friends to get to know each other. When you make the effort to be a part of someone's life, and invite them to share yours, you form a strong bond and from there you build trust, respect, understanding, acceptance, life-long affection and love. We are all made stronger by these things.

NATURAL FIRST AID

Getting plenty of sleep, cooking from scratch, reducing stress, and other points I've touched on in this chapter will help keep you healthy, and next I'll provide recipes and information for drinks, tonics and remedies that may help if you do get sick. But note that sometimes we need something extra to ease symptoms or to help our bodies start the healing process. If your symptoms persist or if you have continued pain, please see your doctor. It's very important to get a professional medical opinion when needed.

Medications, ointments and first-aid treatments should always be used with caution because, like food, they sometimes contain substances you'd rather not consume or have on your skin. For instance, common old VapoRub is made using petroleum-based chemicals. Vaseline contains it too. As a general rule, don't use mineral oil, which is also derived from petroleum, and avoid products containing artificial fragrances. Some tampons contain residue from the cotton processing, so use organic tampons or a menstrual cup instead. It's best to be as vigilant with your personal hygiene products, medications and drinks as you are with your food.

In keeping with a more gentle approach to self-care, I've included information here about natural first aid and home remedies. You're more likely to find honey and lavender oil than plastic bandaids and disposable wipes, and some of the fabric items here can be washed and used again. There are a few products you can make from scratch too, because we try to use that back-to-basics approach in everything we do.

If you don't know much first aid it would be wise to buy an up-to-date St John Ambulance first aid book. There is a general version and one for babies and children. See the Resources section for more information.

Supplies and equipment

To make up your first-aid kit, find a suitable container that can be closed securely, then gather the supplies in this list. Some can be made at home and some should be bought at the chemist or health-food store. (The ice pack should obviously go in the fridge rather than in the container.)

- **Lavender essential oil** – has a mild soothing effect for headaches, bruises and insect bites
- **Tea-tree oil** – has antiseptic and anti-fungal properties
- **Aloe vera gel** – for burns, sunburn, minor cuts and abrasions
- **Arnica** – for bruises, sprains and muscle pain (not to be used when pregnant)
- **Cotton buds**
- **Eye bath**
- **Gauze swabs**
- **Crepe bandages**
- **Triangle sling** – can be made at home using a 1 metre square of cotton or calico cut into two triangles, and washed after each use
- **Homemade rice pack** – place in a microwave or on a tray on top of a wood stove to heat up to treat muscle pain and stiffness
- **Ice pack** – can be a bought gel pack, a zip-lock bag of ice cubes or a packet of frozen peas
- **Small scissors**
- **Surgical tape**
- **Thermometer**
- **Tweezers and needle**
- **Hydrogen peroxide 3 per cent** – use to cleanse a wound before dressing it
- **Paracetamol/ibuprofen** (including the type suitable for children if you have them)
- **Bandaids** – I prefer fabric bandaids to the plastic ones because they let the skin breathe under the strip while completely enclosing the wound

TIP: To make a rice pack, sew together three sides of a rectangle that will comfortably fit around your neck, knee or elbow, fill it with rice, then sew up the fourth side.

Treatments for common complaints

SUNBURN

Add a cup of apple cider vinegar to your bath water and soak for ten minutes or so to ease discomfort. Or apply aloe vera gel to the face and shoulders.

INSECT BITE

If there is tightening in the throat or any other sign of a severe reaction, seek medical attention immediately.

Apply an ice pack to the site for about fifteen minutes three times a day. If the bite is on an arm or leg and there is swelling, elevate the limb as well. After treating with the ice pack, apply a couple of drops of lavender essential oil to the bite.

PAIN AND SWELLING

An ice pack is also good for pain and swelling associated with sports injuries and falls. Apply for fifteen minutes three times a day and then rub with arnica.

MUSCLE AND JOINT PAIN

If you know you've injured yourself, take the weight off the joint. If there's no swelling, apply a warm rice bag for about twenty minutes and repeat that treatment every two hours. If possible, it may be better to have a warm bath to which 2 cups of Epsom salts have been added.

If you have joint or muscle pain and you're not sure why, see your GP.

MINOR BURNS

Please note: honey treatment is for first-degree or minor burns. All severe burns should be treated by a doctor. Honey treatment is not suitable for babies under twelve months.

Honey has been used for medicinal reasons for thousands of years, and recent research has confirmed its effectiveness in the treatment of wounds and burns. It has healing properties, and also works on burns because its viscosity stops bacteria from reaching the vulnerable burned skin. Tea-tree or manuka honey are best, but you can also use raw honey, which is unprocessed and contains many of the essential active components needed for healing. You can buy manuka and tea-tree honey at health-food stores, and you can buy raw honey from any local beekeeper. Don't use supermarket honey, as it doesn't have the healing properties.

As soon as the burn happens, run cold water over it for about fifteen minutes. This will not only relieve the pain; if it's a first-degree burn the water will also reduce the temperature of the burned area and help reduce the effects of the burn. Work out how severe the burn is. You can treat a first degree and a small second-degree burn at home; a large second-degree and all third-degree burns must be treated by a doctor. A third-degree burn is a medical emergency, so call the ambulance and don't remove clothing from the skin or break any blisters. If it's a limb, elevate it and reassure the patient while you wait for help to arrive.

If you can treat the burn yourself, prepare a clean treatment area while the water is running over the burn. For a hand, arm or upper body, this can be as simple as a clean tea towel on a table with the patient sitting on a chair. If the burn is on the feet or legs, you'll need a bed or sofa on which to lay the patient down.

Carefully dry the burn and surrounding skin. Pour honey quite thickly on the burn, spreading it with your hand inside a clean plastic bag, or with the underside of a clean spoon. Cover with a sterile dressing and tape the sides down with surgical tape.

Change the dressing daily until the wound heals. To do this, carefully remove the dressing and discard, taking care not to break any blisters. If the burn looks infected or very swollen, see a doctor. If it looks as if it's healing, add more honey if it's starting to wear thin, then cover with a new dressing and tape down. Don't remove any honey. When the burn heals, gently wash the area and remove all the honey.

Aloe vera gel is an excellent treatment for minor cuts and abrasions. Apply pressure to stop the bleeding then clean the cut with gauze and water. Dab on some aloe vera, then cover with a bandaid or gauze and a bandage, depending on the size of the wound.

If the wound has dirt or gravel in it, or it is a penetrating wound such as one caused by a dirty garden fork or rake, it can be cleaned with hydrogen peroxide 3 per cent. Pour a small amount of peroxide into the wound and leave it to fizz. Often the fizzing will clean out any dirt. Dry the wound carefully with gauze, then cover with clean gauze and tape the edges. Repeat this process with fresh dressings four times a day until the wound has healed.

RECIPES FOR HOME REMEDIES AND TONICS

When I write about remedies and tonics here, I do so as a fellow traveller, not as a professional. If you have any doubts about your health or are unsure about trying a remedy, talk to your pharmacist, doctor or naturopath.

We sometimes forget that many commercial remedies are made using common plants and herbs as a basis. These old remedies are used because they've always been effective and continue to be today. Soups, teas, tonics and a range of other concoctions are easily made at home with none of the additives or preservatives present in over-the-counter medications.

Chicken soup for colds and flu

Some people claim chicken soup cures their colds. I won't go that far, but this soup will boost nutrition levels and increase hydration in someone who probably doesn't feel like eating much.

This recipe has more herbs, garlic, onions and ginger in it than the chicken soup I usually make, to improve its restorative powers. Grate the vegetables or process them in a food processor so that the patient doesn't have to swallow large pieces when they have a sore throat. It's best served in a mug so it can be sipped, with a spoon for the chicken pieces and vegetables. Sick kids might be tempted to drink just the broth without the vegetables. They'll still get the benefit of the vitamins and minerals.

Adding vinegar to the water will help draw minerals from the bones but make sure it's vinegar you'd use on a salad, not cleaning vinegar. If you want to, you can test how much gelatin is in your broth once it's cooked by chilling it in the fridge. When it's cold, a good broth will be like jelly.

1 chicken carcass, chopped into smaller pieces

1 bay leaf

6–8 garlic cloves, skinned and crushed

2.5 cm piece of fresh ginger, skinned and grated

salt and pepper to taste

1 tablespoon apple cider vinegar

2 skinless chicken breasts

2 onions, finely diced

2 sticks celery, finely diced

2 carrots, grated

½ bunch parsley, finely chopped

1. Place the chicken carcass, bay leaf, garlic, ginger, salt and pepper in a large stockpot with 5 litres of water and the vinegar. Bring to the boil and simmer gently with the lid on for 3 hours. Check the level of liquid every hour to make sure it's not boiling away. Add more water if necessary.

2. Pour the liquid through a sieve to remove the bones and herbs and return it to the pot.

3. Cut the chicken breast into small cubes and add to the mix.

4. Bring the broth back to the boil and add the vegetables. Simmer for 20 minutes.

5. Test for seasoning, turn off the heat and add chopped parsley.

Elderberry cold and flu tonic

If you have space for a small tree in your backyard, I encourage you to plant an elderberry tree. They're easy to grow in a wide variety of climatic regions and they grow well from cuttings. Recent research has shown that elderberries made into a syrup help prevent swine and avian flu and may support the immune system. See the Resources for details on where to buy dried elderberries online.

Take two tablespoons once a day as a preventative measure if you've been exposed to a cold or flu, or two tablespoons three times a day if you already have a cold or flu, continuing until the symptoms stop. Do not give this to babies under the age of twelve months. The tonic can be stored in the fridge for up to six months.

elderberries

fresh ginger, grated

honey, preferably raw honey

1. Strip the elderberries from their stem and discard the stems.
2. Wash the berries, then place in a medium saucepan. For every cup of berries, add 1 cup of water and 1 tablespoon of grated ginger. Bring to the boil, then simmer for 30 minutes.
3. Strain the berries through a fine sieve or food mill, collecting the dark elderberry liquid in a jug.
4. When the liquid is warm (not hot), add honey to taste. Allow to cool further, then pour into sterilised glass bottles.

Immunity–boosting tea

This tea can help promote recovery when you have a cold or the flu. Drink the tea hot to raise the core temperature of the body, and keep it warm in a thermos or reheat by adding a small amount of hot water.

1 lemon, washed and finely sliced (including the peel)

½ orange, washed and finely sliced (including the peel)

1 to 2 tablespoons grated fresh ginger

honey to taste

1. Brew 500 ml of strong black tea in a coffee plunger or teapot.
2. Add the lemon, orange, ginger and honey and allow to steep.

Homemade vapour rub

This is a DIY version of Vicks VapoRub, made with essential oils. Mark the jar with 'adult vapour rub' or 'baby vapour rub' and the date, then store in the fridge for up to three months.

Both versions are made the same way. To use, rub about half a teaspoon onto the chest of someone who has a cold to open up the airways and help with breathing.

INGREDIENTS FOR
TEENS & ADULTS

5 drops tea-tree
essential oil

5 drops eucalyptus
essential oil

½ cup coconut oil

2 tablespoons grated
beeswax

INGREDIENTS FOR
BABIES & CHILDREN

2 drops tea-tree
essential oil

3 drops lavender
essential oil

¼ cup coconut oil

1 tablespoon grated
beeswax

1. Melt the beeswax in a heatproof bowl over a saucepan of simmering water.
2. Add the essential oils and the coconut oil and mix thoroughly.
3. Pour into a small jar with lid and allow to sit for 24 hours for the oils to infuse.

Herbal teas

Many people say herbal teas help in various illnesses and conditions, and I believe some of them do. I use herbal teas because they calm and nurture, and I feel good drinking them. Make a few different teas to find the ones you love. Some herbs you can try include lemon balm, borage, mint, calendula, fennel, chamomile, lemon myrtle, rosella and parsley. See the Resources for more information about the benefits of herbal tea.

If you grow the herbs yourself, you'll know that the petals or leaves you use are free from any harmful sprays. Many herbs grow well in pots on a sunny windowsill or in a sunny protected spot outdoors. Drink fresh herb tea when the plants are actively growing, but keep harvesting your herbs so you can dry and store them, giving you plenty of tea over the entire year.

To make up any herbal tea, start by boiling fresh water. Add ¼ cup of a chopped fresh herb or 2 teaspoons of a dried herb to a tea-brewing basket or teapot and allow to infuse for 5–10 minutes. Cover the brew with a saucer (if it's in a cup) or a tea-cosy (if it's in a pot) to keep it warm.

TIP: Herbs can be dried in the oven or a dehydrator, or you can tie them at the stems and hang them indoors.

Herb- and fruit-infused water

Despite what you may read, drinking water infused with herbs and/or fruit isn't going to boost your nutrition levels. It does, however, provide a variety of ways for your family and guests to drink water – the best drink. It's important to stay hydrated, particularly in summer or when doing strenuous work.

Adding citrus slices to a filled water jug and leaving it in the fridge overnight will make a good supply of infused water for the following day. All these fruits make thirst-quenching drinks when added to water: strawberries, raspberries, crushed blueberries, watermelon, mango, crushed pineapple, passionfruit. Experiment to see which herbs team well with which fruit so you can find a drink suited to your taste: for example, thyme goes well with pears, cherries, figs and grapes; mint goes with just about every fruit; and basil goes with any strong-flavoured fruit, especially apricots, figs and plums.

december

A TIME FOR CELEBRATION

*'Do not go where the path may lead,
go instead where there is no path and leave a trail.'*
— RALPH WALDO EMERSON

THE FESTIVE SEASON

December, what a splendid month it can be. It's a time to look back and review what we've done, organise end-of-year gatherings, celebrate the holidays, relax and think about what will change next year. But if you're weighed down by debt and have trouble resisting the temptation of excessive gift shopping, it can also be one of the worst times. If this describes you, don't worry: we'll get through December together.

Let's take this last chance to make the year one to remember. We'll be fine-tuning, planning and celebrating our family feasts – be they Hanukah, Christmas, St Lucia's Day, the Solstice, Festivus or Kwanzaa. And then we'll look ahead and do some planning for the coming year. There's a lot to do, so let's get on with it so we can also sit back and put our feet up for a well-earned break.

Traditions for the holidays

Traditions strengthen families – they reinforce a feeling of belonging and help us to identify with our family culture. Sometimes I hear people regretfully say they have no family traditions. It may be they've grown up with none, or they've moved away from their family and don't see traditions played out in everyday life, or they've forgotten what they used to do. No matter what the circumstances, seasonal traditions can be started in your family, or you can modify the traditions you grew up with. These are your traditions and they should suit you, your family and the values you hold dear. December is the ideal time to think about your traditions, and how you might begin or adjust them if you want to.

Starting a family tradition is as simple as doing whatever it is, and then repeating it at regular intervals to build a sense of expectation and significance among your family. Traditions can be associated with festive occasions, but they can just as easily be ordinary daily rituals such as eating together as a family at the kitchen table, or going camping during the school holidays. Hanno and I have restarted an old tradition in my family by having morning tea on the front verandah most days. We both stop whatever we're doing, I make a pot of tea, serve up a couple of slices of homemade cake or biscuits, and we sit, rest and talk. Christmas Day pavlova has been a tradition here for over thirty years. You can see how deceptively commonplace family traditions can be.

So don't worry if you have no family traditions – just start some. Think about your values, work out how they relate to your family life, and consider activities that reflect and strengthen who you are collectively as a family.

Planning your December feasts

Work out what extra food you need this month so that you'll have enough –but not too much – for your festive days, summer barbecues and those Saturday afternoons when friends and neighbours drop by for a drink. Look in your stockpile and freezer to see what's there, work out your festive-occasion menus plus snacks for more casual or unplanned gatherings, and write a shopping list. We all know how chaotic shopping is in the week before Christmas, so I encourage you to gather what you need as early in the month as you can. You'll be able to buy everything except for the fresh fruit, vegetables and dairy, including wine and beer. Getting organised early is particularly important if you need to order special cuts of meat from the butcher, or if you want organic meat.

> TIP: Ask your butcher early in the month about ordering special cuts of meat for your feasts. If you want organic, free range, extra-large or anything unusual, often they will have to be ordered well in advance.

For me, the cut-off point for going shopping in December is the beginning of the school holidays. By the time school's out, I've already done all my shopping and I won't go back to the shops until the last week of the year. And that will only be for a quick restock of fresh fruit, vegetables and dairy.

> TIP: Put aside an afternoon early in the month to make some pickles and spiced nuts for snack platters and cold meats, as well as ginger syrup and lemon cordial, delicious fresh alternatives to overly sweet and preservative-dense soft drinks. I've included recipes in this chapter.

The spirit of giving

Don't undo any of the valuable frugal work you've done this year by rushing out and buying last-minute gifts. We discussed gifts in January, when you planned your year's gift-giving, and in August, when homemade gifts were made. So during the year I hope you've worked steadily on preparing your gifts and cards. You will, no doubt, also have had a few gifts to buy; if you wrote a list early in the year, perhaps you bought all you needed at the mid-year stocktake sales. You should have a secret gift cupboard to hide all your purchases; it's also a good idea to wrap every gift as soon as you have it so you're less likely to keep looking at it and then use it for something else. (Make sure you attach a note saying who it's for and what's inside.) Planning will definitely help you save money on gifts. Even if you've missed the boat this year, get into the habit of putting aside an amount in your budget for it, attend the after-Christmas sales to begin your gift stash for the coming year, and put time aside for the gifts you want to make yourself.

If you need a couple of last-minute gifts now, the spiced nuts, pickles and chutney recipes later in this chapter can be decorated with ribbons or raffia and might save the day for you. Don't expect your gift-giving to be absolutely perfect the first year – and don't run back to the shops.

Pavlova

6 egg whites

250 g caster sugar

2 teaspoons cornflour

2 teaspoons white vinegar

½ teaspoon vanilla

1. Preheat the oven to 130°C/265°F.
2. Add the egg whites to the bowl of your electric mixer and whisk them at a medium-high setting. Add the sugar a tablespoon at a time, beating well between each addition. When you add the last spoonful of sugar, add the cornflour, vinegar and vanilla as well.
3. Take a small pinch of the mixture between your fingers and rub them together. If you can still feel sugar in the mix, keep beating until you have a smooth mixture.
4. Place a square of baking paper onto a baking tray. For a round pavlova, draw a pencil line around a plate on the paper. Add the pavlova mix inside the circle and straighten the sides of the pavlova with a spatula in an upwards motion; this will create strong walls.
5. Bake for about 90 minutes or until the pavlova feels dry and set, then turn off the heat, leave the oven door ajar and allow the pavlova to cool down in the oven. When cool, it can be topped with whipped cream and fruit.

TIP: It's important that the bowl and beater you use to whisk the egg whites are clean and free from any fat or egg yolk, otherwise the egg whites won't form peaks.

Ginger syrup

While it's a good idea to make ginger beer using the fermentation method, it takes a while to brew. In December, if you have friends dropping in for drinks, you need something you can make, and possibly remake, fairly quickly. A batch of this recipe takes just twenty-four hours to prepare. Mixed with iced sparkling mineral water and a mint leaf, ginger syrup makes a refreshing summer drink – taste-test a small glass to see what ratio of syrup to water you prefer. And it isn't just a once-a-year treat – in winter it's delicious added to black tea.

15 cm piece of ginger

juice of 1 lemon

2 cups sugar

2 cups water

1. Wash the ginger, then grate it into a saucepan with the lemon juice, sugar and water.
2. Bring to the boil with the lid on. Turn down the heat to a slow simmer and cook for an hour.
3. While the ginger syrup cools, leave the lid on and allow the ginger to steep for the rest of the day.
4. Strain the syrup into a container, removing the ginger, and store in the fridge. It will keep in the fridge for a few months.

TIP: You can reuse the ginger for another batch that will be weaker than the first but still delicious.

Lemon cordial

This cordial stores well in the fridge for at least a month. Dilute with cold water to taste and serve with lots of ice.

1.5 kg sugar

8 lemons

1. To make sugar syrup, boil 1.5 L water with the sugar until the sugar has dissolved.
2. Wash the lemons, then grate about 2 tablespoons of lemon rind before you cut them. Add the grated rind and the juice to a large bowl. Pour the sugar syrup over the juice and mix well.
3. Allow to cool and pour into clean bottles.

TIP: If you have a backyard lemon tree, pick the lemons about a week before you want to make the cordial – this will give you more juice.

Spiced nuts

You can choose any of your favourite nuts for this recipe – I usually use cashews, almonds, pecans and macadamia nuts.

2 tablespoons butter

2 tablespoons honey

½ teaspoon salt

1 teaspoon paprika

1 teaspoon chilli powder

4 cups mixed nuts

1. Preheat the oven to 180°C/355°F.
2. Add the butter to a frying pan and melt over a low heat. Add the honey, salt, paprika and chilli powder, mix it together and add the nuts. Stir until the nuts are coated in the sticky butter.
3. Pour the nuts onto a slice tray lined with baking paper. Spread them out with a fork and bake for 10–15 minutes.
4. Remove from the oven and allow to cool. When completely cold, store in an airtight jar.

Pickled onions

Onions are my favourite vegetable – we eat them almost every day. When added to spiced vinegar, they're very difficult to resist. Pickled onions will add interest and crunch to your sandwiches, salads and cheese boards. This recipe can be changed with different spices, so you can make the onions exactly to your taste.

Pickling onions, which are immature brown onions, are available in late spring and all through summer. You can also use white or red onions if you can find small ones. Look for onions that are small and all the same size, with no signs of sprouting.

Pickled onions will last up to twelve months in the cupboard if they're sealed properly.

1 kg small onions

50 g cooking salt

550 ml apple cider or malt vinegar

150 g sugar

2 cm piece of ginger, peeled and crushed

1 teaspoon mustard seeds

1 teaspoon peppercorns

1 fresh chilli, deseeded, or a pinch of dried chilli flakes

2 bay leaves

YOU'LL ALSO NEED:

1 large jar or a few small jars, sterilised, with screw-on lids.

1. Cut the top and bottom off the onions, removing very little of the onion, then peel.
2. Place the peeled onions into a shallow, flat-bottom bowl and pour all the salt evenly over the top of them. With clean hands, move the onions around to make sure they're all coated in salt. Cover with a tea towel and leave overnight.
3. To make the spiced vinegar, place the vinegar, sugar, spices and bay leaves in a saucepan and bring to the boil. Remove from the heat, put a lid on the saucepan and let the mixture infuse overnight.
4. The following day, wash the salt off the onions and pack them in a large jar or several small ones.
5. Strain the vinegar. If you want crunchy onions, pour the cold vinegar over the onions and seal the jars. If you like softer onions, bring the vinegar back to the boil and pour it over the onions and seal. Allow to mature for 4 weeks before eating.

TIP: When you finish eating the onions, use the spiced vinegar in salad dressings.

Spicy pineapple chutney

If you have time during the month, make some quick preserves. Pickling done at the beginning of the month will be ready to eat at your December parties and on Christmas Day, when they can be served with a variety of meats and seafoods. My pickled onions and spicy pineapple chutney are stars of December because they're easy to make and most people enjoy them. Both will store well for many months and can be enjoyed all through the year. They make great little gifts too.

This delicious chutney is ideal with ham on the Christmas menu. It will develop flavour over the first few weeks, so give it 2 or 3 weeks before eating. The jars will store well for at least 6 months. Store in the fridge after opening.

1 tablespoon olive oil

2 large red onions, chopped

2 red cayenne chillies with seeds

small piece fresh ginger, peeled and grated

1 red capsicum, finely chopped

1 teaspoon tumeric

1 teaspoon cumin

1 teaspoon mustard seeds

½ teaspoon salt

½ teaspoon white pepper

1 large pineapple, skinned and chopped into small chunks

200 g brown sugar

1 cup white wine vinegar

1. Add olive oil to a large saucepan on medium heat and add the onions, chilli, ginger and capsicum. Cook for about 3 minutes or until softened.
2. Add the spices, salt and pepper and mix. Add the pineapple, then add the sugar and vinegar and mix thoroughly.
3. Bring to the boil, then turn down the heat. With the lid off, allow to simmer for an hour. Stir occasionally to make sure it's not sticking to the bottom of the pan.
4. When the chutney has darkened and thickened, and while it's still hot, pour into sterilised jars and seal with a lid. Leave on the bench to cool down overnight and check the next morning to make sure all the lids are sealed tight.

TIP: Choose the variety of chilli depending on how hot you want the chutney.

TEN SIMPLE IDEAS FOR DECEMBER

1. Make it a new tradition to take an end-of-year family photo. Ask everyone in the family to dress well and have the photo taken in the same place every year, possibly at the kitchen table or in the garden.

2. Send an email to relatives and friends you won't be seeing over the holidays and attach your family photo.

3. Take part in a community event: attend a school play or concert, tour your neighbourhood to look at the Christmas lights, help to collect donations for a local charity, have a street barbecue for neighbours, look in on elderly relatives or neighbours to see if they need help during the holidays, plan and supervise a pool party for your teens, organise a year's-end morning tea for your kindy kids with help from other parents, bake a few Christmas cakes and take them to the local senior citizens' club or retirement village with your children . . . There are so many things you can do in the community at the end of the year. It's a wonderful time to connect and establish good communal ties.

4. Help serve Christmas lunch at a local charity or volunteer to help a local organisation with their December activities.

5. Make a live wreath for your front door (see the Resources).

6. Bake holiday biscuits, make a gingerbread house or do some traditional baking that supports your cultural celebrations.

7. On Boxing Day, instead of going to the shopping sales, watch the cricket on television and explain the history of the game to the kids. Organise a limited overs game in the backyard or at a local park and celebrate the day with plenty of icy cold homemade ginger beer. If you're not a sporty family or it's too hot or cold to go outside, download or rent a couple of movies and make some popcorn for a movie marathon. Or do all of the above.

8. Read a book. You've probably seen at least one book during the year that you'd like to read – now is the time. Make yourself a drink, find a quiet place to sit and start your book. Make sure you have a bookmark with you, because you'll probably be interrupted a few times.

9. Pick up your needles and knit. December is a great time to sit with your latest project or teach yourself to knit. If you're a new knitter, you'll find many different instructions on how to start knitting on YouTube, as well as a few beginner projects. Or have a look back at the August chapter and in the Resources section for some crafty ideas.

10. Have you ever wondered about your ancestry? Researching your own family tree is an enriching and interesting hobby, and it's easier than you think. You'll need the name and date of birth or death of one of your parents, grandparents or any blood relative. Register on a site such as ancestry.com, type in the name and date, and if they have any information about that person it will appear. And that is your start. You can find Australian, UK, European and US births, deaths and marriages records, as well as military and church records. Often in December, at Easter and on long weekends, the site gives free access to various records. Discovering your own direct relatives from long ago is very exciting, and placing yourself in a family tree helps gives you a sense of who you are. (See the Resources.)

TIP: Giving a framed family tree to a newborn baby in your family is a beautiful and meaningful gift.

LOOKING BACK AND MOVING FORWARD

Look back through the chapters of this book, month by month, and acknowledge the work you've done and the changes you've made. Work out what new skills you need so you can continue to improve what you do in your home. Think about your values and build into the coming year the activities that will continue the improvements you're making. And don't be afraid of change. Everything changes, sometimes through a renewal and sometimes through just fading away. I still change my list every year, adding new things I want to know more about and dropping others to make way for the new. I see this as a sign of vitality and strength, and a way of keeping my home life interesting and enriching.

One thing is for certain: every year will be different to the last. What we've covered in this book is really just the start of what is possible, but it can provide you with a guide to forming the foundation of future growth.

And finally . . .

I hope you have a December full of satisfying activities and entertaining parties, and that you enjoy spending time with your family and friends. I hope you accomplish all you set out to do and feel more comfortable in your home than you ever have before. Right at the end of the month, in those dying days of the year, withdraw from the outside world, stay at home with those you love and imagine what you'll do next year. Our lives aren't dictated by the whims of fashion or what is popular; we travel to the beat of our own drums and because we do, next year can be anything we want it to be.

So kick off your shoes, spend time in that dreamy zone between wakefulness and snoozing, and think of what you can do next year that will enrich your spirit and let you feel you're really alive. When the page turns again, we'll be back to January, our planning month, where anything is possible.

A NOTE FOR NORTHERN HEMISPHERE READERS

The monthly topics in *The Simple Home* match Southern Hemisphere seasons but you can use this book wherever you live. If you live in Europe or the Americas and follow Northern Hemisphere seasons, here is an alternative chapter order:

January: Organise the Year Ahead
February: Your Money and Your Life
March: A Food Revolution
April: Spring Cleaning
May: The Home Dairy
June: Preserving and Food Storage
July: Laundry Love

August: Domestic Crafts, Sewing and Household Linens
September: Food Gardening in Containers
October: Simple Home Bakes
November: Health and Wellbeing
December: A Time for Celebration

CONVERSIONS

LIQUID CONVERSIONS

METRIC	IMPERIAL	STANDARD CUPS
30 ml	1 fl oz	2 tablespoons
60 ml	2 fl oz	¼ cup
80 ml	2¾ fl oz	⅓ cup
125 ml	4 fl oz	½ cup
185 ml	6 fl oz	¾ cup
250 ml	8 fl oz	1 cup

OVEN TEMPERATURES

CELCIUS	FAHRENHEIT	GAS MARK
120°C – very slow	250°F	1
150°C – slow	300°F	2
160°C – warm	315°F	2-3
180°C – moderate	350°F	4
190°C – moderately hot	375°F	5
200°C – moderatey hot	400°F	6
220°C – hot	425°F	7
230°C – very hot	450°F	8
240°C – very hot	475°F	9

DRY WEIGHT CONVERSIONS

METRIC	IMPERIAL
15 g	½ oz
30 g	1 oz
45 g	1½ oz
55 g	2 oz
125 g	4 oz
150 g	5 oz
200 g	6½ oz
225 g	7 oz
250 g	8 oz
500 g	1 lb
1 kg	2 lb

LENGTH CONVERSION

METRIC	IMPERIAL
2.5 cm	1 inch
30 cm	1 foot (12 inches)
91 cm	1 yard (3 feet)
1 metre	3 feet 2 inches

RESOURCES

Paprika Recipe Manager
The best app I've used for recipe collection, menu planning and shopping lists. See paprikaapp.com

Pepperplate
I haven't tried this app, which has similar functions to the Paprika app, but I know it's popular. See pepperplate.com.

http://www.kidspot.com.au/kitchen/articles/budgeting/best-shopping-apps-for-meal-planning
Information about supermarket shopping apps.

apartmenttherapy.com/diy-breadbox-charging-stationbetter-homes-and-gardens-171079
A very clever DIY charging station. If you have an old bread bin or something similar, you'll be able to keep all your charging devices organised and in one place.

FEBRUARY — Your Money and Your Life

Your Money or Your Life by Joe Dominguez and Vicki Robin, Penguin, USA
This book explains ways of dealing with your finances and gives a compelling explanation of selling your life hours. It's a worthwhile read.

Down to Earth: A Guide to Simple Living by Rhonda Hetzel, Penguin, Australia
The way I manage money is explained in detail in the 'Saving and Spending' chapter in my first book.

'Accumulating Poverty? Women's experiences of inequality of the lifecycle', Australian Human Rights Commission
A 2009 report examining the problem of the gender gap in retirement savings. Available at humanrights.gov.au/publications/sex-discrimination.

moneysmart.gov.au
The Australian Government's Moneysmart website is an excellent source of information about writing a budget and managing your money. Click on 'Managing your Money' and browse the topics.

moneysmart.gov.au/managing-your-money/budgeting/how-to-do-a-budget
moneysmart.gov.au/superannuation-and-retirement/retirement-income-planning
The budgeting and retirement income planning information here is excellent.

ingdirect.com.au/home-loans/calculators/extra-loan-repayments.html
There are several mortgage calculators available online. The ING website has one that shows the effects of making extra home loan repayments.

TrackMySPEND: moneysmart.gov.au/tools-and-resources/calculators-and-apps/mobile-apps/trackmyspend
Pocketbook: getpocketbook.com
Mint: mint.com
Three different apps to try that can help you track your spending.

australia.gov.au/content/seniors-card
Information about the seniors card, which you can apply for if you are residing in Australia, sixty years of age or over, and not working more than a set numbers of hours per week in paid employment. The card will give you travel concessions and certain business discounts.

MARCH — A Food Revolution

The Thrifty Kitchen by Suzanne Gibbs and
    Kate Gibbs, Penguin, Australia
Nourishing Traditions by Sally Fallon with
    Mary G. Enig, New Trends Publishing, USA
The Real Food Companion by Matthew Evans,
    Murdoch Books, Australia
*Stephanie Alexander's Kitchen Garden
    Companion*, Penguin, Australia
Once a Month Cooking by Jody Allen,
    Penguin, Australia
Coming Home by Cathy Armstrong,
    Penguin, Australia
All these books support the simple values of local,
seasonal and slow cooking. The first two would be
a solid start for any new cook.

seasonalfoodguide.com
Seasonal food guides and information about local
farmers markets in Australia.

'Unhappy Meals', Michael Pollan, The New York
Times Magazine, 28 January 2007
If you haven't read any of Michael Pollan's books,
this is an excellent article to start with. Available at
michaelpollan.com/articles-archive/unhappy-meals/.

APRIL — Food Gardening in Containers

Organic Vegetable Gardening, Annette
    McFarlane, ABC Books, Australia
Organic Fruit Gardening, Annette McFarlane,
    ABC Books, Australia
Recommended Australian gardening books for
tropical and subtropical gardens.

The Permaculture Home Garden, Linda Woodrow,
    Penguin, Australia
Easy Organic Gardening, Lyn Bagnall,
    6Scribe Publications, Australia
*Stephanie Alexander's Kitchen Garden
    Companion*, Penguin, Australia
*The Postage Stamp Vegetable Garden: Grow
    Tons of Organic Vegetables in Tiny Spaces
    and Containers* by Karen Newcomb, Ten Speed
    Press, USA
Recommended Australian gardening books for
temperate gardens.

Eden Seeds Planting Guide
A planting guide for all areas of Australia, available
at edenseeds.com.au/flux-content/eden/pdf/
EdenSeeds-PlantingGuide.pdf.

instructables.com/id/Tater-Totes-Potato-grow-bags
Tutorial on how to sew your own potato grow bags.

recycledorganics.com/infosheets/3pqc/IS3-09.pdf
Australian standard potting mix info sheet.

themicrogardener.com/how-to-make-bamboo-tepee
Instructions for how to make a bamboo tepee for pots.

down---to---earth.blogspot.com.au/2010/08/
harvesting-and-garden-maintenance.html
This harvesting and garden maintenance post on
my blog has a lot of helpful information.

bunnings.com.au
diggers.com.au
greenharvest.com.au
Good sources of supplies. Weed mat is available
at Bunnings and most nurseries. Seaweed
concentrate, Seasol, is available at Bunnings, and
certified organic seaweed concentrate is available
at both Green Harvest and Diggers. Sturdy grow
bags suitable for potatoes and small fruit trees are
available at Green Harvest.

MAY — Laundry Love

images.marthastewart.com/images/content/web/pdfs/pdf3/stain_removal_basics.pdf
A handy stain removal chart for all types of stains.

burkesbackyard.com.au/home-among-the-gumtrees/around-the-house/clothes-lines
How to make an undercover clothes drying rack.

nwedible.com/diy-wall-mounted-clothes-drying-rack/
DIY recycled wall-mounted clothes drying rack.

down---to---earth.blogspot.com.au/2007/07/how-to-make-cold-pressed-soap.html
Step-by-step instructions for how to make soap.

textileaffairs.com/lguide.htm
Label care guide.

designsponge.com/2012/06/diy-project-simple-wooden-laundry-rack.html
A DIY simple wooden laundry rack.

recyclingnearyou.com.au
PlanetArk's website containing information on the safe disposal of chemicals.

JUNE — Food Preserving and Storage

down---to---earth.blogspot.com.au/2011/11/freezing-and-pickling-vegetables.html
A comprehensive guide to freezing and pickling vegetables.

rivercottage.net/recipes-in/preserves
Some lovely preserves recipes from Hugh Fearnley-Whittingstall's River Cottage.

Preserves: River Cottage Handbook No. 2 by Pam Corbin, Bloomsbury, UK
Fix, Freeze, Feast: The Delicious, Money-Saving Way to Feed Your Family by Kati Neville and Lindsay Tkacsik, Storey Publishing, USA
The Art of Fermentation: An In-Depth Exploration of Essential Concepts and Processes from Around the World by Sandor Ellix Katz, Chelsea Green Publishing, USA
Books on preserving, freezing and fermentation.

JULY — Simple Home Bakes

down---to---earth.blogspot.com.au/2007/06/bread-making-for-beginners.html
My step-by-step tutorial for making bread by hand.

nytimes.com/2006/11/08/dining/081mrex.html
The *New York Times* no-knead bread recipe.

buenavistafarm.com.au
Fiona at the Inner Pickle blog has some wonderful baking recipes.

taste.com.au/recipes/20528/gluten+free+buckwheat+bread
A recipe for gluten-free buckwheat bread.

allrecipes.com.au/how-to/17/standard-australian-cooking-measurements.aspx
Standard Australian cooking measurements.

donnahay.com.au/recipes/conversion
Conversion calculator and Australian measurements.

whatkatiesews.net
A good dressmaking and home sewing blog.

burlapandblue.com/2013/05/28/50-favorite-simple-sewing-tutorials
50 simple sewing tutorials.

New Complete Guide to Sewing,
Readers Digest

craftsy.com/blog/2013/10/choosing-fabric-for-clothes/
How to choose the right fabric for clothes.

folksyblog.tumblr.com/post/42347711014/choosing-the-right-fabric-for-your-craft-project
How to choose fabric for craft projects.

tessuti-shop.com
To buy linen or hemp in Australia online.

dmc-usa.com/Education/How-To/Learn-the-Stitches/Embroidery-Stitches.aspx
textileschool.com/articles/541/hand-stitch-types
Two good guides to embroidery stitches for beginners.

ravelry.com
A knitting and crochet community.

knitty.com
An online knitting magazine with free tutorials and patterns.

tandemknits.com/2015/01/16/top-10-knitting-blogs-2015-edition/
A list of very good knitting blogs.

theaussieknittingco.com/conversion-charts-abbreviations
A list of knitting needle sizes.

britishcraftnetwork.tv
The British Craft Network has a wide range of free craft tutorials.

threadsmagazine.com/how-to
Threads online magazine has many how-to articles and videos for all sorts of sewing.

youtube.com/watch?v=mhYUU3solac&spfreload=10
Basic leather-carving videos on YouTube.

youtube.com/watch?v=Pa50Ag_bv6w&spfreload=10
Basket-making videos on YouTube.

biology.clc.uc.edu/fankhauser/cheese/cheese.html
Dr Fankhauser's cheese-making site. Click on 'cheese press, home made' for info on how to make a cheese press.

instructables.com/id/A-Simple-and-Inexpensive-Cheese-Press/step3/Making-the-Mold
How to make a cheese mould at home.

cheesemaking.com/includes/modules/jwallace/onlinenews/newsfiles/cave/cave1.html
How to provide a humid area for maturing cheese and how to set up a cheese cave.

culturesforhealth.com/storing-aging-homemade-cheese
Information on how to store and age cheese.

betterhealth.vic.gov.au/bhcv2/bhcarticles.nsf/pages/Milk_the_facts_and_fallacies
Learn more about milk.

down---to---earth.blogspot.com.au/2007/07/homemade-condensed-milk.html
An easy homemade condensed milk recipe.

Green Living Australia: greenlivingaustralia.com.au/cheesemaking_ingredients_cultures.html
Ascott Dairy UK: ascott-dairy.co.uk/dairy/cheese-cultures-rennets
New England Cheesemaking Supply Company USA: cheesemaking.com
Where to buy starter cultures online.

OCTOBER – Spring Cleaning

abc.net.au/local/stories/2009/02/16/2492837.html
Shannon Lush's method for cleaning mould can be heard on this radio program.

You can buy beeswax online at **Etsy (etsy.com)** or **eBay (ebay.com)**.

Essential oils can be found at most health food shops.

Oil of cloves can be bought online at **biome.com.au** or in some chemists.

Microfibre cloths can be bought at the supermarket or hardware stores.

NOVEMBER – Health and Wellbeing

abc.net.au/health/healthyliving/mindmood/meditation
A series of audio relaxation meditation exercises

abc.net.au/health/consumerguides/stories/2006/06/19/1837215.htm
How to choose a GP.

First Aid Fast for Babies and Children Australian First Aid, shop.stjohn.org.au/first-aid-signage-publications.
Essential first-aid books for the home, available online at the St John shop.

articles.mercola.com/sites/articles/archive/2012/02/20/the-natural-way-to-speed-wound-healing.aspx
More info about medicinal honey.

naturaltherapypages.com.au/article/Herbal_Tea_Benefits
The benefits of herbal teas.

australherbs.com.au
Buy dried elderberries online.

DECEMBER – A Time for Celebration

artofmanliness.com/2013/10/09/creating-a-positive-family-culture-the-importance-of-establishing-family-traditions
Some insightful, useful information about creating family traditions.

taste.com.au/menus/christmas+menu+plans
Christmas menu planner.

buzzfeed.com/peggy/cheap-and-easy-last-minute-diy-gifts-theyll-actually-want#.dlKoVMoZDZ
Last-minute cheap and easy gift ideas.

youtube.com/watch?v=cuIXH6Qzz6Q
How to make a fresh Christmas wreath.

betterreading.com.au/book_list
Some lists to help you find a book to read.

youtube.com/watch?v=MCZXZiThKoA
Learn how to knit.

ancestry.com.au or ancestry.com
To start your family tree, just type in the name of someone in your family, with their birth date, and if anyone has been researching them, that family tree will appear.

ACKNOWLEDGEMENTS

Although there is a common perception that a book is written by a solitary person, this book is the product of a writer with a magnificent support team. My family keeps me going and makes all things possible. My husband, Hanno, continued his support of my creative efforts by doing the housework I didn't have time for, making the dinners I missed and hanging out the laundry that kept us in clean clothes. My sister, Tricia de Chelard, provided encouragement, laughter and a practical eye for quality and detail when we worked together on the craft projects. My sons, step-son, daughters-in-law and nephews all played their part by being interested in what I do and giving praise and reassurance along the way.

The fine people at Penguin have continued to nurture and support me as a writer. I have great respect and a warm place in my heart for my publisher, Andrea McNamara. With a rare blend of creativity and pragmatism, Andrea inspired me to write what I hope has resulted in a useful and practical book. My ever-patient editor, Jo Rosenberg, has a deep understanding of my message, so her gentle encouragement throughout the writing process kept me committed to producing a book that will help those who, like me, are living their simple values in a complex world.

I thank designer Laura Thomas, who has crafted such a beautiful book, Caroline Jones, who did a splendid job cooking and baking my recipes so they presented beautifully on the pages, and photographer Julie Renouf, whose work brought the food and ideas to life for you to see. I don't meet these people but I am grateful for their work and their commitment to excellence.

Thanks also to Rose Marshall, who has been a faithful and dear friend to me since she started reading my blog many years ago. Rose's wisdom and support kept me going during some very busy hours and I'm thankful she's been there. Rose and Alison Smith help me run the Down to Earth Forum, and our team of Sue, Michele, Becci, Sherri, Rhonda, Judy and Jenny help moderate. Together we keep it a dynamic, ever-changing and interesting place to share information, learn and socialise. Thanks to all these wonderful women who kept the forum together during the months I was writing, and for so much more.

I would be negligent if I failed to mention my first book, *Down to Earth*. It was constantly on my mind while I wrote and the thought of it kept me tapping away on the keyboard until I found the right words and told the full story. That book has been such a part of me for the past few years and I didn't want to let it down by making *The Simple Home* less than it could be. In the end I think I've written the sister of *Down to Earth* and I hope the connection of the two books and the message they contain will allow them to sit side by side, in your bookshelf and in your heart.

INDEX

CLEANING PRODUCTS

RECIPES

HOME REMEDIES

VIKING

UK | USA | Canada| Ireland | Australia
India | New Zealand | South Africa | China

Penguin Books is part of the Penguin Random House group of companies
whose addresses can be found at global.penguinrandomhouse.com.

Penguin
Random House
Australia

First published by Penguin Group (Australia), 2016

10 9 8 7 6 5 4 3 2 1

Text copyright © Rhonda Hetzel 2016

Photographs copyright © Julie Renouf 2016

The moral right of the author has been asserted.

Design by Laura Thomas © Penguin Group (Australia)
Internal photography styling by Cherise Pagano
Home economy by Caroline Jones
Cover photographs licensed through Shuttersock.com: Tangarine and teaspoon
by bogdandimages, spool of thread by Garsya, rolling pin by Picsfive, bobbins and
thimble by gourmetphotography, leaves by VICUSCHKA, texture by alexkar08.
Line drawings licensed through Shuttersock.com: AKaiser, bioraven, Canicula,
Doremi, Digiselector, Hein Nouwens, Liliya Shlapak, Lynea, Mila Petkova, Morphart
Creations, Olga Korneeva, Pim, Roberto Castillo, Sketch Master, Strejman.
Typeset in Adobe Caslon by Laura Thomas
Colour separation by Splitting Image Colour Studio, Clayton, Victoria
Printed and bound in China by Toppan Leefung Printing Limited

National Library of Australia Cataloguing-in-Publication data:

Hetzel, Rhonda, author.
The simple home: a month-by-month guide to self-reliance,
productivity and contentment/Rhonda Hetzel.
9780670079025 (hardback)
Self-reliant living–Australia.
Sustainable living–Australia.
Home economics–Australia.
Quality of life–Australia.
Conduct of life.

640

penguin.com.au